Transforming Historical Trauma through Dialogue

I dedicate this book to my partner, Tami Derezotes.
As the therapist tells Will in the film Good Will Hunting,
a soul mate is someone who challenges you. In that sense, Tami,
you have always challenged me to be the best person I can be,
and I always appreciate that.

Transforming Historical Trauma through Dialogue

David S. Derezotes

University of Utah

Los Angeles | London | New Delhi
Singapore | Washington DC

Los Angeles | London | New Delhi
Singapore | Washington DC

FOR INFORMATION:

SAGE Publications, Inc.
2455 Teller Road
Thousand Oaks, California 91320
E-mail: order@sagepub.com

SAGE Publications Ltd.
1 Oliver's Yard
55 City Road
London EC1Y 1SP
United Kingdom

SAGE Publications India Pvt. Ltd.
B 1/I 1 Mohan Cooperative Industrial Area
Mathura Road, New Delhi 110 044
India

SAGE Publications Asia-Pacific Pte. Ltd.
3 Church Street
#10-04 Samsung Hub
Singapore 049483

Printed in the United States of America

A catalog record of this book is available from the Library of Congress.

978-1-4129-9615-0

This book is printed on acid-free paper.

MIX
Paper from
responsible sources
FSC® C014174

Acquisitions Editor: Kassie Graves
Editorial Assistant: Elizabeth Luizzi
Production Editor: Libby Larson
Copy Editor: Gillian Dickens
Typesetter: C&M Digitals (P) Ltd.
Proofreader: Susan Schon
Indexer: Jean Casalegno
Cover Designer: Edgar Abarca
Marketing Manager: Lisa Sheldon Brown
Permissions Editor: Karen Ehrmann

13 14 15 16 17 10 9 8 7 6 5 4 3 2 1

Brief Contents

Preface   xiv

Acknowledgments   xv

Introduction   xvi

**SECTION I: SOCIOHISTORICAL TRAUMA, TRANSFORMATION, AND DIALOGUE:
DIALOGUE MODELS FOR TRANSFORMING SOCIOHISTORICAL TRAUMA**   1

1. What Is Sociohistorical Trauma? What Is Historical Trauma?   5

2. What Is Transformation?   27

3. Dialogue Practice   43

4. The Development of the Dialogue Facilitator   67

5. Basic Dialogue Phases, Tasks, and Issues   87

SECTION II: DIALOGUE MODELS   101

6. Psychodynamic Dialogue: Telling Our Stories   103

7. Cognitive-Behavioral Dialogue: Exploring Attitudes and Behaviors   123

8. Experiential-Humanistic Dialogue: Talking From the Heart   137

9. Transpersonal Dialogue: Talking From Spirit   149

10. Biological and Environmental Dialogue: Communicating
    With Our Bodies and Nature   161

SECTION III: DIALOGUE APPLICATIONS   171

11. Bridging Divides Through Dialogue: Transforming Our
    Spaces of Misunderstanding   173

12. Dialogue in Social Justice Work   181

13. Dialogue in Peace and Conflict Work   195

14. Dialogue Across the Life Span   207

15. Community Therapy: Transforming Mental
    Health Challenges Through Dialogue   219

Index   239

About the Author   251

Detailed Contents

Preface   xiv

Acknowledgments   xv

Introduction   xvi

**Section I: Sociohistorical Trauma, Transformation, and Dialogue:
Dialogue Models for Transforming Sociohistorical Trauma**   1
   Introduction to Section I   1

1   What Is Sociohistorical Trauma: What Is Historical Trauma?   5

   Multiple Theoretical Perspectives   7
      A Theory of Theories   7
      A Brief History of the Science of Trauma   8
      Developmental Systems Perspective on Evolution and Historical Trauma   10
      Human Evolution and Historical Trauma   11
      Evolution of Memory   12
      The Neurobiology of Historical Trauma   13
      Historical Trauma and Cultural Evolution   14
      Historical Trauma in World History   15
      Studies in Political Science   15
      Historical Trauma in Modern Literature and Film   15
      Human Diversity and Cultural Contexts of Trauma   16
      Intergenerational Transmission   17
      Interdisciplinary Studies   19
      Ecobiopsychosocialspiritual Elements of Sociohistorical Trauma   19
   Assessment of Sociohistorical Trauma in Dialogue Facilitation   21
   Vignette 1: Ashes of Mother Earth   21
   Vignette 2: Two Halves Make a Whole   22
   References   23

2   What Is Transformation?   27

   Empowerment   28
      Empowerment and Transformational Learning Theory   29
      Transformation and Empowerment in Oppressed, Minoritized,
        or Non-Western Populations   30

Posttraumatic Growth   31
    Resilience   32
    Spirituality, Religion, and Transformational Growth   32
    Transpersonal Psychology and Transformation   33
Relational Transformation   34
    Relational Transformation With Self   34
    Developmental Dimensions   35
    Body Parts   35
    Relational Transformation Between People   36
    Transformation of Relationship With the Ecosystem   38
Vignette: Dialogue   39
References   40

3 Dialogue Practice   **43**

Introduction and Definitions   43
Rules for Dialogue Participants and Facilitators   46
Interdisciplinary Theory and Research   47
    Historical Context of Dialogue   47
    Dialogue and Education   48
    Religion and Dialogue   50
    Dialogue in Political Science   51
    Dialogue in Social Work   51
    Psychological Studies of Dialogue Process and Intergroup Prejudice   52
    Philosophy and Dialogue   53
    Peace and Conflict Studies and Dialogue   53
    Organizations and Dialogue   54
    International Examples of Dialogues   55
Intergroup Dialogues   56
Ecobiopsychosocialspiritual Development   59
    Physical   59
    Emotional   59
    Cognitive   60
    Social   60
    Spirituality   60
Vignette 1: What Is Dialogue?   61
Vignette 2: How Has Dialogue Transformed Participants?   62
References   63

4 The Development of the Dialogue Facilitator   **67**

The Importance of Facilitator Development   67
The Facilitator's Ability to Shift From "Me" to "We"   68
Relationship and Dialogue   70
Conscious Use of Self in Relationship   71

Multidimensional Development   73
    Physical Maturity   73
    Emotional Maturity   74
    Cognitive Maturity   74
    Social Maturity   75
    Spiritual Maturity   75
Assessing Dialogue Outcomes: An Artistic and Scientific Process   75
Multidisciplinary Perspectives on Facilitator Development   78
Countertransference in Social Work   78
    Facilitator Training   79
    Group Work   79
    Psychology   81
    Business   81
    Participatory Facilitation   82
Author's Dialogue With the Reader   82
Vignette 1: Effective Dialogue Facilitator   83
Vignette 2: A Dialogue   83
References   85

5   Basic Dialogue Phases, Tasks, and Issues   87

Introduction and Orientation   87
Engagement and Assessment   89
    Identifying Need   89
    Inviting Participants   90
    Setting Goals   90
    Commitment   90
    Ground Rules   91
Relationship and Community-Building Work   91
    Creating Space   91
    Opening Up   92
    Managing Difficult Conversations   93
    Action-Processing-Action   94
    Bigger and Smaller   94
    Checking In and Checking Out   94
Evaluation and Follow-up   94
    Following Up With Social Action   94
    Renegotiating   95
    Referring   95
    Re-searching   95
Additional Dialogue Issues   96
    Participants Are Supervisors   96
    Dialogue Training Groups   96
    Co-facilitation   97
    Structure   97
    Dealing With Challenging Participants   97

Mistakes	98
Debriefing	98
Vignette: What Is Dialogue?	99
References	100

SECTION II: DIALOGUE MODELS   **101**
Introduction to Section II   101

6 Psychodynamic Dialogue: Telling Our Stories   **103**

A General Psychodynamic Approach to Dialogue   103
What Is the Psychodynamic Approach?   105
Scientific Evidence for Psychodynamic Approaches   106
Psychodynamic Dialogue   107
The Role of the Facilitator in Psychodynamic Dialogue   108
Internal Dialogue: An Ego State Model   109
Internal Dialogue: Working Through Transference and Projections   111
Collective Dialogue With Couples   113
Collective Dialogue With Families   115
Collective Dialogue With Institutions   117
Collective Dialogue With Cultures   119
The Psychodynamically Oriented Dialogue Facilitator's Self Work   121
References   122

**7 Cognitive-Behavioral Dialogue: Exploring
Attitudes and Behaviors**   **123**

Two "Kinds" of Cognitive Conversation   123
Behaviors   125
What Is the Cognitive-Behavioral Approach?   126
Scientific Study of CBT   128
CBT Dialogue   129
Beginning Dialogue With an Intellectual "Warm-up"   129
Work With Values   131
Development of Nonjudgmental Awareness Through Detachment
From Negative Thoughts   132
Awareness of Alternative Views   132
Development of Communication Skills   133
Behavioral Experiments   134
References   135

8 Experiential-Humanistic Dialogue: Talking From the Heart   **137**

What Does It Mean to Talk From the Heart?   137
How Are Cognitions, Emotions, and Feelings Different and Related?   137

What Comes First, Emotions or Thoughts?   138

Experiential-Humanistic Theory and Research   138

Psychodrama   139

The Neurology of Emotions   142

EH Techniques for Dialogue: Using "Real Plays" to Experience and Express Emotion   143

     Simple Sharing of Sensations and Emotions   143

     Listening With Presence: Genuineness, Empathy, and Warmth in Dialogue   144

     One-Person Psychodrama Between Internal Voices ("Vertical")   145

     Two-Person Psychodrama Between External Voices ("Horizontal")   145

     Two-Person Psychodrama Involving Both Internal and External Voices
         ("Two-Dimensional")   145

     Whole-Group Psychodrama Involving Both Internal and External Voices
         ("Three-Dimensional")   146

     Theatrical Psychodrama and Dialogue   147

References   147

9   Transpersonal Dialogue: Talking From Spirit   **149**

Transpersonal Dialogue   149

Spirituality and Religiosity   149

What Are the Differences and Relationships Between Religion and Spirituality?   150

Evidence for the Transpersonalist Approach   151

Spirituality in Social Work   152

Spiritual Interventions From the World's Wisdom Traditions   152

Mindfulness   153

Transpersonal Exercises for Dialogue   155

     Sharing Intentions   155

     Sharing Imagination   155

     Mindfulness   157

     What Do You Know to Be True?   157

     Living Funeral   157

     Giving Blessings   157

References   158

**10   Biological and Environmental Dialogue: Communicating
With Our Bodies and Nature**   **161**

Whole-Body Dialogue   161

     Body-Mind Connection   162

     Dance and Movement   162

Whole-Body Exercises for Dialogue   163

     Movement Between Whole Group and Small Group   163

     Expressing With the Whole Body   164

     Listening With the Whole Body   165

     Body Image Dialogue   165

     Sexuality as Dialogue   165

Deep Ecology Dialogue   166
Deep Ecology   167
    Conversations Between Local Wildlife, Ecosystems, and Humans   168
    Dialogue With Pictures of Living Things   168
    Dialogue of Sacred Landscapes   168
    Sensing the Seasons   168
References   169

SECTION III: DIALOGUE APPLICATIONS   **171**
Introduction to Section III   171
What Is the Inclusive Approach?   171

11 Bridging Divides Through Dialogue: Transforming Our Spaces of Misunderstanding   173

Gender Divides   175
Religious Divides   175
Political Divides   176
Divides About Sexual Orientation   177
Divides About Job Rankings   178
Following Up Dialogue With Action for Social Change   179
References   179

12 Dialogue in Social Justice Work   181

What Is Social Justice Work?   181
Social Justice Work and Sociohistorical Trauma   182
    Research in Social Justice Work   182
    Why Do Social Justice Work?   182
Beginnings   184
    Warm-ups   184
    Finding Commonalities and Reasons for Commitment   184
    Practice Dialogues   184
    Anticipating Challenging Reactions   185
Dialogues of Privilege   187
    What Is Privilege?   187
    Intergroup Dialogue   187
    Intragroup Dialogue   188
Dialogues of Oppression   188
    Sharing Stories of Sociohistorical Trauma   188
    Transforming Challenging Reactions   190
Developing Multicultural Competence   191
    What Is Multicultural Competence?   191
    Understanding Motivations   191
    Understanding Obstacles   192

Becoming Allies 192
   Understanding What an Ally Is and Is Not 192
   Allies in Social Justice Dialogue 192
Cooperative Social Action 193
   Planning Cooperative Actions 193
   Dialogue During Events 193
   Debriefing 193
References 194

13   Dialogue in Peace and Conflict Work   195

What Is Peace? 195
   Dialogue Is Peace Practice 195
   Peace and Sociohistorical Trauma 196
   Peace and Conflict Studies 196
Approaches to Peaceful Conflict Resolution 197
   Psychodynamic Dialogue Approaches 197
   Cognitive-Behavioral Dialogue Approaches 197
   Experiential-Humanistic Dialogue
      Approaches 198
   Transpersonal Dialogue Approaches 199
   Bioecological Dialogue Approaches 199
Mediation 200
Reconciliation 201
Major PCS Curriculum Areas 202
A Dialogue Models Class in Support of PCS or Diversity Curriculum 203
   Purpose and Context 203
References 205

14   Dialogue Across the Life Span   207

Children 207
   Basics 207
   Examples of Dialogue With Children 209
Adolescents 210
   Basics 210
   Examples of Adolescent Dialogue 211
Young Adults 212
   Basics 212
   Dating Issues 213
Middle Age 214
   Basics 214
   Bridging Transgenerational Divides 214
   Midlife Parent–Younger Child Dialogue 214
   Midlife Child–Aging Parent Dialogue 215
   Partners Dialogue 215

Aging   216
     Basics   216
     Transgenerational Dialogue   216
     Dialogue Training Groups   217
     Dialogues of Life and Death   217
References   218

15   Community Therapy: Transforming Mental Health Challenges Through Dialogue   219

What Is Mental Health and Illness?   220
Community Therapy Is a Transformative Response to Sociohistorical Trauma   221
     What Is Community Therapy?   222
     The Community Therapist   223
Community Therapy Applications   224
Individual Applications   224
     Depression   225
     Anxiety   225
     Personality Disorder: Borderline and Narcissistic   225
     Bipolar Disorder   226
     Psychosis   226
     Pervasive Developmental Disorder   227
Family Applications   227
     Ideological Divides   227
     Helping Families Deal With Sexual Minorities   228
     Multiple Family Dialogue   229
     Child Custody Issues   229
Local Community Applications   229
     Conflicts Between Pedestrians, Bicyclists, and Motorists   230
     Dialogue as an Alternative to the Legal System   230
     Treatments for Community Poverty   230
     Dialogue and Public Health   231
     Bridging Intergenerational Divides   231
Applications in Working With Institutions   232
     Dialogue in School Curricula   232
     Dialogue in Church Curricula   232
     Large Organizations   232
Applications in Working With the Ecosystem   234
     Dialogue on Environmental Issues   234
     Dialogue With Other Living Things and Dialogue With Ecosystem Elements   235
     Combined Dialogue   235
Applications in Working With the Global System   235
References   237

Index   239

About the Author   251

Preface

I believe that we need more leaders who see their role as dialogue facilitators. Such leaders are likely to help transform the sociohistorical trauma in our families, institutions, and local and global communities. Such leaders are not reluctant to stand up to violence when necessary, but they also recognize that violence tends to lead to more violence, creating ongoing cycles of sociohistorical trauma. I believe we can co-create a world where people can be both passionate about we think, feel, and want and yet remain compassionate toward those who think, feel, and act differently.

Acknowledgments

I want to express my gratitude to Kassie Graves, Senior Acquisitions Editor, Human Services at SAGE Publications. Thank you, Kassie, for believing in this project and giving me the opportunity to write and publish this text.

I also need to acknowledge some of the people who were especially helpful to me as I researched and wrote this book. Thank you to Candace Christensen and Sui Zhang for your help in the literature reviews. Thanks to AuDeane Cowley; you have always been willing to let me discuss my ideas with you. I am thankful to Kilo Zamora, for your help in developing the chapter on social and economic justice issues. I also acknowledge George Cheney and Mark Owens and Debra Daniels; I value you as co-developers and co-facilitators of dialogue, and I have learned valuable lessons from all of you. Finally, thanks to all of the people who have allowed me to facilitate dialogue spaces for you; you have all also been important teachers for me as well.

Introduction

*T*ransforming Historical Trauma is written for both professional helpers and for the general public, although professionals may be more familiar with some of the concepts in the text. This text is divided into three sections.

Section I: Sociohistorical Trauma, Transformation, and Dialogue

The five chapters in this section provide a background into the research and theories that inform the three main topics of the text. The population at risk includes people who experience sociohistorical trauma (described in Chapter 1). The practice goal with this population is transformation (described in Chapter 2). The method used to treat this population is dialogue (described in Chapters 3, 4, and 5). Section I is the most academic section and has the heaviest use of citation, which gives the reader a summary of the most recent and relevant literature on these subjects. The author has used female pronouns throughout most of Section I.

Section II: Dialogue Models

The five chapters in this section provide dialogue models that can be used to help transform sociohistorical trauma. The psychodynamic model (Chapter 6), cognitive-behavioral model (Chapter 7), experiential model (Chapter 8), and transpersonal model (Chapter 9) are informed by the four "forces" of psychology that have been developed over the past 150 years. The ecological and biological models (Chapter 10) are drawn from more recent approaches to professional helping that have especially emerged in the past decades. These chapters are a blend of literature review and model building. The chapters are heavily referenced but not necessarily as extensively as in the first five chapters of Section I. The author has used a mixture of female and male pronouns in Section II.

Section III: Dialogue Applications

The last five chapters of the text provide readers with dialogue methods that can be used with groups commonly encountered in today's practice settings. These methods are drawn from the models described in Section II. Chapter 11 describes dialogue methods that can be used to help bridge community divides. The use of dialogue to help address social and economic justice issues is addressed in Chapter 12. Dialogue models for peace and conflict resolution work is the focus of Chapter 13. Chapter 14 provides methods for children, youth, adults, and the elderly across the life span. Finally, the last chapter (Chapter 15) offers a community therapy model of dialogue for work with mental health issues. Chapters in this last section include shorter literature reviews and devote relatively more attention to the description and philosophy of practice in dialogue methods. Chapters in this section use primarily male pronouns.

Sociohistorical Trauma, Transformation, and Dialogue

Dialogue Models for Transforming Sociohistorical Trauma

INTRODUCTION TO SECTION I

Interpersonal violence is a monologue—a disconnection from self and the world, a one-way conversation that silences the other and makes dialogue unsafe. The silencing can continue well after the initial violence ends, as recipients of violence and even their descendants become disempowered, lose their ability to grow and develop, and become disconnected from the world.

Interpersonal violence often leads to further violence. Recipients seek revenge and retaliate, creating ongoing cycles of perpetration and victimization. Perpetrators of violence may be no more well off than victims, often living in a state of disconnection, fear, uncertainty, and hypervigilance.

Interpersonal violence creates sociohistorical trauma, which is any ongoing reaction to the initial violence. On the individual level, sociohistorical trauma is characterized by any physical, emotional, cognitive, and spiritual reactions that usually vary with each individual context. When a child is maltreated by a parent, for example, she may become unable to defend herself, express her pain, ask for what she wants, learn in school, or even experience her own memories and other emotions. Another maltreated child may deal with her pain by victimizing other children in school or by abusing her own children when she becomes a parent.

On the collective (or "macro") level, sociohistorical trauma is characterized by the substitution of power, aggression, and control for relationship. Aggression and control can be inflicted on the community or on other communities. Throughout history, for example, when slavery has been perpetuated upon populations of people, they may experience loss of self-respect and dignity and sometimes respond with behaviors that are destructive to

1

themselves and to others. Sociohistorical trauma can lead to ongoing cycles of revengeful violence between large groups, such as what we see today in ethnic conflicts, for example, in the Balkans, Central Africa, and the Middle East. Or women have historically been oppressed by men in many families, institutions, and communities, and many women may still carry "internalized oppression" and understandably hold resentment toward men.

Sociohistorical trauma may be the most dangerous form of trauma. Humans seem to naturally want to make sense out of suffering. When our pain seems to come from "natural" causes, such as earthquakes, storms, or even wild animals, we may view the events as "acts of God" (if religious) or perhaps as "events in a chaotic world" (if not so religious). When suffering seems to be caused by other people, we are tempted to react with anger and seek revenge toward those we see belonging to the perpetrator-group. Such reactions can lead to cycles of retaliation lasting years, decades, and even centuries.

Members of trauma-recipient groups may remain silenced and unable to engage in constructive dialogues. They may also justify their own self-destructive behaviors as well as their retaliatory behaviors. Obviously, our human tendency to seek revenge is an individual, family, community, and global problem that, with the development of weapons of mass destruction, now threatens the development and even survival of humanity. Such trauma, when still not transformed, inhibits the cooperation required to ensure our collective survival and postsurvival growth. When people go "out of relationship" and into cycles of self-destruction, violence, retaliation, and hatred, they cannot work together to find common solutions to such global survival threats as overpopulation, preparations for war, ecosystem destruction, and water and air pollution.

There is reason for hope. Our capacity to destroy each other through violence is matched by our current ability to also co-create a better world. We have the technology to reduce such global survival threats as overpopulation, global warming, ecosystem destruction, and urban poverty. Our global priority now must be to learn how to live cooperatively, so we can co-create the best world our descendants could receive from us.

Following sociohistorical trauma, a person or community can experience transformations toward greater empowerment, growth, and connection. Dialogue can help build the kind of relationships necessary for cooperation, even between trauma-recipient and trauma-perpetrator groups. Dialogue puts the value of relationship higher than the value of what we create with our hands (e.g., wealth, power, status) and minds (e.g., beliefs, ideologies).

This text is about dialogic transformation of sociohistorical, or human-caused, trauma. Dialogue, as presented here, is the self-reflective and relationship-building process that can help transform violence into peaceful, mutual cooperation. Sociohistorical trauma is violence perpetuated by people on other people and may be primary (experienced firsthand) and/or secondary (experienced through my friends, family, ancestors).

Section I, with five chapters, provides a foundation for the dialogue models presented in the rest of the book. Each chapter summarizes the multidisciplinary literature on the featured subject. Although these first chapters are some of the most heavily referenced in the text, these subjects cannot be completely covered in any single chapter.

The first chapter presents a summary of the current relevant literature on *sociohistorical trauma*. Since most of the literature on trauma is not specifically about sociohistorical trauma, much of this chapter covers the current literature on trauma. A multidisciplinary review of the literature on *transformation* follows in Chapter 2. Chapter 3 presents a summary of the literature on *dialogue*. Chapter 4 presents the personal/professional *development of dialogue facilitators*. Finally, Chapter 5 offers a review of the basic phases, tasks, and issues in dialogue.

EXPERIENTIAL LEARNING I.1

(1) Have you experienced any kind of violence perpetuated by other people upon you? Did it tend to silence you, either at the time or later on in your life?

(2) What conditions in a relationship or larger group make you feel safe enough to have dialogue? Has dialogue ever helped you positively transform your own sociohistorical trauma?

(3) Why is sociohistorical trauma a particularly dangerous form of trauma, especially in our world today?

CHAPTER 1

What Is Sociohistorical Trauma?

What Is Historical Trauma?

Historical trauma is a reaction to violent experience that challenges the person to develop new ways of thinking and behaving. There are many kinds of traumatizing events, of course, and individuals may respond very differently to the same event. The kinds of experiences that may traumatize us include life-threatening events such as violent crime, a tsunami, or a serious accident. People can also be traumatized by loss or anticipated loss of a loved one, a job, physical or mental health, or lover. Trauma is sociohistorical when perpetrated by people on people, such as in child maltreatment, domestic violence, or war.

Historical trauma has helped design the architecture of human beings. Probably everything we feel, think, and do reflects at least in part the ways our ancestors responded to challenges they faced in the past. Our current theories suggest that human responses to trauma influence not only the individual across the life span but also the traits of our descendants.

Nature tends to create especially powerful memories of threatening events. This is because organisms that respond effectively to threats in the environment tend to survive, and powerful memories are more likely to be remembered. Threatening events often challenge us to develop new ways of thinking or acting that may help us cope with future challenges.

In a human being, historical trauma seems to be stored in an evolving "memory complex," which contains many forms of information. Each person responds to these memories in unique ways that reflect her own internal and external world. Thus, we can say that historical trauma is an *"ecobiopsychosocialspiritual"* process, in that ecological, biological, psychological, social, and spiritual elements are all involved. Another way to express this is that trauma is a body-mind-spirit-environment process. Ecological processes include influences of family, culture, community, and the local ecosystem. The biology of trauma includes evolution, neurological processes, and overall physical health. The person's formal and informal social supports, psychological well-being, and spiritual beliefs about herself and her world also affect the trauma process.

The many impacts of historical trauma are influenced or mitigated not only by the nature of the traumatizing threat but also by a multitude of other genetic, epigenetic, environmental, and "epi-environmental" influences.

Genetic influences are potential traits that can be passed on to a person by her parents through her genome. Although scientists do not yet even agree on what a "gene" is, we know that complex traits can be expressed through combinations of genes. Many so-called personality traits are considered to be largely genetic; one example would be the tendency toward what we call introversion or extroversion, which can be modified across the life span but tends to be fairly stable.

Epigenetic influences are those that may influence the expression of genetic traits. Most epigenetic influences can also be viewed as being associated with environmental conditions. Scientists have discovered that some genetic traits can be expressed or repressed when humans experience prenatal or postnatal trauma. For example, if a mother experiences extreme stress during a pregnancy, she may activate epigenetic processes that express genetic material that creates a heightened state of preparedness for stress in her child's life.

Environmental influences are any life experiences that result in physiological, emotional, cognitive, social, and other changes in the person. Common environmental influences include factors in the family, culture, and community such as child maltreatment, poverty, or racism.

Finally, *epi-environmental* influences are those that mitigate environmental influences. Many epi-environmental influences are at least in part associated with genetic tendencies. For example, the person's self-motivation, life experiences, and perseverance would likely modify how she responds to the death of a family member.

Historical trauma has multiple "causes" that are difficult to assess precisely. However, as in any other complex system, small changes can ultimately lead to larger scale shifts in people's behavior. Another way to say this is that small changes in genetic, epigenetic, environmental, or epi-environmental influences may change the behavior of large groups of people. This potential of course supports the possibility that dialogue may ultimately lead to gradual, significant change and thus another reason for hope.

EXPERIENTIAL LEARNING 1.1

(1) Describe historical trauma in your own life. What are the causes of this trauma?

(2) Describe the story of someone you know who has suffered historical trauma and who now seems to be doing well and someone who has never been able to recover from historical trauma. Why do you think they handled their trauma differently?

(3) What group of people do you belong to that has suffered collective historical trauma? How does that trauma still affect your own thoughts and behaviors?

MULTIPLE THEORETICAL PERSPECTIVES

A Theory of Theories

Since historical trauma has multiple causes, and since the relative weight of these causes can vary, the best theory of historical trauma is a multidisciplinary approach that equally values all perspectives. These perspectives include such disciplines as history, neurobiology, sociobiology, anthropology, social work, psychology, and medicine. Further enriching our understanding of historical trauma, any discipline may have multiple schools of thought that can contribute to our understanding of trauma. For example, many theories of human behavior in the discipline of psychology could be applied to the same case of historical trauma, such as psychodynamic, cognitive-behavioral, experiential, and transpersonal theory. In many cases, a synthesis of these perspectives can be developed.

The Western medical model has dominated the historical trauma literature in the past decades, emphasizing the diagnosis and treatment of such individual mental disorders as posttraumatic stress disorder (PTSD) and acute stress disorder (ASD). However, the most advanced theory is also the most inclusive, and theories of historical trauma are required that are *both* individual and collective (having to do with families and communities), oriented to *both* strengths and pathologies, and able to incorporate all ecobiopsychosocialspiritual elements.

Concerns have been raised that the clinical focus of the Western mental health industry on trauma uses a technical rather than moral approach that is too focused on the individual's "emotional catharsis" and "chemical imbalances" and too removed from social contexts. Experts point out that the majority of refugees, for example, have historically been able to function throughout life without expert mental health treatment (Summerfield, 2000). Similarly, clinical approaches to treating historical trauma symptoms (such as substance abuse) in American Indian and Alaskan Native populations have been largely ineffective without the addition of approaches that build on the cultural and tribal strengths (Yellow Horse Brave Heart & DeBruyn, 1995).

The nature of historical trauma for any individual can be expressed mathematically through a multiple regression expression that contains all the interrelated elements of the ecobiopsychosocialspiritual model.

$$HxT = aE + bB + cP + dS + eSp + fU + gI - gO,$$

where

HxT is historical trauma;

E includes environmental factors such as shared history, ecosystem health, and conditions of war and peace;

B includes biological factors such as genetics, epigenetics, and disease;

P includes psychological factors such as meaning, will, focus, and personality;

S includes sociological factors such as family, culture, religion, health of government, social justice, and economic equality;

Sp includes spiritual factors such as a sense of meaning, purpose, and ethics;

U includes all other still unknown factors influencing historical trauma;

I includes interactive effects, when factors interact in ways that either increase or decrease total historical trauma;

O includes overrepresented factors (since *E, B, P, S,* and *Sp* are at times interrelated to some degree, the *O* factor represents the extent to which certain factors may have been overexpressed [by being included more than once] and thus need to have their power subtracted); and

a, b, c, d, e, f, and *g* are "intensity factors" that show the relative influencing power of *E, B, P, S, Sp,* and *U.*

EXPERIENTIAL LEARNING 1.2

(1) Plug in your own experiences into the mathematical formula for trauma. Share your results.

(2) What are the individual and collective issues in your own historical trauma?

(3) What is your perspective on the Western approach to trauma?

What follows is a series of interrelated perspectives on historical trauma, all represented by one or more of the elements of our inclusive theory of historical trauma. These perspectives are summarized in Table 1.1.

A Brief History of the Science of Trauma

Scientists have increasingly seen trauma as an unavoidable life experience. Living things are understood to have evolved strategies to reduce the risks of trauma and maximize the potential benefits. Like many more "advanced" animals, humans have evolved the ability to create emotionally charged memories of trauma that can help us avoid similar experiences again. However, trauma can also be associated with destructive patterns that may persist in the lives of individuals, families, communities, and nations, across single or multiple lifetimes (Goodman & West-Olatunji, 2008).

Some common symptoms of trauma have been identified. Many trauma survivors oscillate between the two opposite extremes of what Herman (1997) called the "dialectic of trauma." In this dialectic, the human psyche seems to avoid painful memories and future trauma by either withdrawing into a numbing depression of mind and body (constriction) or compulsively recalling (intrusion) and even reenacting the original traumatic experience in what Freud (1920/2007) called the "repetition compulsion." In a third common symptom, the psyche at least initially may keep the mind and body alert and constantly prepared for new threats (hyperarousal).

Table 1.1   Perspectives on Trauma Literature

Perspective	Content
History of science of trauma	How our views of trauma continue to change
Developmental systems	Genetic, epigenetic, environmental, and epi-environmental issues
Human evolution	How trauma informs evolution
Human memory	Why we have memory
Neurology of trauma	What happens in the traumatized brain
Cultural evolution	How cultural change is related to trauma
World history	Trauma in world history
Literature and film	How trauma is a theme in our art
Cultural context	Cultural factors in trauma
Intergenerational	What is intergenerational trauma?
Interdisciplinary studies	Integration of trauma studies across academic disciplines
Biopsychosocialspiritual	Integrated theory of trauma
Assessment	Assessment of trauma in dialogue process

This dialectic of trauma, in both individual and collective forms, has been rediscovered by scientists in successive generations. For example, Freud (1896) observed constriction and intrusion in his female patients and initially realized that his "hysterical" patients suffered from "premature sexual experience," which today we might call sexual trauma. Many soldiers who survived the trauma of serving in the world wars were observed to develop dialectical symptoms, in a syndrome first called "shell shock" and later diagnosed as "neurotic illness" (Kardiner & Spiegel, 1947). U.S. veterans of the Vietnam War had similar trauma-related symptoms, complicated by their country's political ambivalence about that war (Lifton, 1973). One of the key insights of the women's liberation movement was the realization that large numbers of civilian women are traumatized (as Freud originally thought) by physical and sexual violence perpetrated within their own families (Herman, 1997). These women also often experience the dialectical symptoms of constriction and intrusion, as well as hyperarousal.

Until recently, the literature has primarily described these negative trauma effects, using a clinical model of assessment and analysis. Trauma can disempower people when they experience no control over the events that harm them and can also disconnect people from their own identity, other people, and the world around them when the trust they had in those meanings are betrayed. Families, communities, and nations can also experience constriction, intrusion, and hyperarousal, and these symptoms can become chronic when the traumatic conditions are ongoing (such as ongoing war, oppression, or poverty).

We now know, however, that historical trauma can either help inform our cooperative efforts to co-create the highest good or divide us from our best judgment, from each other, and from the world we all live in. Trauma can evoke both self-destructive and resilient responses from individuals and families (Denham, 2008). When, for example, an individual experiences sexual assault as a child, she can continue to make decisions that create unnecessary suffering for herself, by avoiding all relationships (constriction) or becoming sexually active with untrustworthy men (intrusion and repetition compulsion). However, she might also choose to develop healthier relationships throughout her life. Similarly, if a minority population suffers discrimination and oppression, some members of that community might develop antisocial or addictive behaviors, while others may participate in community service work. Contemporary (current) trauma can also interact with historical trauma to intensify lifetime or intergenerational reactions to trauma (Evans-Campbell, 2008).

Since 1980, the diagnosis of PTSD has been used to describe the symptoms of trauma in the *Diagnostic Statistical Manual of Mental Disorders* (*DSM*). The definition of PTSD has changed significantly since 1980 and continues to change. Often the underlying trauma is not well understood by helping professionals, and considerable work remains to be done in basic research as well as in the education of professionals about PTSD assessment and treatment (Rosenbaum, 2004). Although the standard definitions of PTSD require the etiology of a life-threatening event, recent evidence suggests that the majority of events (up to 87.5%) associated with PTSD are not life-threatening (Alessi, 2010).

In the literature, *historical trauma* has most typically been defined as a collective experience, in contrast with the term *psychic trauma,* which is typically defined as an individual experience. However, historical trauma is known to involve complex interactions between the individual, family, and culture (Denham, 2008). The term *psychosocial trauma* (Martin-Baro, 1994) was introduced to describe this complex interaction of individual and collective experiences and meanings.

The diagnosis of complex posttraumatic stress disorder was developed in the past decades to describe observed reactions to prolonged and repeated social trauma, as might be experienced, for example, in a war, in captivity, or in slavery. Complex PTSD is usually associated with social structures that allow for the exploitation and abuse of weak or minority populations, such as in abusive families, impoverished inner-city slums, and regions of political repression and genocide. Symptoms include somatization, disassociation, and affect dysregulation (Herman, 2009).

Developmental Systems Perspective on Evolution and Historical Trauma

The developmental systems perspective is especially useful in work with historical trauma because it provides a theoretical framework that integrates the consideration of genetic, epigenetic, environmental, and epi-environmental influences. The developmental systems perspective suggests that changes in human traits are always caused by a combination of genetic and environmental factors that are all essentially of equal influence (Moore,

2002). When humans encounter certain intense environmental conditions, such as trauma, they might react with novel behaviors, physiological responses (e.g., fight-or-flight response), and even anatomical changes. Such developmental changes can interact with genetic factors to influence both individual development and intergenerational evolution.

Thus, for example, as a woman reduces her anxiety by learning a meditation technique, her body is activating and deactivating certain genetic traits, and these traits are more likely to be expressed in her lifetime, as well as in the lives of her descendants. Although scientists do not understand the mechanisms behind these complex interactions, there is increasing evidence that supports the developmental systems perspective.

Epigenetic factors are increasingly thought to play an important role in the expression of genetic material in every human being. Epigenetic mechanisms in DNA molecules respond to prenatal and postnatal environments by expressing genes that are most likely to deal effectively with new threats and opportunities. For example, the presence of maternal PTSD predicts low cortisol levels in the children of Holocaust survivors (Yehuda, Teicher et al., 2007). Psychiatric heredity was found to be not necessary for soldiers who experience severe war-related stress to develop PTSD symptoms (Plasc et al., 2007).

Recently, scientists have learned that the standard causal theory about protein production may need to be modified. Essentially, we have thought that DNA creates RNA, which then creates proteins. However, studies of adaptations in octopus species suggest that RNA can be modified directly by enzymes that respond to current ocean temperature. Thus, through such "RNA editing," RNA can be modified before it makes proteins. Octopuses and other invertebrates even seem to be able to edit their RNA editing, or "meta-edit." This discovery suggests that humans may also have similar mechanisms (Harmon, 2012).

EXPERIENTIAL LEARNING 1.3

(1) What symptoms show up in your own historical trauma?

(2) Do you know anyone who has complex historical trauma? Explain.

(3) Do you think that any historical trauma of your ancestors (including parents) has been passed on to you? Explain.

(4) Can you see any evidence of epigenetic factors operating between the generations in your own family?

Human Evolution and Historical Trauma

The architecture of humanity was in large part designed by historical trauma experienced by our human and nonhuman (earlier) ancestors. This statement is not meant to imply that historical trauma has not caused incredible suffering, because our ancestors have suffered, often severely, through the ages. However, it is hoped that historical trauma can continue to inform both individual development and collective evolution.

Many of our developed traits may have begun as initial responses to difficulties in our environment (Dawkins, 2004; Neihoff, 1999). For example, one theory of human aggressiveness and war suggests that humans learned to dehumanize enemy tribes by viewing them much like they viewed nonhuman predators and that males are most aggressive because they learned to compete over females (Smith, 2007). These kinds of theories are not meant to excuse human behaviors but rather help us understand and hopefully begin to replace aggressiveness with assertive cooperation.

Evolutionary theorists now offer explanations for many common human traits observed today. For example, all of our basic emotions that shape all human activity probably also had roots in traumatic events (sad, mad, glad, scared, excited, disgust) and are rooted in our mammalian past ("6 Basic Emotions," 2006). Human intelligence appears to be rooted in refinements in brain structure that evolved at least in part to give our ancestors advantages over powerful and often dangerous nonhuman animals in their environment (Dicke & Roth, 2008). What we might call the "art instinct" may have evolved in humans as a way to court and even entertain our lovers and perhaps to compete with other suitors (Dutton, 2009).

Another theory suggests that conservative political tendencies in some people may be rooted in a history of traumatic environments when joint action and obedience to the group authority were required for survival, whereas liberal tendencies may at times originate from behaviors learned in more stable past environments ("Human Evolution," 2008). Sexual shame and the need for domestic privacy may have evolved from the need to protect the family from threatening tribal conditions (DeWaal, 2009). Kissing is a way for prospective lovers to exchange pheromone messages and test the major histocompatibility complex that regulates immune systems (Fields, 2009). Finally, cultural explanations for human selflessness suggest that moral codes developed as a means to trade between tribes, as well as form tribal unity and religious identity against outside threats ("Fair Play," 2010).

All of these theories are based on evidence but remain unproven. However, most researchers agree that most if not all human traits have some connection with ancient genetic themes.

Evolution of Memory

What we call historical trauma today could be viewed as an alarm system that evolved in our distant past that, once activated, would not easily go back off. Traumatic memory probably started to evolve at least 500 million years ago in bivalves and other early animal ancestors as a means of self-protection (Russell, 2000). Organisms that could "recall" what elements in their environment were threatening might be more likely to avoid similar threats.

There is increasing scientific evidence that emotions evolved at least in part to intensify and maintain our traumatic memories (Doidge, 2007). Although there continues to be scientific debate over which nonhuman animals (if any) have emotions, human memory seems to be intensified by the strength of the original emotional response to the precipitating event.

Humans seem to have two types of memory. Explicit (or declarative) memory is intentional recall of a past experience and is stored initially in the hippocampus for months or years and then eventually may go on to more permanent cerebral cortex locations. Implicit (or nondeclarative) memory is experienced through actions rather than through conscious recall (Linden, 2007). Although historical trauma seems to be associated more with implicit (nonintentional) memory, elements of explicit memory also seem to contribute to the process.

Implicit memory of even very ancient historical trauma may be associated with current attitudinal and behavioral patterns. For example, since women need stability for reproduction, they may have evolved a more peaceful biology that produces less of the testosterone often associated with more violence in men (Hand, 2003). This need for social stability may contribute to the much lower rates of violent behavior observed today in women.

Humans now can take medications that may enhance or inhibit explicit and implicit memories. Obviously, such medications may assist in "treating" PTSD symptoms. However, some scientists worry that the treatment of long-term memories may interfere with short-term functioning, and the treatment of short-term memories may interfere with long-term functioning as well (Baker, 2010).

Increasing evidence (from studies of glutamate receptors) suggests that memories themselves are not meant to stay stable and may be designed to be slightly modified each time the mind recalls them, so that the person can blend new experiences with older experiences in a "reconsolidation" process (Nader, Schafe, & LeDoux, 2000).

The Neurobiology of Historical Trauma

The human brain appears largely to be governed by inherited history recorded in neurological circuits and modified by the individual's life experiences. Development could be thought of as the further development of synaptic connections in the brain, learned through trial and error, that result in more useful perceptions and behaviors (Purves, 2010).

Researchers have found linkages between human neurobiology and historical trauma. These discoveries help link measurable physical processes with the thoughts, feelings, and behaviors experienced by trauma survivors and descendants. Our neurobiology thus may be thought of in part as an internal historian that seeks to protect us from the many threats our ancestors encountered.

Our neurobiology may, for example, be associated with the difficulties we still have in the "contact zones" where people of different cultures and beliefs interact. Since our human ancestors lived in isolated communities for 80,000 to 100,000 years, we may still have a neurological imperative to live with people who are similar to us and reflect the internal structure of culture and ideology we grew up in (Wexler, 2008). Brain imaging reveals that the amygdala is associated with a fear response to people who look different but that this fear can be overcome by a frontal lobe view of a "bigger we" (Begley, 2008). Although neurobiology may help us explain and even "treat" the physical mechanisms of trauma, such findings do not of course excuse any violent behavior.

Researchers have found that the classic PTSD symptoms (avoidance, hyperarousal, reexperiencing) are associated with the dominance of what is called the "survival brain" (that serves to protect a person from danger) over the "learning brain" (that strives for growth, healing, and self-development). Again, brain imaging suggests that underactive ventromedial areas of the prefrontal cortex and an "overactive" right amygdala are usually found in the brains of traumatized people. When the survival brain is dominant, emotions and information processing are not well regulated, and the person may experience persistent distress, rapid body reactions to triggers, and inhibited emotional-cognitive development (Ford, 2009).

In addition to having substructures, our brains also use many neurotransmitters that assist in sending "signals" across the many synapses that connect nerve cells together. Researchers, for example, now also believe that some people with violent criminal records have a biology of aggression that is linked to low levels of serotonin, high rates of alcoholism, and hypoglycemia. The neurochemical self-control necessary to control their violence seems to sometimes be impaired by past trauma (Rossby, 2002). Low levels of gamma-aminobutyric acid (or GABA, an inhibitory neurotransmitter) and neuropeptide Y (or NPY, a peptide neurotransmitter that in part regulates energy balance and memory formation) have been found to be associated with PTSD symptoms (Ford, 2009). More than 100 neurotransmitters have already been identified in the human brain, and scientists now know that they all seem to be involved in multiple complex interactions with other biological agents and structures. There still is little if any evidence that historical trauma (or any other "disorder") is "caused" simply by a "chemical imbalance" of one or two of these neurotransmitters in the brain (Breggin & Cohen, 2000). In addition, there are probably few if any unitary and isolated functions of brain structures in relation to human behavior; brain structures seem rather to function together.

Indeed, although significant advances have been made in understanding brain functions, much more remains unknown about how the brain actually works. The actual neurobiology of historical trauma appears to be very complex, and given the fact that humans have about 100 billion neurons with 500 trillion synapses, all of our brain functions are housed in the most complex structures currently known in the universe.

Historical Trauma and Cultural Evolution

Some theorists have studied the role that human communication may play in intergenerational historical trauma. In addition to transmission through human reproductive biology, historical trauma may be transmitted in part through the meme, the basic unit of cultural transmission of human traits (Brodie, 1996). At the same time that memory evolved in individual organisms, perhaps a half billion years ago, the first memes may have also developed, as awareness of the environment and associated habits were passed on from the brain of one bivalve to another (Russell, 2000).

According to theories of cultural evolution, memes "replicate" today through such communication technologies as television, the Internet, and film. Viewers can now watch live coverage of war scenes, terror attacks, natural disasters, and other traumatic events. Conversations about politics, religion, and other ideologies probably also transmit memes through local, national, and global communication networks. People all over the planet can co-experience traumatic events through our communications technologies, when, for example, video of mass-casualty terrorism is distributed on television and online.

Another theory suggests that, at least partly in response to the complex problems we face, we create beliefs and behaviors that comfort us. These beliefs and behaviors are based more on emotional needs than facts and are called "supermemes" (Costa, 2010). The danger of such supermemes, according to this theory, is that they can lead to a society that refuses to deal with the real issues that challenge us today. For example, we may focus more on accumulating wealth and cheering on our local sports teams than on the challenges of overpopulation and global warming.

Historical Trauma in World History

We know that our ancestors also experienced historical trauma. Historians have found evidence of this historical trauma in ancient texts. For example, stories of historical trauma and its aftermath can be found in the Old Testament of the Christian Bible (Birnbaum, 2008). Indeed, a study of recorded history shows a record of ongoing trauma experienced by different populations, including wars, periods of poverty and starvation, widespread fatal illnesses, and natural disasters. This trauma can persist in a society over decades or even longer. Historians have, for example, argued that British society as a whole still suffers from the historical trauma that originated in the collective horrors experienced on the Western Front during World War I.

In recent decades, researchers have paid particular attention to the historical trauma suffered by minority populations, through such experiences as colonialism, slavery, and war. The historical experience of Mexicans living in what is now the United States, for example, has been described as parallel to the intergenerational historical trauma experienced by American Indian, African American, and Pacific Islander populations (Estrada, 2009). These populations, as we will see, have often passed on the trauma across generations of descendants.

Studies in Political Science

Political scientists have also been interested in the relationship between historical trauma and political processes. When populations of people have experienced oppression or violence at the hands of other peoples, the politics of both populations may be influenced by collectively held stories. For example, a political-cultural analysis has identified themes of historical trauma in the histories of African Americans (Gump, 2010).

In historical trauma, large-scale political processes seem to interact with individual and family processes. For example, political scientists have found that a family history of political persecution seems to alter the coping styles of family members (Yakushko, 2008). Political pressure from the state, community, and family can silence the memory and voice of war survivors (Liem, 2007). Political and ethnic violence can result in negative psychological impact on children, although individual, familial, and cultural factors all mitigate the nature and extent of the impact (Cairns & Dawes, 1996).

Historical Trauma in Modern Literature and Film

Literary scholars have also contributed to our understanding of historical trauma. The argument could be made that many of our favorite novels, plays, short stories, films, and poems describe at least in part the processes of historical trauma. Studies of North American literature, for example, have identified common themes of historical trauma experienced by American Indians during European colonization (Van Styvendale, 2008).

Films are arguably the most influential art forms of our era. Themes of historical trauma can be identified in most of the top films of the first decade of the 21st century (by unadjusted domestic gross totals), including *Avatar* (2009), *The Dark Knight* (2008), *Shrek 2* (2004), *Pirates of the Caribbean: Dead Man's Chest* (2006), *Spider-Man* (2002), *Transformers: Revenge of the Fallen* (2009), *Star Wars: Episode III—Revenge of the Sith* (2005), *The Lord of the Rings: The Return of the King* (2003), *Spider-Man 2* (2004), *The Passion of the Christ* (2004), and *Toy Story 3* (2010) (for list of "top films," see Dirks, 2010).

People have been able to not only survive trauma but also continue to live meaningful lives. Some literatures describe these creative responses people have made to historical trauma. Drama education scholars have written about how historical trauma is described in theater through the technique of using witness testimony in community (Cox, 2008).

Human Diversity and Cultural Contexts of Trauma

Many scholars who study and promote human diversity have also become interested in historical trauma theory. The experience of social collective historical trauma has been associated with many of the life difficulties of oppressed peoples. When trauma is inflicted upon a population of people who share an ethnic, a national, a cultural, or other common identity, this collective historical trauma can be transmitted across generations as descendants continue to identify with the pain of their ancestors (Brave Heart, 1999). Indigenous scholars have, for example, found evidence of historical trauma and associated mental, sexual, and substance abuse issues in American Indian people in both Canada and the United States (Pearce et al., 2008).

A growing number of researchers have been studying historical trauma across different cultures. Many of these studies look scientifically at the historical trauma associated with such global events as slavery, holocaust, war, colonization, economic exploitation, and the unequal distribution of wealth and power.

Each population will experience historical trauma in the context of their own beliefs, rituals, and other contexts. A wide range of PTSD symptoms, for example, were found among traumatized populations from four different countries, suggesting that expression of PTSD following historical trauma is influenced by local, environmental factors (de Jong et al., 2001).

Professional helpers have found that historical trauma must always be assessed in the context of such cultural differences. For example, nurses have been advised to use traditional approaches when addressing historical trauma in American Indian populations, including holistic medicine, relational focus, and spirituality (Struthers & Lowe, 2003). American Indian women cope from the effects of historical trauma through the use of such cultural "buffers" as strong identity, spirituality, enculturation, and traditional healing practices (Walters & Simoni, 2002).

Cultural differences processes may be complex and hard to understand. Latino veterans of the Vietnam War, especially Puerto Rican veterans, have had a higher risk of PTSD and a higher risk of severe PTSD symptoms than did Caucasian veterans. Since functioning levels were not influenced by ethnicity, the symptoms may be more related to cultural differences in expressive style rather than in levels of pathology (Ortega & Rosenheck, 2000). Japanese American World War II internees tended to not have the family communication necessary to help descendants sort out race-related trauma, historical trauma, and unique familial factors (Nagata & Cheng, 2003).

Studies of Holocaust survivors and their descendants have provided evidence of the interaction of genetics and environment in historical trauma. Evidence that maternal PTSD is related to increased risk of PTSD in offspring of Holocaust survivors suggests that epigenetic factors may contribute (Yehuda, Bell, Bierer, & Schmeidler, 2007). Psychological distress has been found in both second- and third-generation Holocaust survivors (Scharf, 2007), and the presence and severity of these symptoms seem to be related across generations (Yehuda, Schmeidler, Giller, Siever, & Binder-Brynes, 1998). However, adequate parenting, genetic strengths, and social supports may explain the lack of clinical evidence for maladaptive behavior in some second-generation populations (Van Ijzendoorn, Bakermans-Kranenburg, & Sagi-Schwartz, 2003).

The collective experience of colonial holocaust seems to affect the majority of American Indians. One researcher uses the term *historical unresolved grief* to describe the intergenerational trauma experienced by American Indians following their own North American holocaust. This unresolved grief is linked to such issues as suicide, homicide, child maltreatment, domestic violence, and substance abuse (Yellow Horse Brave Heart & DeBruyn, 1995). Individual factors also interact with culture to influence the process of historical trauma. The severity of PTSD symptoms in descendants of Holocaust survivors was also related to a personal history of additional stressful events (Yehuda et al., 1995).

Professional helpers may struggle to be sensitive to the presence and symptoms of historical trauma in clients from unfamiliar cultures. Formal measures are being developed for practitioners to assess historical trauma among various populations, including American Indians (Whitebeck, Adams, Hoyt, & Chen, 2004). More attention is being given to the initial formal training and continuing education of professionals. The family systems literature, for example, suggests that multigenerational effects of historical trauma must be included in assessments (Abrams, 1999).

Minority populations can also experience historical trauma when exposed to the microaggressions commonly experienced in the "contact zones" between cultures. Ethnic harassment has also been shown to result in PTSD-like symptomatology with Latino populations (Schneider, Hitlan, & Radhakrishnan, 2000). Racist incidents can be traumatizing, particularly among people of color, and can result in psychological and physical symptoms (Bryant-Davis & Ocampo, 2005). The same environmental conditions that are symptomatic of populations that suffered historical trauma can further traumatize descendants of trauma survivors. Children living in inner cities can experience loss of self-acceptance, trust, morals, and security associated with their traumatic experience of violence, drugs, guns, and violence (Parson, 1994).

Intergenerational Transmission

Although scientists know that historical trauma can be transmitted across generations, the complex mechanisms involved in the transmission process are still not well understood.

Research suggests that many factors are associated with transmission of trauma, including factors located outside the family (such as cultural and political factors) as well as inside the family (such as psychological and biological factors). Intergenerational transmission of trauma can also be bidimensional, in the sense that the traumatization of children can also affect their parents and families. The family and the culture can be a transmitter of trauma as well as a buffer and healer of trauma. When families and cultures are able and willing to talk about and process what happened, when issues of justice are addressed, and when adapted belief systems add to resiliency, the chances of healing seem to be improved for descendants (Danieli, 1998).

Most people who experience war trauma today are civilians, and exposure to military violence can interfere with the protective qualities of the family, as studies of Palestinian children have confirmed (Qouta, Punamaki, & El Sarraj, 2003). PTSD symptoms were identified in two generations of Cambodian refugees following their survival in the Pol Pot war (Sack et al., 1994). Similar findings were discovered in Sudanese and Ugandan war refugees (Karunakara et al., 2004).

Military veterans, of course, can experience historical trauma from active service in a war. Children of fathers who participated in abusive violence during the Vietnam War showed more behavioral disturbance than children of other Vietnam War vets (Rosenheck & Fontana, 1998). The children and grandchildren of historical trauma survivors seem to often experience higher rates of health and mental health challenges than other children. The intergenerational historical trauma of aboriginal youth in Canada has been linked to suicidal behaviors, mental illness, physical problems, human immunodeficiency virus (HIV) risk, and substance abuse (Pearce et al., 2008).

Wives of war veterans have experienced more psychological distress than women in a control group (Westerink & Giarrantano, 1999). The secondary traumatization of wives of former prisoners of war (POWs) was aggravated by their husbands' aggression and mitigated by the ability of the women to self-disclose (Dekel & Solomon, 2006). When traumatized children have good perceived parenting, they are more protected from developing poor self-esteem and other psychological distress, and they are able to engage in political activity without increased risk of more distress (Punamaki, Qouta, & El Sarraj, 1997).

The source of secondary traumatization is the collection of symptoms now often called PTSD, not participation in combat. Emotional numbing, detachment, and avoidance may affect parenting effectiveness. Symptoms include eating and communication disorders, academic and behavior problems, and emotional issues, but not self-esteem. Overall, secondary trauma is strongly associated with the father's level of PTSD and violent behavior. The children's gender, age, and birth order, as well as family, culture, and support systems, also are associated with secondary trauma symptoms (Dekel & Goldblatt, 2008).

Attachment theory offers another perspective on trauma across generations. From this perspective, trauma experience may affect the ability of the parent to care for, protect, and give meaning to the child. When the family and society emphasize only strength and courage in the face of trauma, children may not be able to grieve in a healthy way (Bar-On et al., 1998). From a psychodynamic perspective, secondary traumatic stress disorder involves at least in part such unconscious processes as projection by parents and introjection by their children (Rowland-Klein & Dunlop, 1997).

EXPERIENTIAL LEARNING 1.4

(1) Is there a trait you have that you believe evolved out of historical trauma? Explain.

(2) Do you find that your most vivid memories are associated with trauma? Do you know anyone who has complex historical trauma? Explain.

(3) In what unique ways does your family or culture seem to deal with historical trauma?

Interdisciplinary Studies

Eventually, all professional disciplines that contribute to the historical trauma literature could be integrated to help generate more inclusive and advanced theories. Some examples of the integration of some disciplines already exist in the literature.

For example, biopolitics has been advanced as a new approach to understanding political science, based on an interdisciplinary approach to understanding the long-term biological bases of behavior (Blank & Hines, 2001). Sociobiology seeks to understand the biology of social behavior by drawing from ecology, ethology (zoological study of animal behavior), and genetics (Wilson, 1998). Researchers who draw from such a combination of perspectives may be able to be especially helpful in informing helping professionals, policymakers, and the general public about the etiology and dynamics of trauma.

Ecobiopsychosocialspiritual Elements of Sociohistorical Trauma

Humans have many interrelated developmental dimensions, including the physical, emotional, cognitive, social, and spiritual. The person is also always interconnected with her environmental systems, which includes her family, local community, and global community, and the life-supporting ecosystems that sustain her. In this text, this complex system of internal and external systems will be called *ecobiopsychosocialspiritual.*

Like every human process, historical trauma is complex, with many interrelated causes, elements, and results. Scientists believe that all trauma is at the same time physical, emotional, psychological, sociological, and political (Kirmayer, 1996). An ecobiopsychosocialspiritual approach to historical trauma is the most advanced theory because it is the most inclusive theory, with all the elements of the system of systems.

Sociohistorical trauma is always individual, in the sense that it is experienced or expressed by an individual, and interacts with the person's own strengths and limitations. Individual experiences and characteristics influence the historical trauma process. For example, the sudden unexpected death of a loved one was found to be the most important predictor of PTSD in a Detroit neighborhood, with women at higher risk of symptoms than men (Breslau et al., 1998).

Trauma is also always collective, in that collective factors such as shared history, genetic material, and cultural memes are always involved in the process (Boehnlein, 2001). Social support networks, for instance, may be a protective factor for keeping a high level of perceived self-efficacy in Bosnian and Croatian refugees (Ferren, 1999).

Spirituality can be defined here as the individual's experience of connectedness, purpose, peace of mind, and all the other "highest" levels of human development. In contrast, religion can be understood as a collective experience of shared rituals, doctrines, and beliefs.

The world's wisdom traditions offer many spiritual and religious perspectives that offer explanations and approaches to what we are calling sociohistorical trauma.

Some concentration camp inmates during World War II were able to survive the terrible ordeal at least in part because of the belief systems they held about the world. Those that had a strong belief system, perhaps in a god or in a life purpose, were able to experience what we now might call posttraumatic growth (Frankl, 2006). A similar theory has been presented about war veterans; those men who are able to find a shared or community meaning for their combat experiences seem to survive the trauma of war and do better in their posttraumatic life (Tick, 2005).

Researchers have found that mindfulness techniques can quiet the emotional response to traumatic pain. When people use mindfulness techniques, which usually involve some kind of nonjudgmental awareness of internal or external events in the here and now, people are able to notice the sensations of physical or social pain without the emotional reactions. Apparently, the thalamus first helps process the sensory quality of traumatic suffering, and then the cingulate cortex is involved with processing the emotional response. Mindfulness can increase sensory awareness and "decouple" that awareness from such unpleasant emotional reactions as fear and anger (Heller, 2010).

Although world religions have different doctrines, rituals, and beliefs, they do share some common approaches to trauma. Many religions suggest that "normal" consciousness is often unhealthy and can lead to unnecessary pain and suffering, and they offer such solutions as enlightenment (Hinduism), salvation (Christianity), or an end to suffering (Buddhism) (Tolle, 2006). Versions of the golden rule ("You shall love your neighbor as yourself.") can be found in all of the world's major religions (Religious Tolerance, 2010). Most religions teach essentially that forgiveness is the ultimate goal in the traumatic process.

EXPERIENTIAL LEARNING 1.5

(1) Invent a name for a new interdisciplinary field of study that could help us understand the etiology and dynamics of sociohistorical trauma.

(2) What is the spiritual dimension of sociohistorical trauma in your own life?

(3) If people were assessed from an ecobiopsychosocialspiritual perspective in some institutional setting, such as the medical clinic, the unemployment office, or the university, what might be different?

(4) What is sociohistorical trauma?

ASSESSMENT OF SOCIOHISTORICAL TRAUMA IN DIALOGUE FACILITATION

Assessment in dialogue facilitation is an ongoing process, as it is in psychotherapy. However, the dialogue facilitator will often not have the opportunity to meet individually with participants and make thorough assessments. In clinical work, assessments can incorporate the use of formal and informal measures, and a growing variety of valid and reliable formal instruments for assessing PTSD continue to become available to clinicians (Keane, Weathers, & Foa, 2000).

In dialogue facilitation, assessment data about participants will emerge from two major sources: in the stories they tell about themselves as well as in the social interactions that the participant has with others in the actual dialogue process. The dialogue facilitator looks for congruence and incongruence between how the participant describes her past and how she acts in the present.

VIGNETTE 1: ASHES OF MOTHER EARTH

I met historical trauma many years ago as a young child. I did not know its identity at that time but felt that it had several names that affected the most innocent. Historical trauma came to me in many forms; the most obvious were through my fears. It was during my boarding school days that historical trauma became most evident, with fears of inadequacies, loneness, isolation, and guilt. Soon after, I was again taken away from my natural family to be sent away into foster care. I was 8 years old. I slept on a comfortable bed and had the luxuries of electricity and running water, and plenty to eat. The guilt that engulfed me was overwhelming, as though these tokens of gifts were for my benefit but actually paralyzed me and stunted my growth both mentally and physically. I began to eat too much, feeling as though food could fill me with love that I so much desired. Historical trauma followed me, intimidated me, hid me from my true self, and gave me no option but to hate myself. I began to be controlled through a replacement that carried out those abuses as I learned to hate those that abused me. I was intimidated, controlled, and battered until my dreams became nightmares with knives piercing my most private parts and for most of my life continued to haunt me simply because of its effect on my life. I did not know the full meaning the cycle it brought me into, but knew all these behaviors and its intent were the same, to control me. Whenever I tried to deny the existence of historical trauma, it was evident that I could not erase it from my mind without some sort of support or spiritual intervention. Historical trauma had other allies, its close friend, "the unconscious," that laid the groundwork for the secrets, the untold stories of abuse that happened on a daily basis as a child, leading to the cycle of violence into adulthood.

For now, I will call historical trauma the Ashes of Mother Earth. I cannot say that historical trauma and I had ever become friends, yet we grew up side by side, and were aware of each other in our behaviors, feelings, and even actions. I had always felt like dust in the sand, the mud of the earth, in which nothing could grow. It was a parallel to how my life had been as I was thrown down upon dirt floors to be hushed and abused. Yet, it was the story of Mother

Earth that brought me back to life, resurrecting me with new life as I educated myself, arose to new accomplishments, restored my soul with spiritual experiences to rid myself of trauma that held me back and had almost destroyed me. I can say now that having gone through these experiences has strengthened me and provided me with the knowledge I need to help those in our Native communities and surroundings, especially in my own life.

VIGNETTE 2: TWO HALVES MAKE A WHOLE

As I began to think about historical trauma in my own life, I can tell you that many questions have been answered through *dialoguing,* bringing me new understanding and insight into my life. I have met individuals, coworkers, friends, and even clients, who have all played a part in putting the pieces of my puzzle together, whether they know it or not. I can be honest and say that I do not have all the answers, but that I am beginning a journey in finding out many unanswered questions, especially those that I do not remember. This has become an important quest for me, *lost memories.*

As difficult as dialoguing has been for me on occasion, I find that by communicating my thoughts and feelings, some memories return and become real and my emotions are once again brought to the surface. I see my other half brought to the here and now to the point I become a more holistic person. The other half being the person I once was, filled with pain, hardships, and a loss of identify I could never quite understand.

Dialoging has become a conversation with myself. It has become that *voice* I never had. I am allowed to ask questions and even allowed to hear the answers to those questions, whether they are supportive or constructive criticisms. I had always been quiet, shy, and an easily intimidated person. Through my boarding school experiences, foster homes, and traumatic home experiences, my voice was never heard or accounted for. Dialoguing brought those experiences forward to understand, interpret, be angry, sad, happy, and rejoice in knowing I am the person who controls my future. It is a transformation that enables me to move forward and accomplish those things that I feel are important for myself and for my family.

Vignettes Author: Renee Harrison

Renee Harrison is from Shiprock, New Mexico, a small town in the Four Corners region in northern New Mexico. She attended the University of Utah, where she received a bachelor's degree and a master's degree. She is currently in her second year as a PhD student in the School of Social Work. Renee previously worked as a behavioral health counselor for the Indian Walk-In Center in the Salt Lake City area. She has six beautiful children who have accomplished much in their lives.

REFERENCES

Abrams, M. S. (1999). Intergenerational transmission of trauma: Recent contributions from the literature of family systems approaches to treatment. *American Journal of Psychotherapy, 53*(2), 225–231.

Alessi, E. (2010, September 27). Presentation on unpublished research. College of Social Work, University of Utah.

Baker, S. (2010, Fall). Rx for genius. *Discover: The Brain,* pp. 18–25.

Bar-On, D., Eland, J., Kleber, R. J., Krell, R., Moore, Y., Sagi, A., et al. (1998). Multigenerational perspectives on coping with the Holocaust experience: An attachment perspective for understanding the developmental sequelae of trauma across the generations. *International Journal of Behavioral Development, 22*(2), 315–338.

Begley, S. (2008, March 3). How your brain looks at race. *Newsweek,* pp. 26–27.

Birnbaum, A. (2008). Collective trauma and post-traumatic symptoms in the biblical narrative of ancient Israel. *Religion and Culture, 5,* 533–546.

Blank, R. H., & Hines, S. M. (2001). *Biology and political science.* London: Routledge.

Boehnlein, J. K. (2001). Cultural interpretations of physiological processes in post-traumatic stress disorder and panic disorder. *Transcultural Psychiatry, 38,* 461–466.

Brave Heart, M. Y. H. (1999). Oyate Ptayela: Rebuilding the Lakota Nation through addressing historical trauma through Lakota parents. *Journal of Human Behavior in the Social Environment, 2*(1–2), 109–126.

Breggin, P. R., & Cohen, D. (2000). *Your drug may be your problem: How and why to stop taking psychiatric medications.* New York: Da Capo Press.

Breslau, N., Kessler, R. C., Chilcoat, H. D., Schultz, L. R., Davis, G. C., & Andreski, P. (1998). Trauma and posttraumatic stress disorder in the community. *Archives of General Psychiatry, 55,* 626–632.

Brodie, R. (1996). *Virus of the mind: The new science of the meme.* Seattle, WA: Integral Press.

Bryant-Davis, T., & Ocampo, C. (2005). Racist incident-based trauma. *The Counseling Psychologist, 33*(4), 479–500.

Cairns, E., & Dawes, A. (1996). Children: Ethnic and political violence—a commentary. *Child Development, 67,* 129–139.

Costa, R. (2010). *The watchman's rattle: Thinking our way out of extinction.* Philadelphia: Vanguard.

Cox, E. (2008). One refugee's story. *Research in Drama Education, 13*(2), 193–198.

Danieli, Y. (1998). Conclusions and future directions. In Y. Danieli (Ed.), *International handbook of multigenerational legacies of trauma* (pp. 669–689). New York: Plenum.

Dawkins, R. (2004). *The ancestors tale.* Boston: Houghton Mifflin.

de Jong, J. T. V. M., Komproe, I. H., Van Ommeren, M. V., El Masri, M., Araya, M., Khaled, N., et al. (2001). Lifetime events and posttraumatic stress disorder in 4 postconflict settings. *Journal of the American Medical Association, 286*(5), 555–562.

Dekel, R., & Goldblatt, H. (2008). Is there intergenerational transmission of trauma? The case of combat veterans' children. *American Journal of Orthopsychiatry, 78*(3), 281–289.

Dekel, R., & Solomon, Z. (2006). Secondary traumatization among wives of Israeli POWs: The role of POWs' distress. *Social Psychiatry & Psychiatric Epidemiology, 41*(1), 27–33.

Denham, A. R. (2008, September). Rethinking historical trauma: Narratives of resilience. *Transcultural Psychiatry,* pp. 391–414.

DeWaal, F. B. M. (2009). Bonobo sex and society. *Scientific American Mind, 20*(3), 4–11.

Dicke, V., & Roth, G. (2008). Intelligence evolved. *Scientific American Mind, 19*(4), 70–77.

Dirks, T. (2010). Filmsite: All-time box office hits (domestic) by decade and year. http://www.filmsite.org/boxoffice2.html

Doidge, N. (2007). *The brain that changes itself: Stories of personal triumph from the frontiers of brain science*. New York: Penguin.

Dutton, D. (2009). *The art instinct: Beauty, pleasure, and human evolution*. New York: Bloomsbury.

Estrada, A. (2009). Mexican Americans and historical trauma theory: A theoretical perspective. *Journal of Ethnicity in Substance Abuse, 8*(3), 330–340.

Evans-Campbell, T. (2008). Historical trauma in American Indian/Native Alaska communities: A multilevel framework for exploring impacts on individuals, families, and communities. *Journal of Interpersonal Violence, 23*, 316–338.

Fair play: The origins of selflessness. (2010, March 20). *The Economist*, pp. 88–90.

Ferren, P. M. (1999). Comparing perceived self-efficacy among adolescent Bosnian and Croatian refugees with and without posttraumatic stress disorder. *Journal of Traumatic Stress, 12*(3), 405–420.

Fields, R. D. (2009). Sex and the secret nerve. *Scientific American Mind, 20*(3), 33–39.

Ford, J. D. (2009). Neurobiology and developmental research: Clinical implications. In C. A. Courtois & J. D. Ford (Eds.), *Treating complex stress disorders: An evidence-based guide* (pp. 31–58). New York: Guilford.

Frankl, V. (2006). *Man's search for meaning*. New York: Beacon. (Original work published 1946)

Freud, S. (1896). The aetiology of hysteria (Standard ed., Vol. 3; J. Strachey, Trans.). London: Hogarth.

Freud, S. (2007). Beyond the pleasure principle (J. Reddick, Trans.). London: Penguin. (Original work published 1920)

Goodman, R. D., & West-Olatunji, C. A. (2008). Transgenerational trauma and resilience: Improving mental health counseling for survivors of Hurricane Katrina. *Journal of Mental Health Counseling, 30*(2), 121–136.

Gump, J. P. (2010). Reality matters: The shadow of trauma on African American subjectivity. *Psychoanalytic Psychology, 27*(1), 42–54.

Hand, J. L. (2003). *Women, power, and the biology of peace*. San Diego, CA: Questpath.

Harmon, K. (2012, January 5). Octopuses reveal first RNA editing in response to environment. Octopus chronicles: Adventures and discoveries with the planet's smartest cephalopods. *Scientific American*. http://blogs.scientificamerican.com/octopus-chronicles/2012/01/05/octopuses-reveals-first-rna-editing-in-response-to-environment/

Heller, R. (2010, Fall). Buddhism's pain relief. *Buddhadharma: The Practitioner's Quarterly*, pp. 34–38.

Herman, J. (1997). *Trauma and recovery: The aftermath of violence-from domestic violence to political terror*. New York: Basic Books.

Herman, J. (2009). Foreword. In C. A. Courtois & J. D. Ford (Eds.), *Treating complex stress disorders: An evidence-based guide* (pp. xiii–xvii). New York: Guilford.

Human evolution: Moral thinking. (2008, February 23). *The Economist*, p. 98.

Kardiner, A., & Spiegel, H. (1947). *War, stress, and neurotic illness*. New York: Hoeber.

Karunakara, U. K., Neuner, F., Schauer, M., Sing, K., Hill, K., Elbert, T., et al. (2004). Traumatic events and symptoms of post-traumatic stress disorder amongst Sudanese nationals, refugees and Ugandans in the West Nile. *African Health Sciences, 4*(2), 83–93.

Keane, T. M., Weathers, F. W., & Foa, E. B. (2000). Diagnosis and assessment. In E. B. Foa, T. M. Keane, & M. J. Friedman (Eds.), *Effective treatments of PTSD: Practice guidelines from the International Society of Traumatic Stress Studies* (pp. 18–36). New York: Guilford.

Kirmayer, L. (1996). Confusion of the senses: Implications of ethnocultural variations in somatoform and dissociative disorders for PTSD. In A. Marsella, M. Friedman, & R. Scurfield (Eds.), *Ethnocultural aspects of postraumatic stress disorder* (pp. 131–163). Washington, DC: American Psychological Association.

Liem, R. (2007). Silencing historical trauma: The politics and psychology of memory and voice. *Peace & Conflict: Journal of Peace Psychology, 13*(2), 153–174.

Lifton, R. J. (1973). *Home from the war: Vietnam veterans, neither victims nor executioners.* New York: Simon & Schuster.

Linden, D. J. (2007). *The accidental mind: How brain evolution has given us love, memory, dreams, and God.* Cambridge, MA: Harvard University Press.

Martin-Baro, I. (1994). *Writings for a liberation psychology* (A. Aron & S. Corne, Eds.). Cambridge, MA: Harvard University Press.

Moore, D. T. (2002). *The dependent gene: The fallacy of 'nature vs. nurture.'* New York: Freeman.

Nader, K., Schafe, G. E., & LeDoux, J. E. (2000). Fear memories require protein synthesis in the amygdala for reconsolidation after retrieval. *Nature, 406,* 722–726.

Nagata, D. K., & Cheng, W. J. Y. (2003). Intergenerational communication of race-related trauma by Japanese American former internees. *American Journal of Orthopsychiatry, 73*(3), 266–278.

Neihoff, D. (1999). *The biology of violence: How understanding the brain, behavior, and environment can break the vicious circle of aggression.* New York: Free Press.

Ortega, A. N., & Rosenheck, R. (2000). Posttraumatic stress disorder among Hispanic veterans. *American Journal of Psychiatry, 147*(4), 615–619.

Parson, E. R. (1994). Inner city children of trauma: Urban violence traumatic stress response syndrome (U-VTS) and therapists' responses. In J. P. Wilson & J. D. Lindy (Eds.), *Countertransference in the treatment of PTSD* (pp. 157–178). New York: Guilford.

Pearce, M. E., Christian, W. M., Patterson, K., Norris, K., Moniruzzaman, A., Craib, K. J. P., et al. (2008). The Cedar project: Historical trauma, sexual abuse and HIV risk among young aboriginal people who use injection and non-injection drugs in two Canadian cities. *Social Science and Medicine, 66,* 2185–2194.

Plasc, I. D., Peraica, T., Grubisic-Llic, M., Rak, D., Sakoman, A. J., & Kozaric-Kovacic, D. (2007). Psychiatric heredity and posttraumatic stress disorder: Survey study of war veterans. *Croatian Medical Journal, 48,* 146–156.

Punamaki, R., Qouta, S., & El Sarraj, E. (1997). Models of traumatic experiences and children's psychological adjustment: The roles of perceived parenting and the children's own resources and activity. *Child Development, 64*(4), 718–728.

Purves, D. (2010). *Brains: How they seem to work.* Saddle River, NJ: Pearson.

Qouta, S., Punamaki, R., & El Sarraj, E. (2003). Prevalence and determinants of PTSD among Palestinian children exposed to military violence. *European Child & Adolescent Psychiatry, 12,* 265–272.

Religious Tolerance. (2010). Religious information. http://www.religioustolerance.org/reciproc.htm

Rosenbaum, L. (2004). Post-traumatic stress disorder: The chameleon of psychiatry. *Nordic Journal of Psychiatry, 58*(5), 343–348.

Rosenheck, R., & Fontana, A. (1998). Transgenerational effects of abusive violence on the children of Vietnam combat veterans. *Journal of Traumatic Stress, 11*(4), 731–741.

Rossby, P. (2002). *The biology of violence: Serotonin, alcoholism, hypoglycemia.* New York: American Bar Association.

Rowland-Klein, D., & Dunlop, R. (1997). The transmission of trauma across generations: Identification with parental trauma in children of Holocaust survivors. *Australian and New Zealand Journal of Psychiatry, 31,* 358–369.

Russell, P. (2000). *Global brain: The evolution of mass mind.* New York: John Wiley.

Sack, W. H., McSharry, S., Clarke, G. N., Kinney, R., Seeley, J., & Lewinsohn, P. (1994). The Khmer Adolescent Project: Epidemiologic findings in two generations of Cambodian refugees. *Journal of Nervous and Mental Disease, 182,* 387–395.

Scharf, M. (2007). Long-term effects of trauma: Psychosocial functioning of the second and third generation of Holocaust survivors. *Development and Psychopathology, 19,* 603–622.

Schneider, K. T., Hitlan, R. T., & Radhakrishnan, P. (2000). An examination of the nature and correlates of ethnic harassment experiences in multiple contexts. *Journal of Applied Psychology, 85*(1), 3–12.

6 basic emotions. (2006, December 23). *The Economist,* pp. 4–7.

Smith, D. L. (2007). *The most dangerous animal.* New York: St. Martin's.

Struthers, R., & Lowe, J. (2003). Nursing in the Native American culture and historical trauma. *Issues in Mental Health Nursing, 24,* 257–272.

Summerfield, D. (2000). Childhood. War, refugeedom and 'trauma': Three core questions for mental health professionals. *Transcultural Psychiatry, 37*(3), 417–433.

Tick, E. (2005). *War and the soul: Healing our nation's veterans from post-traumatic stress disorder.* Wheaton, IL: Quest Books.

Tolle, E. (2006). *A new Earth: Awakening to your life's purpose.* New York: Penguin.

Van Ijzendoorn, M. H., Bakermans-Kranenburg, M. J., & Sagi-Schwartz, A. (2003). Are children of Holocaust survivors less well-adapted? A meta-analytic investigation of secondary traumatization. *Journal of Traumatic Stress, 16*(5), 459–469.

Van Styvendale, N. (2008). The trans/historicity of trauma in Jeannette Armstrong's *Slash* and Sherman Alexie's *Indian Killer. Studies in the Novel, 40*(1/2), 203–223.

Walters, K. L., & Simoni, J. M. (2002). Reconceptualizing Native women's health: An 'indigenist' stress-coping model. *American Journal of Public Health, 92*(4), 520–524.

Westerink, J., & Giarrantano, L. (1999). The impact of posttraumatic stress disorder on partners and children of Australian Vietnam veterans. *Australian and New Zealand Journal of Psychiatry, 33,* 841–847.

Wexler, B. E. (2008). *Brain and culture: Neurobiology, ideology, and social change.* Cambridge: MIT Press.

Whitebeck, L. B., Adams, G. W., Hoyt, D. R., & Chen, X. (2004). Conceptualizing and measuring historical trauma among American Indian people. *American Journal of Community Psychology, 33*(3/4), 119–130.

Wilson, E. O. (1998). *Consilience: The unity of knowledge.* New York: Knopf.

Yakushko, O. (2008). The impact of social and political changes on survivors of political persecutions in rural Russia and Ukraine. *Political Psychology, 29*(1), 119–130.

Yehuda, R., Bell, A., Bierer, L. M., & Schmeidler, J. (2007). Maternal, not paternal, PTSD is related to increased risk for PTSD in offspring of Holocaust survivors. *Journal of Psychiatric Research, 42,* 1104–1111.

Yehuda, R., Kahana, B., Schmeidler, J., Southwick, S. M., Wilson, S., & Giller, E. L. (1995). Impact of cumulative lifetime trauma and recent stress on current posttraumatic stress disorder symptoms in Holocaust survivors. *American Psychiatry, 152,* 1815–1818.

Yehuda, R., Schmeidler, J., Giller, E. L., Siever, L. J., & Binder-Brynes, K. (1998). Relationship between posttraumatic stress disorder characteristics of Holocaust survivors and their adult offspring. *American Journal of Psychiatry, 155*(6), 841–843.

Yehuda, R., Teicher, M. H., Seckl, J. R., Grossman, R. A., Morris, A., & Bierer, L. M. (2007). Parental post-traumatic stress disorder as a vulnerability factor for low cortisol trait in offspring of Holocaust survivors. *Archives of General Psychiatry, 64*(9), 1040–1048.

Yellow Horse Brave Heart, M., & DeBruyn, L. M. (1995). The American Indian holocaust: Healing historical unresolved grief. *American Indian and Alaska Native Mental Health Research, 8*(2), 60–76.

CHAPTER 2

What Is Transformation?

In this chapter, we will explore multidisciplinary perspectives on personal transformation. Transformation is viewed as an intentional process in which the person gradually uses her trauma as an opportunity for increased growth and service to others. Although transformation can occur after any kind of trauma, this chapter will focus particularly on the transformation of sociohistorical trauma.

Especially for oppressed populations, transformation is associated with the empowerment necessary to protect and improve their lives. For more privileged populations, transformation also provides opportunity for people to use their privilege in ways that support the self-empowerment of others less fortunate. In the transformation process, growth is most significant in those whose development was frozen in response to sociohistorical trauma. Transformation is particularly relational (or reconnecting) for those who have lived their lives alienated from their own bodies, from other people, or from their world. As someone becomes empowered, she begins to experience her own capacity to help herself.

The process of individual and collective transformations may be especially important to humans during the era we happen to live in today. Most, if not all, of our ancestors experienced some kind of interpersonal historical trauma, and our ancestors have also faced extinction in our distant past. However, now for the first time in our history, our own technologies can either destroy our world or help us co-create a transformed and increasingly better world. To the extent that our sociohistorical trauma remains largely untransformed, we are likely to remain in a state of fear, mistrust, disconnection, competition, and ultimately violence. As we can transform our sociohistorical trauma, we become more capable of developing the kinds of relationships necessary for cooperation and survival.

Transformation is more than resilience, although resilience may be associated with the transformation process. Resilience can be thought of as the ability to withstand trauma without significant (especially negative) change. When a person is more resilient to trauma, she may be less vulnerable. Transformation involves positive change, sometimes radical positive change, in any or all of the ecobiopsychosocialspiritual dimensions of human development.

Transformation is more than healing, although healing may also be involved in the process of transformation. The Roman and Teutonic peoples thought of healing as "wholing," which involves the recovery of lost "parts" of the person. From the Old English word *hal,* we now have the related words *whole, health,* and *holy.* Our ancient shamanic ancestors talked about "soul loss" when they looked at the consequences of life trauma. A "soul recovery" or "soul retrieval" was the shaman's way of healing trauma and was also understood to involve the recovery of lost parts and energy of the person. The soul retrieval could also lead to transformation, if there was an essential change in the character of the person or tribe.

Perhaps the term *transformation* has become more popular because at least in Western culture, we have lost the original meaning of the word *heal*. One could argue that we have replaced true healing with allopathic (Western) medicine, which emphasizes symptom reduction rather than wholeness. Instead of seeking reconnection with body, mind, spirit, other people, and environment, we perhaps seek to relieve the painful symptoms of our fragmentation and disconnection with pills and our popular short-term therapies.

The Greek word for transformation is *metamorphoo,* which is a complete or radical change, as in the metamorphosis of a caterpillar becoming a butterfly. In recent decades, Ferguson (1980) popularized the word *transformation* in the West to suggest a "change in consciousness" or "paradigm shift" in thinking. The term *transformation* remains quite popular in many subcultures, including in "New Age" circles and in the "neo-evangelistic church" (Leslie & Leslie, 2005). In the following sections, the ecobiopsychosocialspiritual elements of transformation will be explored in association with the themes of empowerment, growth, and relationship.

The transformation of sociohistorical trauma is in some ways different from the transformation of trauma caused by nature (such as floods, diseases, or earthquakes). If my ancestors suffered during a severe forest fire, for example, I am unlikely to hold a special hatred for forests. However, when other people hurt me, I seem to have such lingering responses as fear, competition, rebellion, anger, or retaliation (usually directed at the perpetrating population).

Anger is a natural human reaction to suffering; as Mark Twain said 150 years ago, most of us silently wish revenge about something. When my trauma has been "caused" by other people, my anger may result in behaviors that are destructive to myself and others. As the Dalai Lama famously observed, resentment is the poison meant for the other that ultimately can destroy myself. As Martin Luther King Jr. noted, revenge is an ineffective transformative strategy; hate cannot drive out hate—only love can do that.

As our great wisdom traditions all teach us, the medicine for violence is the realization of connection and relationship. In our increasingly crowded and technologically advanced civilization, more of humanity than ever before is aware of the ways that each of us is connected not only with our families and local communities but also with our global community and with the ecosystems that support all life.

In this chapter, transformation is described as a process that involves three key elements: empowerment, growth, and relationship.

EMPOWERMENT

Empowerment can be thought of as a self-advocacy practice that can occur on any of the personal, social, local, and global levels. The transformation of sociohistorical trauma may thus be associated with individual, family, local community, and even global levels of empowerment (Gawain, 2000).

Researchers have recorded many situations where individuals, families, and communities have generated an empowerment response to trauma. Empowerment has been, for example, a response to mass-casualty terrorism, genocide, poverty, war, and political imprisonment (see Bussey & Wise, 2007). Through transformation, people can gradually gain the safety, opportunities, resources, will, and skills that can help them improve their lives.

Empowerment and Transformational Learning Theory

The transformation of sociohistorical trauma may incorporate elements of transformational learning. Transfomational learning is a model developed by educational theorists that can help describe the conditions and nature of the empowerment process. This process may happen in many contexts, including in the formal classroom, in the family, or on an individual level.

In transformational learning, the individual engages in critical reflection, changes her frame of reference, and develops new assumptions about her world. This kind of learning may be most likely to occur when the person engages in conversations with others about how they think and feel (Mezirow, 1994). In other words, as will be further described in Chapter 3, transformational learning can happen when people engage in dialogue with each other. Transformation, like dialogue, has both individual and collective elements.

The word *educate* literally comes from the Latin root *ducare* ("to lead") and prefix *e* ("out"), and thus to educate is to draw out. However, Western education has arguably become a process where the "expert" teacher tends more to "fill in" knowledge and skills and values for the student. Milojevic (2005) has argued, for example, that students in contemporary state education in the United States are essentially fed one future, which is the expected ongoing growth of the global marketplace. Similarly, education in nations across the globe has also been critiqued as incorporating corporate and "consumerist" themes (see "Carnivalesque Rebellion Week," 2010).

In contrast, in transformational learning, self-reflection and creativity are encouraged by the teacher, who strives to share power with students in her classroom. Many possible futures are possible. In this process, learning is especially facilitated when the class is learner centered; the instructor provides an atmosphere of safety, openness, and trust, and students are encouraged to engage in critical reflection (Taylor, 1998). Students find their own meanings in the process. Transformational learning tends to be self-directed but does not have to be problem solving or practical. In fact, sources of information may include feelings, dreams, and imagination. Artistic activities such as film, poetry, and music may especially assist in promoting experiential learning (Cranton, 2006).

Transformational learning is thus potentially both individual and collective. Participants engage in a "praxis" that incorporates both reflection and action. Such transformation involves self-reflection followed up by social action and more self-reflection, in an ongoing process. In such social transformation, the learners engage actively in their learning, they rediscover their own empowerment, and society itself hopefully changes. People's engagement in self-education may lead to their active opposition to oppression (Freire, 1970).

In the transformation process, people may have to master and thus "pass through" a "threshold concept" that helps open them to viewing their world in new ways. Individuals and groups are best facilitated in passing through such a threshold when their teacher uses experiential approaches that empower the student's control over her own learning. Such transformation is not just about a cognitive breakthrough, however, but also involves the development of new ways of feeling and acting in the world. In this process, participants may engage in original reflection, problem-solving skills, wisdom, and creativity (Hays, 2008).

Transformation and Empowerment in Oppressed, Minoritized, or Non-Western Populations

When non-Western people become more empowered, their transformation may not fit with Western theories about trauma and transformation (Hoshmand, 2006). Every individual and every population in the world may have unique transformational experiences. As noted above, trauma has become a very popular subject in Western psychology. However, since ethnocultural factors strongly influence the person's reactions to traumas, Western psychology does not necessarily explain the coping styles of people across the world (Wong, Wong, & Lonner, 2005).

Some researchers report that a blend of mainstream psychology, ethnic indigenous healing, and sociopolitical action can lead to individual and collective transformation for oppressed populations (Comas-Diaz, 2007). For example, a four-generation American Indian family has maintained family identity and developed a "narrative of resilience" that emphasizes service to family and others and the development of hope for the future (Denham, 2008). In another study, Cherokee people were reported to cope through a style of self-reliance based on self-discipline, self-confidence, and personal responsibility. The researchers reported that style was best understood through the stories people told about how they dealt with stress (Lowe, Riggs, Henson, & Liehr, 2009). For Canadian aboriginal peoples, "residential school syndrome" is hypothesized to be associated with forced attendance in Canadian residential schools (similar to the boarding schools used in the United States with American Indians). In response to such trauma, some aboriginal people have transformed their community culture, using their own traditional cultural approaches (Robertson, 2006).

Not surprisingly, each person's worldview and social consciousness seem to interact with their transformational processes. As social consciousness grows, the person moves from awareness "embedded" in the self to an engaged and collaborative global citizen (Schlitz, Vieten, & Miller, 2010). When trauma-recipients believe that they have a shared experience of oppression within their culture, they seem to be able to make effective sense of their suffering, and they become more empowered to resist and respond effectively to oppression (Johnson, Thompson, & Downs, 2008). Social transformations in such areas as immigration, wages, and housing have been organized through "religious collaboratives" such as the National Farm Worker Ministry or Evangelicals for Environmental Responsibility (Harper, 2009).

EXPERIENTIAL LEARNING 2.1

(1) What is the difference between a "positive" and "negative" transformation? Describe a situation in your life when you have experienced one and a situation when you experienced the other.

(2) What is empowerment? Can someone else empower another person? To what extent do you feel empowered?

(3) What does the root of the word *educate* actually mean? Has your educational experience in your life conformed to this meaning?

(4) What is transformational learning? Have you had transformational learning experience in your life? Describe one.

(5) How might non-Western people experience empowerment and transformation differently than Western people?

POSTTRAUMATIC GROWTH

Posttraumatic growth is usually associated with the transformation process. Posttraumatic growth is physical, emotional, cognitive, social, and/or spiritual development following the traumatic experience. Although there has been growing enthusiasm for this subject in the recent literature, posttraumatic growth is not a new concept. Themes of growth following suffering have appeared in literatures and philosophies throughout history.

In the 1990s, domains of posttraumatic growth were theorized, including self-perception, relationships, and life philosophy (Tedeschi & Calhoun, 1995). Researchers found that trauma survivors can experience a variety of positive outcomes, including new purpose and priorities, better relationships, improved personal resources, more positive life view, greater personal strength, and spiritual development (Tedeschi & Calhoun, 1996, 2004). A factor analysis of data collected from trauma survivors provided five factors associated with posttraumatic growth, including enhanced personal strength, opening to new possibilities, developing healthier relationships, greater life appreciation, and spiritual growth (Calhoun & Tedeschi, 2006).

A study of 16 parents whose children were murdered, for example, showed that even this kind of trauma can ultimately result in a positive transformation for the parent as well as for the larger society. These parents showed such characteristics as an increased gratitude for life, strong belief system, social supports, self-care, and compassion (Parappully, Rosenbaum, van den Daele, & Nzewi, 2002). In another study, adolescent Cambodian refugees in Montreal with posttraumatic stress disorder (PTSD) were found to have developed developmental strengths as a result of their refugee experiences (Rousseau, Drapeau, & Platt, 1999). About 83% of women living with human immunodeficiency virus (HIV) infections reported that their illness had helped bring about at least one positive change in their lives. These changes included relationships, self-view, value of life, new healthy behaviors, spirituality, and career goals (Siegel & Schrimshaw, 2000).

Posttraumatic growth can be supported by both interpersonal and intrapersonal factors. Clinical interventions that focus on such internal processes as the development of personal strength and appreciation of life can help facilitate posttraumatic growth (Ickovics et al., 2006). Posttraumatic growth interacts with such personal traits as evolving life wisdom and life narratives and is an ongoing process. Posttraumatic growth seems to be associated with a number of processes, including the gradual reduction of initial automatic rumination, increased self-disclosure through writing and talking, enhanced spiritual activity and social support, reduction of emotional distress, and positive schema change (Tedeschi & Calhoun, 2004).

Resilience

Resilience is a process in which the person learns to adapt successfully to suffering and may include the elements of simple recovery, resistance, and future reconfiguration. Resilience may be promoted through such personal qualities as coping skills, intelligence, and optimism as well as environmental qualities such as social support and a safe physical environment (Lepore & Revenson, 2006). In resilience theory, posttraumatic growth could be thought of as especially related to the "future reconfiguration" element noted above, when the individual starts to develop in new and positive ways.

The concept of resilience was first used to describe the ability of some children who were able to overcome traumatic experiences in urban neighborhoods and became high-functioning adults (Garmezy & Nuechterlein, 1972). Resilience is different from simple recovery, in that in resilience, the person may not experience even temporary symptoms following trauma. Such resilience is relatively common and can be associated with such strategies as hardiness, self-enhancement, positive emotion, laughter, and repression of negative emotion and thought (Bonanno, 2004). Five elements have been identified in coping styles related to resilience, including family support, individual acceptance and striving, religion and spirituality, ability to use avoidance and detachment, and emotional outlets (Heppner et al., 2006). Resilience to physical and mental health, trauma stress, and PTSD severity has been found to be associated with spiritual beliefs and ability to control anger. Individual resilience is associated with physical health and PTSD severity (Connor, Davidson, & Lee, 2003).

Spirituality, Religion, and Transformational Growth

William James (1902) was the first modern Westerner to write about spiritual transformations in association with what he called the "varieties of religious experience." In the century since the time of James, researchers have found that both spiritual and religious growth can be stimulated by trauma and that both can also support posttraumatic growth (Ai & Park, 2005). For example, a systematic review of 11 empirical studies shows that religion and spirituality are often helpful in trauma, that trauma can lead to a deepening of belief, and that posttraumatic growth is usually associated with religious openness, religious coping, ability to face existential questions, and participation in religion (Shaw, Joseph, & Linley, 2005).

The Spiritual Transformation Scientific Research Program (STP, 2010) has found evidence of psychosocial, biological, and cultural factors associated with spiritual transformation. For example, people may incorporate new rituals in their lives, develop greater empathy for others, and draw on the courage to experience new forms of consciousness. Researchers have also found that although spiritual transformation is not always experienced as positive, people may come to discover and value what is most sacred to them (Koss-Chioino & Hefner, 2006).

There are neurobiological correlates to spiritual transformation. What one theorist calls the practice of "mindsight," or the use of one's mind to analyze its own thought processes, can help change brain function and thus enable personal transformation (Siegel, 2010). Mindsight takes advantage of the brain's neuroplasticity to develop intuition (thought to be centered in the middle prefrontal cortex) and empathy and moral awareness (in the middle prefrontal region). Increasing evidence of human brain plasticity in children and adults confirms that such transformations can occur across the life span (Koerth-Baker, 2009). Researchers have found increases in radical empathy (experiencing the suffering of the other as if it is one's own) and in other elements of spiritual transformation to be linked with neuroplasticity (Koss-Chioino & Hefner, 2006). Even changes in beliefs can measurably alter brain structures (Schwartz & Begley, 2002).

Transpersonal Psychology and Transformation

Transpersonal psychology (see Chapter 9) is the study of the spiritual dimension of human development. Many transpersonalists have commented on the association of spiritual development with traumatic life experiences (Wilber, 1997). Largely building on the integral philosophy of Ken Wilber, Combs (2009) offered a view of transformation that involves all parts of the body-mind-spirit system. Transpersonal transformation is a change in consciousness characterized by shifts in how the person sees herself and the world (Mandala-Schlitz, Vieten, & Amorok, 2007).

Wilber (2006) compares and contrasts transformation with what he calls translation. Translation is actually a defense in which the self protects its continued existence by substituting radical change with cognitive change. Current beliefs may be "translated" into new beliefs that may seem to be revolutionary. In other words, translation is mostly a cognitive, frontal lobe process, used to "protect" lower, more limbic (emotional) processes. In transformation, however, the self itself is examined, and the person's identification with self is gradually diminished (Wilber, Engler, & Brown, 1986).

EXPERIENTIAL LEARNING 2.2

(1) What is posttraumatic growth? Describe one way that you have experienced posttraumatic growth.

(2) What is resilience? In what ways have you been resilient, in the face of a life difficulty? What do you believe made you resilient?

(3) Can you relate personally to the idea of spiritual (and/or religious) transformation? Explain.

RELATIONAL TRANSFORMATION

Transformation of sociohistorical trauma is always relational. Since the trauma was relational, the healing process must also be relational. Relational transformation involves in part a dialogue with the self, in which the person becomes gradually more aware and accepting of all her parts. Relational transformation also involves dialogue with the Other (who may be one person, a group of people, or larger aspects of my world). In this process of relating, I hope to create healthier relationships not only with my own self but also with other people and the larger world I live in and with their ecosystems (see, e.g., Calhoun & Tedeschi, 2006).

Relational Transformation With Self

In relational transformation, the person becomes increasingly skilled at intrapersonal dialogue, which is effective "conversation" with and expression of all the "parts" of self (see Chapter 5). As the person becomes more whole or healthy, she seeks to better understand all her parts and share them with others in each moment. What are the "parts" of self in this dialogue? Several models may be especially useful in describing our intrapsychic world and understanding transformation.

Elements of transpersonal psychology (Wilber, 1997, 2006) and transactional analysis (Berne, 1958) can be combined to describe a model useful for understanding internal dialogue (see Derezotes, 2006). Study of the great wisdom traditions of the world suggest that people can relate at the prepersonal, personal, and transpersonal levels of consciousness (Wilber et al., 1986). These levels can be thought of as three essential "ego states" or parts of the self that work best when they are in good dialogic relationship with each other.

The prepersonal is the consciousness of a child, before ("pre") the adult personality is developed, and includes the ability to be spontaneous, enjoy pleasure, and play. The personal is the consciousness of the adult and includes the responsibilities, roles, belongings, beliefs, and so on that people develop as they mature. Perhaps most difficult to understand, the transpersonal is the ego state from which a person can "watch" the rest of her self and the world. In the transpersonal ego state, the person is capable of more objective awareness, contemplation, and meditation, and it includes the ability to "disidentify from" or "go beyond" (trans) the roles, belongings, and beliefs of the adult personality. Disidentification from the personality (or "mask") of the adult simply means that the person realizes that there is more to her than her personality and refuses to value her own roles, belongings, and beliefs more than her connection with others.

These three "ego states" are illustrated in Figure 2.1. Since, in the prepersonal ego state, the child is dominant, the child is drawn in the largest circle. Similarly, the parent is inside the largest circle in the personal ego state, where it is dominant. Finally, the observing self (OS) is inside the largest circle in the transpersonal ego state because the observing self is dominant there.

Thus, in one day, a person may choose to relate to the world and herself from any and all of these three levels of consciousness. For example, when it is time to get up in the morning, the prepersonal child may want to lie in bed because she still feels tired from the night before. However, eventually, the personal adult will coax the child out of bed, knowing that she has to get to work. Later on in the day, the observing self may dominate and simply observe the child and adult interact during some reflective time after lunch.

Figure 2.1   Levels of Consciousness

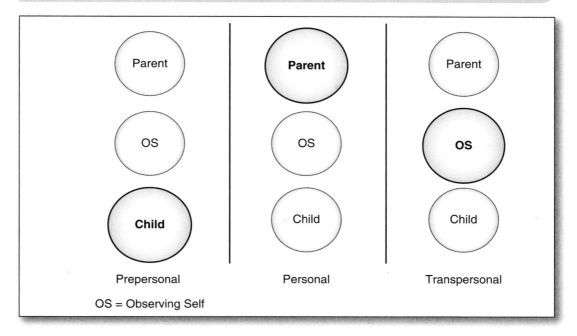

Developmental Dimensions

Human development includes the physical, emotional, cognitive, social, and spiritual dimensions. Transformation also involves an increasing dialogue between these "parts" of the self (see Derezotes, 2000). In this intrapsychic dialogue model, the observing self is drawn in the middle, facilitating conversation between these elements of human development (see Figure 2.2).

Body Parts

The human body has many physical "parts" or "members." Relational transformation can also include an increasingly effective dialogue with these body parts as well. Each part or member of the body can be considered to have its own wisdom (Johnson, 1991). For example, we often say we have a "gut" feeling, referring to the wisdom of our digestive system. Obviously, our body parts do not always agree on every subject. For example, while the heart may not love someone, the genitals may lust after them. A dialogue between different body wisdoms may help the person make life decisions. In this model, the observing self is also drawn in the middle, facilitating conversation between various body "parts" (see Figure 2.3; only a few examples of body parts are shown).

The general goal of relational transformation can be thought of as the ability of a person to move her awareness and expressions intentionally between levels of consciousness, developmental dimensions, or sources of body wisdom (see Chapter 10).

Figure 2.2   Developmental Dimensions Dialogue

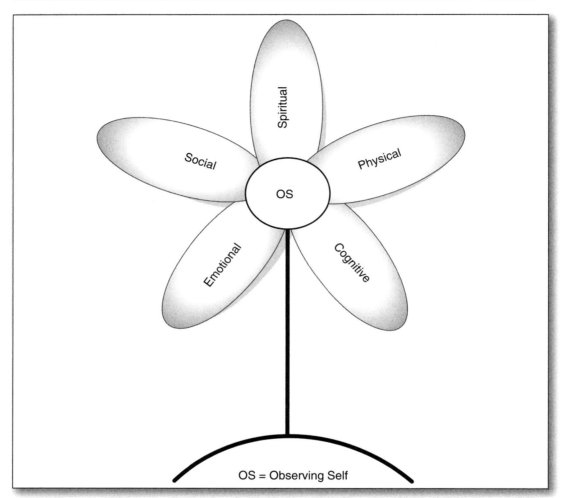

OS = Observing Self

Relational Transformation Between People

In relational transformation, intimate relationships are co-created where people are empowered to share any or all the levels of consciousness (prepersonal, personal, and transpersonal), the dimensions of human development (physical, emotional, cognitive, social, spiritual), and the body wisdoms. The establishment of healthy relationships, or relational transformation, may however go through a relatively turbulent and uncharted process involving hurt, fear, anger, and ultimately forgiveness.

What is forgiveness? Forgiveness is a long-term goal of transformation of sociohistorical trauma. Nonviolent empowerment and posttraumatic growth may initially be "fueled" by anger toward the perpetrators of trauma. For example, a battered woman may need to get

Figure 2.3   Body Parts Dialogue

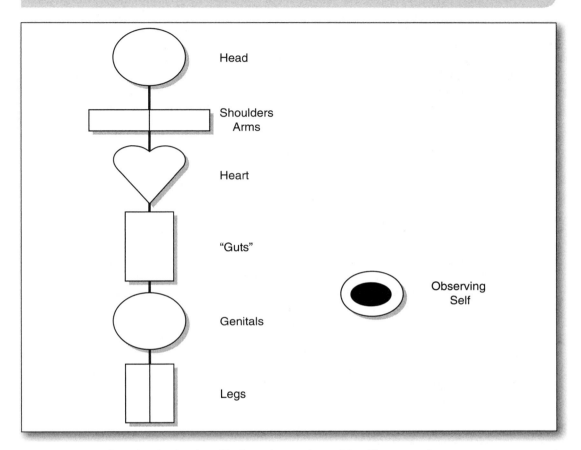

angry at her abusive husband before she can leave him. However, she may not want to stay angry her whole life, simply because her resentment poisons her own life more than it harms her perpetrator. Forgiveness is the "letting go of anger" so that there is room for peace. Forgiveness is about the trauma recipient's decision to live free of resentment and hatred and is not about acceptance of the trauma perpetrator's behavior.

Forgiveness is one of the ultimate goals of the process of relational transformation. Worthington's (1998) pyramid model of forgiveness has five stages, including recollection of the original trauma and suffering, empathizing with the perpetrator of the trauma, offering the gift of forgiveness, committing to forgive, and holding onto forgiveness.

Forgiveness may well also have a neurological basis. Forgiveness seems to involve processes, at least in part, in the parietal lobes, where we create our sense of self, distinct from others. Some researchers have found evidence that positive, loving, and compassionate beliefs are associated with health and happiness (Newberg & Waldman, 2009).

The development of healthy relationships also requires in part the ability to be empathic with and listen to others. One physiological correlate for social mirroring, collective consciousness, and transformation may be in mirror neurons in premotor and posterior parietal cortices that respond to actions and intentions of others as well as mirror neurons in the anterior insula and anterior cingulate cortices that seem to be related to empathy and language (Combs & Kripper, 2008). Brain imaging has recently shown that people who listen well to each other actually have measurable parallel brain activities (Barth, 2011).

As described in Chapter 1, epigenetic changes in trait expression can occur from one generation to the next. DNA traits can be expressed in new ways from one generation to the next (Church, 2008). Change in consciousness and belief can alter genetic expression through epigenetic processes during a life span (Lipton, 2005). The frontal lobe, which directs higher order, purposeful behavior, can create new brain structures and decide what information (including traumatic histories and associated meanings) is most useful (Goldberg, 2001). Even the aging brain develops wisdom, seeks social contacts, optimizes challenges, and wants to serve others (Cozolino, 2008).

As will be further described in Chapter 3, relational transformation can occur through dialogue. The experiences of listening and responding, mutual empathy, authenticity, mutuality, and sensitive humor (all elements of dialogue) can help transform relationships (Hartling, Rosen, Walker, & Jordan, 2000). Service to others is one way for people to experience transformation in relationships. Dialogic conversation in the classroom is especially transformative when students are involved in and reflect on a service activity and develop personal values and civic responsibility (Sutton, 2010). Relationship building usually takes time. Research of intergroup dialogue with college students suggests that personal transformation varies from person to person but can begin in a surprisingly small number of group meetings (Messer, 2008).

Changes in relationship can be described, for example, through story inquiry, an approach that can be used to understand transformation following trauma (Rateau, 2010). Elements in story inquiry include what matters most to the person, the meanings the person gives to her experience, the general plot, the resolution process, and a synthesis of findings that inform the research question (Liehr & Smith, 2008). There is also a literature about the transformation of romantic relationships through a commitment to love (Wade, 1999).

EXPERIENTIAL LEARNING 2.3

(1) Do you agree with the author when he says that transformation of sociohistorical trauma is always relational? Explain.

(2) Describe a transformation you have had in relation with your self.

(3) Can you describe a transformation you have experienced in your relationships with other people?

(4) Would you like to have a transformation in your relationships with other living things and the ecosystems that support life? How could dialogue help that process?

Transformation of Relationship With the Ecosystem

Transformation can also occur with the relationships that the person has with other living things and with the ecosystems that support all life. The philosophy of deep ecology is dialogic in the sense that environmentalism needs to consider not only the well-being of humans but also the welfare of other living things (Naess, 1973). Many authors extend this concern to the well-being of the ecosystems that sustain us, such as "Mother Earth" (Snyder, 1990). This concern for other living things and ecosystems has been framed as being consistent with the major wisdom traditions of the world (Fox, 1988). Some authors believe that if we listen to the ancient ways of knowing, languages, and stories of our hunter-gatherer ancestors, then 21st-century people can gain a reconnection with the "natural" world (Abram, 1996).

VIGNETTE: DIALOGUE

One definition of dialogue is to take part in a conversation in order to resolve a problem. However, for me dialogue is taking part in a conversation in order to resolve the self. It is the exploration of oneself that allows us to effectively engage in dialogue with others. Dialogue is the ability to express one's paradigm while allowing the space for others to express theirs as well. In order to do so, one must go beyond the need to have a definitive right and wrong. The desire to be right and make others wrong is typical behavior of a debate or argument. Rather, dialogue is not to debate, argue, or even agree with one another. It is not to get others on your side or to take the last word. Dialogue is a transformation from the conversations of debate to a higher level of communication whose main purpose seeks to understand. Dialogue shows respect. It is humble, gracious, even in a fit of anger. It does not mock or judge. It does not attack or cower at the same time.

In my work with people who have come to the United States as refugees, I have witnessed transformations through dialogue. Refugees are victims of the most horrendous violations of human rights. They are survivors of torture, trafficking, and exploitation. Each refugee brings with them their own experiences from war and trauma, value systems, politics, ethics, and processes of gathering, communicating, and addressing conflicts within their community in order to heal and rebuild their lives.

As a result of vulnerability, upon arrival in the United States, refugees can find themselves again the target of abuse and are taken advantage of, marginalizing them further to the outskirts of society. As parents, refugees find themselves looking to their English-speaking children to keep the family going, causing a power shift among their roles as the provider. This results in refugee men feeling ashamed, helpless, and stripped of their power. Their children feel confused, cheated out of their childhood with pressures and responsibilities piling up. Refugee women fear what will happen to their families as time goes on and children leave the home. The entire family structure, once familiar, turns on its head. Such conflicts can be addressed through developing the skills and knowledge of how to bring the voices of mom, dad, and child together in dialogue. In-depth discussions on spousal/parent-children relationships, ethnic conflicts, religion, gender differences, and war and trauma can rebuild families and begin the process of healing.

When dialogue is successful, value systems within self and community surely increase, creating stronger community structures. The love and commitment between equal marriage partners; the respect shared between neighbor, parent, and child; and reverence for self can help derail us from the paths of conflict. As a member of our global community, I feel strongly that dialogue is not only helpful in bridging community divides—it is essential for the cultivation of understanding oneself.

Vignette Author: Emily Perry

Emily began her work in the refugee community 5 years ago when she became a Refugee Family Mentor. She worked extensively among the refugee community for several years as a Refugee Job Developer for both Catholic Community Services and the Asian Association of Utah before coming to the Utah Refugee Coalition as the Director of Development. Her background is in International Studies with an emphasis in Global Justice and Human Rights, as well as Peace and Conflict Resolution.

REFERENCES

Abram, D. (1996). *Spell of the sensuous: Perception and language in a more-than-human world*. New York: Pantheon.

Ai, A. L., & Park, C. L. (2005). Possibilities of the positive following violence and trauma: Informing the coming decade of research. *Journal of Interpersonal Violence, 20*(240), 241–250.

Barth, A. (2011, January/February). Good listeners get inside your head. *Discover,* p. 71.

Berne, E. (1958). Transactional analysis: A new and effective method of group therapy. *American Journal of Psychotherapy, 12,* 735–743.

Bonanno, G. A. (2004). Loss, trauma, and human resilience: Have we underestimated the human capacity to thrive after extremely aversive events? *American Psychologist, 59*(1), 20–28.

Bussey, M., & Wise, J. B. (Eds.). (2007). *Trauma transformed: An empowerment response*. New York: Columbia University Press.

Calhoun, L. G., & Tedeschi, R. G. (2006). The foundations of posttraumatic growth: An expanded framework. In L. G. Calhoun & R. G. Tedeschi (Eds.), *Handbook of posttraumatic growth: Research and practice* (pp. 3–23). Mahwah, NJ: Lawrence Erlbaum.

Carnivalesque rebellion week. (2010, November 22–28). *Adbusters*.

Church, D. (2008). *Epigenetic medicine: The new biology of medicine: The genie in your genes*. Santa Rosa, CA: Energy Psychology Press.

Comas-Diaz, L. (2007). Ethnopoliticalpsychology: Healing and transformation. In E. Aldarondo (Ed.), *Advancing social justice through clinical practice* (pp. 91–118). Mahwah, NJ: Lawrence Erlbaum.

Combs, A. (2009). *Consciousness explained better: Towards an integral understanding of the multifaceted nature of consciousness*. New York: Omega Books.

Combs, A., & Kripper, S. (2008). Collective consciousness and the social brain. *Journal of Consciousness Studies, 15*(10–11), 264–276.

Connor, K. M., Davidson, J. R. T., & Lee, L. (2003). Spirituality, resilience, and anger in survivors of violent trauma: A community survey. *Journal of Traumatic Stress, 16*(5), 487–494.

Cozolino, L. (2008). *The healthy aging brain: Sustaining attachment, attaining wisdom*. New York: W. W. Norton.

Cranton, P. (2006). *Understanding and promoting transformative learning*. San Francisco: Jossey-Bass.

Denham, A. R. (2008, September). Rethinking historical trauma: Narratives of resilience. *Transcultural Psychiatry,* pp. 391–414.

Derezotes, D. S. (2000). *Advanced generalist social work practice*. Thousand Oaks, CA: Sage.

Derezotes, D. S. (2006). *Spiritually oriented social work practice*. Boston: Pearson.

Ferguson, M. (1980). *The Aquarian conspiracy.* New York: J. P. Tarcher.

Fox, M. (1988). *The coming of the cosmic Christ: The healing of Mother Earth and the birth of a global renaissance.* San Francisco: Harper & Row.

Freire, P. (1970). *Pedagogy of the oppressed.* New York: Continuum.

Garmezy, N., & Nuechterlein, K. (1972). Invulnerable children: The fact and fiction of competence and disadvantage. *American Journal of Orthopsychiatry, 42,* 328–329.

Gawain, S. (2000). *The path of transformation: How healing ourselves can change the world.* New York: New World Library.

Goldberg, E. (2001). *The executive brain: Frontal lobes and the civilized mind.* New York: Oxford University Press.

Harper, N. (2009). *Journeys into justice: Religious collaborative working for social transformation.* Minneapolis, MN: Beacon Hill.

Hartling, L., Rosen, W., Walker, M., & Jordan, J. (2000). *Shame and humiliation: From isolation to relational transformation* (Work in Progress 88). Wellesley, MA: Stone Center for Developmental Services and Studies.

Hays, J. M. (2008). Threshold and transformation. *European Journal of Management, 8*(3), 24–46.

Heppner, P. P., Heppner, M. J., Lee, D., Wang, Y., Park, H.-J., & Wang, L. (2006). Development and evaluation of a collectivist coping styles inventory. *Journal of Counseling Psychology, 53*(1), 107–125.

Hoshmand, L. T. (2006). Culture-informed theory, research, and practice in global trauma work. *Asian Journal of Counseling, 13*(1), 145–160.

Ickovics, J. R., Meade, C. S., Kershaw, T. S., Milan, S., Lewis, J. B., & Ethier, K. A. (2006). Urban teens: Trauma, posttraumatic growth, and emotional distress among female adolescents. *Journal of Counseling and Clinical Psychology, 74*(5), 841–850.

James, W. (1902). *The varieties of religious experience.* New York: Longmans, Greens & Company.

Johnson, H., Thompson, A., & Downs, M. (2008). Non-Western interpreter's experiences of trauma: The protective role of culture following exposure to oppression. *Ethnicity & Health, 14*(4), 407–418.

Johnson, M. (1991). Knowing through the body. *Philosophical Psychology, 4*(1), 3–18.

Koerth-Baker, M. (2009, November/December). Monitoring live brains reveals plasticity. *Scientific American,* p. 6.

Koss-Chioino, J. D., & Hefner, P. (2006). *Spiritual healing and transformation: Anthropological, theological, neuroscientific, and clinical perspectives.* Lanham, MD: AltaMira Press.

Lepore, S. J., & Revenson, T. A. (2006). The foundations of posttraumatic growth: An expanded framework. In L. G. Calhoun & R. G. Tedeschi (Eds.), *Handbook of posttraumatic growth: Research and practice* (pp. 24–46). Mahwah, NJ: Lawrence Erlbaum.

Leslie, L., & Leslie, S. (2005). What is transformation? http://www.crossroad.to/articles2/05/sarah-leslie/transformation.htm

Liehr, P. L., & Smith, M. J. (2008). Story inquiry: A method for research. *Archives of Psychiatric Nursing, 21*(2), 120–121.

Lipton, B. H. (2005). *The biology of belief: Unleashing the power of consciousness, matter, and miracles.* Carlsbad, CA: Hayhouse Inc.

Lowe, J., Riggs, C., Henson, J., & Liehr, P. (2009). Cherokee self-reliance and word-use in stories of stress. *Journal of Cultural Diversity, 16*(1), 5–9.

Mandala-Schlitz, M., Vieten, C., & Amorok, T. (2007). *Living deeply: The art and science of transformation in everyday life.* Oakland, CA: New Harbinger.

Messer, R. A. (2008). *The mystery and the sacred: A phenomenological case study of personal transformation through reflective intergroup dialogue.* Unpublished dissertation, Gonzaga University. http://gradworks.umi.com/33/27/3327688.html

Mezirow, J. (1994). Understanding transformation theory. *Adult Education Quarterly, 44*(4), 222–232.

Milojevic, I. (2005). *Educational futures: Dominant and contesting visions.* London: Routledge.

Naess, A. (1973). The shallow and the deep, long-range ecology movement: A summary. *Inquiry, 16,* 95–100.

Newberg, A., & Waldman, M. R. (2009). *How God changes your brain: Breakthrough findings from a leading neuroscientist.* New York: Ballantine.

Parappully, J., Rosenbaum, R., van den Daele, L., & Nzewi, E. (2002). Thriving after trauma: The experience of parents of murdered children. *Journal of Humanistic Psychology, 42*(33), 32–70.

Rateau, M. (2010). A story of transformation following catastrophic loss. *Archives of Psychiatric Nursing, 24*(4), 260–265.

Robertson, L. H. (2006). The residential school experience: Syndrome or historic trauma. *Pimatisiwin, 4*(1), 1–28.

Rousseau, C., Drapeau, A., & Platt, R. (1999). Family trauma and its association with emotional and behavioral problems and social adjustment in adolescent Cambodian refugees. *Child Abuse & Neglect, 23*(12), 1263–1273.

Schlitz, M. M., Vieten, C., & Miller, E. M. (2010). Worldview transformation and the development of social consciousness. *Journal of Consciousness Studies, 17*(7–8), 18–36.

Schwartz, J. M., & Begley, S. (2002). *The mind and the brain: Neuroplasticity and the power of mental force.* New York: Harper.

Shaw, A., Joseph, S., & Linley, P. A. (2005). Religion, spirituality, and posttraumatic growth: A systematic review. *Mental Health, Religion & Culture, 8*(1), 1–11.

Siegel, D. J. (2010). *Mindsight: The new science of personal transformation.* New York: Random House.

Siegel, K., & Schrimshaw, E. W. (2000). Perceiving benefits in adversity: Stress-related growth in women living with HIV/AIDS. *Social Science and Medicine, 51,* 1543–1554.

Snyder, G. (1990). *The practice of the wild.* San Francisco: North Point Press.

STP. (2010). The Spiritual Transformation Scientific Research Program. http://www.spiritual transformationresearch.org/about/index.html

Sutton, S. B. (2010). Experiencing dialogue: Conversation as transformation. *Practicing Anthropology, 32*(3), 49–53.

Taylor, E. W. (1998). *The theory and practice of transformative learning: A critical review* (Contract No. RR93002001). Columbus, OH: Center on Education and Training for Employment. (ERIC Document Reproduction Service No. ED423422)

Tedeschi, R. G., & Calhoun, L. G. (1995). *Trauma and transformation: Growing in the aftermath of suffering.* Thousand Oaks, CA: Sage.

Tedeschi, R. G., & Calhoun, L. G. (1996). The Posttraumatic Growth Inventory: Measuring the positive legacy of trauma. *Journal of Trauma Stress, 9,* 455–471.

Tedeschi, R. G., & Calhoun, L. G. (2004). Posttraumatic growth: Conceptual foundation and empirical evidence. *Psychological Inquiry, 15*(1), 1–18.

Wade, B. (1999). *Love lessons: A guide to transforming relationships.* New York: Harper.

Wilber, K. (1997). *The eye of the spirit: An integral vision for a world gone slightly mad.* Boston: Shambhala.

Wilber, K. (2006). *Integral spirituality: A startling new role for religion in the modern and postmodern world.* Boston: Shambhala.

Wilber, K., Engler, J., & Brown, D. (1986). *Transformations of consciousness.* Boston: Shambhala.

Wong, T. P., Wong, L. C., & Lonner, W. J. (2005). *Handbook of multicultural perspectives on stress and coping.* New York: Springer.

Worthington, E. L. (1998). The pyramid model of forgiveness: Some interdisciplinary speculations about unforgiveness and the promotion of forgiveness. In E. L. Worthington (Ed.), *Dimensions of forgiveness: Psychological research & theological forgiveness* (pp. 107–138). West Conshohocken, PA: Templeton Press.

Dialogue Practice

INTRODUCTION AND DEFINITIONS

Dialogue helps make us human. We humans are relational mammals who seem to be designed to seek connection with each other and our larger world. Through dialogue, we can learn to better understand ourselves and others, and we can develop sustainable cooperative and intimate relationships. Dialogue challenges us to do some of the most difficult work humans can do, so that we can achieve the highest levels of development humans can reach. Such work requires uncovering our personal and collective histories as well as the complex emotional, cognitive, physical, and spiritual reactions we experience in our interactions with others. In dialogue, we can ultimately learn to know and love ourselves and others, make meaning out of suffering, and ultimately co-create healthier communities.

In Chapters 1 and 2, the concepts of sociohistorical trauma and transformation are explored. In the United States, most approaches to trauma emphasize the treatment of the individual's symptoms. Dialogue is an approach that emphasizes relationship and community building. Although dialogue can be used in work with most forms of trauma, in this text the focus is on the use of dialogue in transforming sociohistorical trauma. In Chapter 3, the foundations of dialogue are described. In subsequent chapters, more specific theories, knowledge, values, and skills for dialogue are described.

A working theory of dialogue is summarized in Figure 3.1 and further expanded in the text below.

(1) Dialogue is a nonviolent relationship-building practice . . .

The purpose of dialogue is to build relationships. Dialogue is a practice because it involves the use of relationship-building skills that must be practiced.

Nonviolent means that every voice in the dialogue is equally valued and that no attempt to silence voices is tolerated, including the use of psychological, economic, or physical abuse or the threat of any abuse. Nonviolent does not mean that dialogue will necessarily be comfortable or easy. Nonviolent also does not mean that participants cannot express the full range of emotions. Anger, for example, is as acceptable of an emotion as any other, but in dialogue, participants are learning how to express anger nonviolently and in ways that build sustainable relationships.

Figure 3.1 A Theory of Dialogue

Dialogue

(1)   is a nonviolent relationship-building practice . . .

(2)   . . . with shared commitment to parallel intrapersonal and interpersonal (or ecological) work . . .

(3)   . . . directed toward increasing mutual understanding, acceptance, and empowerment . . .

(4)   . . . necessary for our collective transformation from "trauma-repetition" toward sustainable, equitable, and peaceful communities.

> (2) . . . with shared commitment to parallel intrapersonal, interpersonal, and ecological work . . .

Shared commitment means that participants recognize that relationships take time to develop, particularly across cultural, racial, ideological, and other difficult divides, and therefore agree to continue to meet together through both easy and difficult sessions.

Parallel work refers to how individual (intrapersonal) work and relationship-building (interpersonal and ecological) work are interdependent and mutually reinforcing processes in the dialogue. Individual, couple, family, group, community, ecosystem, and global well-being are all understood to be interrelated, and dialogue can be focused on any or all of these levels.

Intrapersonal work includes the person's development of her own interrelated physical, emotional, cognitive, social, and spiritual dimensions. In such work, the person becomes more aware of her body, feelings, thoughts, reactions to others, and spiritual experiences. Physical development brings the ability to understand and express the wisdom of the brain and the rest of the body. Emotional maturity is a process of learning to understand and accept emotions and to effectively control or express them. Cognitive development brings the increasing ability to understand the origins and results of one's thinking patterns. Social maturity is about the understanding and mastery of the complex reactions that every person has to other people in her environment. Spiritual development could be said to include each person's unique and gradual understanding of the meanings, values, and connections that the person has with her world.

In intrapersonal work, the person develops what could be called vertical intimacy, which is increasing reverent connection with self. Interpersonal work includes development of relationship-building skills with other people that facilitate horizontal intimacy (reverent connection with others). She is able to express these internal experiences with others in a proactive (rather than reactive) manner, in ways that enhance her relationships.

Ecological work refers to dialogue with other living things and ecosystems. Dialogue facilitators can create exercises designed to give "voices" to living things and ecosystems. Obviously, the relationship between a person and other living things is different than interpersonal relationships, but dialogue theory suggests that humans can have relationships with other living things and ecosystems and that these relationships are important to well-being.

Dialogue theory suggests that intrapersonal and relationship-building work always go hand in hand. The participant who is working on listening to others will also become better at listening to her self, for example, and participants who become more empathic toward others will likely find more empathy for themselves as well.

> (3) . . . directed toward increasing the mutual understanding, acceptance, and empowerment . . .

Participants learn that in successful dialogue, participants value mutual understanding, mutual acceptance, and mutual empowerment. Understanding and acceptance go hand in hand. Increased understanding without acceptance can become an informed hatred, and increased acceptance without understanding is a form of blind love.

Mutual empowerment is about increasing self-reflection, self-acceptance, critical thinking, and assertive actions of group participants. Empowerment practice includes building on strengths, fighting oppression, multicultural respect, use of cooperative roles, responding to needs, equalizing power differences, and integrating support from others (e.g., Bussey & Wise, 2007; Lee, 2001; Wise, 2005).

> (4) . . . necessary for our collective transformation from "reactive violence" toward sustainable equitable and peaceful communities.

Dialogue participants and facilitators share the common goal of sustainable, creative, and peaceful communities and view dialogue as one tool we can use to transform ourselves and our world toward that goal. Since a peaceful world requires ongoing relationships, transformation requires an ongoing lifestyle of dialogue.

When sociohistorical trauma is not transformed, individuals and communities tend to live with "reactive violence." In such a state, people are more motivated by such negative emotions as fear, anger, and the desire for revenge.

The goals and methods of dialogue are relational. Dialogue may take place on the couple, family, tribal, institutional, community, national, ecosystem, and global levels. Such relationship building is best built upon such values as mutual interest, mutual commitment, and reciprocal caring.

EXPERIENTIAL LEARNING 3.1

(1) What is your reaction to the statement "dialogue helps make us human"? Explain.

(2) Have you found that as you work on your relationships with others that there is also a parallel process of self work that needs to occur? Explain.

(3) What is a sustainable equitable and peaceful community? Have you ever been in a community like this? Explain.

RULES FOR DIALOGUE PARTICIPANTS AND FACILITATORS

In general, participants and facilitators can design their own ground rules, so that everyone can "own" the rules. The following rules are some suggestions that can help groups get started.

Do:

(1) Listen to other people when they talk.

(2) Listen to what goes on inside of me as others speak (such as my body sensations, emotions, and thoughts).

(3) Take the risk to increasingly speak as honestly and directly as I can.

(4) Speak for myself (rather than speaking for others by making statements such as, "All men think that. . . ." or "Everyone in the group feels the same way I do").

(5) Be respectful toward others (honor their right to exist and to have their own viewpoint).

(6) Allow at least several other people to speak before taking another turn.

Do not:

(1) Express judgments (judgments make other people or their expressions wrong; for example, "That is a bad idea" or "You are misguided").

(2) Debate (try to "win" in interactions with others).

(3) Act aggressively (either through verbal or physical violence, bullying, or making threats).

(4) Interrupt others.

(5) Speak longer than a few minutes at a time.

(6) Analyze or diagnose other people (e.g., "You have a narcissistic personality" or "That statement is very borderline").

(7) Insist on agreement (or some other outcome) between members (dialogue may sometimes lead to consensus, but it often does not).

Additional rules for facilitators:

(1) Seek to find the ever-shifting best balance between (a) creating a safe dialogue space where the ground rules are supported and (b) encouraging participants to take risks to be increasingly honest and direct with each other.

(2) Facilitate when necessary, but no more than necessary (the best group runs itself).

(3) The most important "role" is to be myself. After that, in descending order, beginning with the next most important role, is facilitator, participant, and expert.

(4) Move back and forth between the roles of facilitator, expert, and participant in concert with the purpose and prior agreements of the group.

INTERDISCIPLINARY THEORY AND RESEARCH

In the next sections, theories and research findings on dialogue from a variety of disciplines are provided. Table 3.1 summarizes these multidisciplinary perspectives.

Historical Context of Dialogue

In the West, the word *dialogue* has its origin in the Greek word *dialogos*. *Dia* can refer to "through" or "between" or "among," and *logos* refers to "meaning," which suggests that dialogue was seen as a movement of meanings between people. Plato's literary dialogue developed from Sicilian plays (mimes) that probably involved two speakers relating with each other. Other dialogues through the centuries built on these early origins and often involved intellectual conversation through which the author or playwright made her points. Martin Buber (1958) helped develop the modern philosophy of dialogue in which a man might develop an authentic relationship with other people or God. His biographer, Friedman (1983), identified the spirit of Buber's dialogue as the "confirmation of otherness."

A parallel dialogue tradition in the East is Renga, or collaborative, linked-verse poetry. Renga developed in Japan, recorded in the "Collection of Ten Thousand Leaves" perhaps as early as AD 347 (a similar tradition is said to have developed in China at about the same time). In Renga, participants co-create a kind of poetic dialogue, as they respond back and

Table 3.1 Multidisciplinary Perspectives on Dialogue

Perspective	Literature Review Topic(s)
History	Dialogue has been reinvented by cultures throughout our history
Education	Dialogues teach social responsibility, diversity, and bridging social divides
Religion	Interfaith dialogues and community making theory
Political science	Dialogues on international and intranational conflicts, critical thinking
Social work	Dialogues that promote economic and social justice and morality
Psychology	Research of dialogue process and attitudinal/behavioral change
Philosophy	Studies of dialogue traditions and approaches
Peace and conflict	Dialogue in nonviolent conflict resolution, communication approaches
Organizations	Transactional-participatory approach, stages of group development
Diversity work	Deep listening, community relations
Health	Relationship building, education

forth to the sorrow or joy they hear in the poetry of other participants (Schelling, 2007). Many forms of Renga developed over the years, and Renga has become popular again as instant long-distance communication has made the form possible over the Internet (Wilson, 1996).

A more recent dialogue form was created by a Brazilian, in response to concerns about colonialism and oppression. Paulo Freire's (2000) dialogue was a radical teaching approach that emphasized not only understanding the other in an educational setting free from oppression but also fostering positive social change. Freire's approach frees colonized people through the use of such dialogic methods as cooperation and social action rather than such "antidialogic" approaches as conquest, manipulation, and control.

Patrick DeMare's (1972) work on group psychotherapy influenced many dialogue theorists, including David Bohm (1996), who thought that most communication was reflexive (rather than proactive) and superficial and led to widespread social isolation. Bohm advocated for dialogic "free spaces" where people were viewed as equals and engaged in deeper and more creative interactions. Bohm emphasized "proprioception," which is the ability of the person to self-reflect and thus not necessarily react unconsciously or with overt hostility during difficult conversations.

A significant increase in publications by communication theorists in the 1990s tended to broaden the meaning of dialogue to include most efforts by humans to make meaning out of our world. More recently, some scholars have argued for a more limited and "prescriptive" understanding of dialogue as an ethically based practice where the person holds her own ground while "letting the other happen to me" (Stewart & Zediker, 2000).

There has also been a significant increase in support for dialogue in such domains as education, politics, and religion. Examples of organizations that currently promote the use of dialogue in many institutional and community settings include the National Coalition for Dialogue and Deliberation, the World Café, the International Institute for Sustained Dialogue, Search for Common Ground, National Issues Forum, the Public Conversation Project, and Public Dialogue Consortium. The National Issues Forum, a typical example of this growing list of organizations, provides opportunities for citizens to dialogue about national political issues. The goal is not to change opinions or reach agreements but rather to foster understanding of the complexity of issues, an appreciation of the values that people with different stances may hold, and a desire to continue the dialogues (Pearce & Littlejohn, 1997).

Dialogue and Education

Most high schools and colleges in the United States have a debating team. Few, if any, have a dialogue team. One could argue that in our current world, when people do use the term *dialogue,* what they are really talking about is a debate, during which adversaries compete to "win" a conversation. Televised conversations between political candidates or between experts on opposite sides of issues, for example, are often called "dialogues" but are more often debates (with little if any mutual listening, understanding, and acceptance).

The collaborative theory of communication suggests that people in conversation create together the meanings of their words (which reminds us again of the Greek origin of the word *dialogue*). Studies have suggested that dialogue actually does facilitate such co-creation of meaning, while monologues (such as lectures, speeches, etc.) inhibit meaning co-creation (Tree, 1999). *Serial monologue* is contrasted with *interactive dialogue* in the educational literature. In the former, group members are most influenced by the dominant speaker, who delivers a series of monologues to the rest of the group. In interactive dialogue, participants are most influenced by those with whom they interact. Researchers have found that in groups larger than about 10 members, serial monologue becomes more prevalent (Fay, Garrod, & Carletta, 2000).

Dialogic learning is slowly becoming more accepted in mainstream education. Using a broader definition of dialogue than that used in this text, researchers found that reasoning and conceptual shifts can be fostered in computer-based lab settings that use dialogic educational designs (Ravenscroft & Pilkington, 2000). Dialogue is often linked with transformative learning, when students become aware of their own unconscious beliefs, roles, and assumptions. Students use some of the same methods employed in dialogue, such as self-reflection, to create spiritual transformation that can benefit them the rest of their lives (Duerr, Zajonc, & Dana, 2003).

In higher education settings, intergroup dialogue is used to promote social responsibility, the bridging of cultural and social divides, and learning about inequality and social diversity.

The theory behind these dialogues is that campus intergroup relationships are a result of the histories and current state of intergroup relations in the world and that dialogue can have a positive effect on resolving these ongoing conflicts (Zuniga, Nagda, Chesler, & Cytron-Walker, 2007).

Dialogue groups typically include 12 to 18 participants. The content is experiential, rather than the "banking" approach in almost all other college classes (where students passively receive deposits of knowledge from their professors). Participants develop the ability to deepen personal and social identity consciousness, bridge differences across groups, maintain relationships, and promote social justice.

The stages of intergroup dialogue are forming and building new relationships, finding commonalities and differences across groups, exploring difficult topics, and building alliances for action. Facilitators structure conversation that includes dialogue about social structures as well as personal experience. Students are also encouraged to connect their reflection with action that promotes social justice (Zuniga et al., 2007). Some experts credit such educators as Montessori, Dewey, and Freire in moving the field of conflict resolution education forward. Such education is seen as more than just a preparation for positive change but actually a process where people make positive change (Hedeen, 2005).

Some feminist educators have critiqued the dialogic, participatory, and experiential (DPE) approach to teaching and learning. DPE incorporates all three elements into a dialogic teaching style that works best when instructors share space and power with participants (Chow, Leck, Fan, Joseph, & Lyter, 2003). Critics of educational dialogue methods question whether this approach would necessarily work in all situations and with all populations. They point out that some "positions" may still be left out of dialogic conversations, particularly in so-called third spaces where semantic meanings may not be shared across cultures (Burbules, 2006). Other critics question whether dialogue is scientifically measurable, whether it should be associated with social change agenda, and whether it leads necessarily to true knowledge (Rule, 2004).

The effectiveness of dialogue can be limited when instructors do not understand what dialogue is, develop loving relationships but fail to promote social change, are unable to truly transform traditional teacher-student relationships, and fail to consider complex local culture in the classroom (Bartlett, 2005). Adult education projects can be "dialogic spaces" where participants receive skill training, consciousness raising, literacy and income generation work, and other benefits (Rule, 2004).

Cross-cultural education began in the 1940s, with education about similarities and, later, differences across different social groups. Universities can respond to student diversity by changing the structure and composition of the student body, staff, and faculty; by changing curricula; and by promoting student interaction across differences. Intergroup dialogues use student interaction to develop student self-awareness, awareness of cultural differences, dialogue skills, greater cross-group collaboration, and future structural and curricular changes in the university. These dialogues help create sustained communication, consciousness raising, and the bridging of differences.

Religion and Dialogue

In interreligious dialogue, adherents of different religions respond to each with empathy, humility, and hospitality (Panikkar, 1999). Interfaith dialogues have been held successfully in Northern Ireland, the Balkans, the Middle East, Africa, and Southeast Asia for the purposes of promoting peace (Smock, 2002). A review of the literature and case study research suggests that dialogues of oral history can support a "spirit" for justice and peace (Bischoff & Moore, 2007).

A key component of dialogue is personal contemplation, involving reflection on inner feelings, motivations, and beliefs. Contemplative methods of knowing can be formally or informally incorporated into dialogic processes. Hundreds of studies show that contemplative practices can lead to self-awareness, stress reduction, and higher performance in many academic and athletic and artistic skill areas (Hart, 2010).

Three interfaith dialogue models (Phelps, 1996a, 1996b) have made contributions to dialogic process. The common ground network of life and choice works toward finding common ground between groups in opposition. Volunteer facilitators from each group are trained to help participants share their experiences in small groups. The Whitsitt experiment offered dormitory students who live together an opportunity to co-create better understanding and cooperation across their political and religious differences. The Interfaith Health Program built on the Whitsitt experiment to bring together people of various religious backgrounds to work together on public service projects.

Peck's (1987) theory of community making suggests that people go through predictable stages of group interaction. Community, according to this theory, begins with "pseudo-community," in which participants pretend to be more similar than they are, usually for the purpose of protection and safety. Although this stage may be unavoidable, it must be passed through if true community is to be reached. The second stage is best called "chaos" and begins when participants begin to realize they have differences but are unsure of how to deal with them. People may want to run away during this stage, not realizing that it must be gone through to reach true community. After chaos comes emptiness, when people are challenged to let go of the illusions they may have held when they entered the group. Such illusions as a sense of separateness, specialness, or entitlement have to be dropped so that participants can move toward more intimacy and responsibility. In true community, the last stage, people have learned to understand and accept each other. At this point, participants now realize that they are all responsible for the well-being of the community.

Dialogue in Political Science

Dialogue has been used in political negotiations designed to foster relationships between representatives of different countries. Dialogue has been credited with helping negotiators reduce the nuclear arms race and ultimately end the cold war (Yankelovich, 2001).

International and intrastate negotiators can use a four-stage dialogue process. The decision to engage is followed by Stage 2, which involves identifying the issues, setting ground rules, and setting up a plan for sustained conversation. Third, the two groups come to a deeper understanding of each other through dialogue. The fourth stage involves group problem solving and common actions (Chufrin & Saunders, 1993).

Although cross-cultural dialogues have been tried, some international negotiators note that the zero-sum frameworks and ideological divides still persist, for example, in Middle East arms control talks. The "realist model" is offered as an explanation for this perceived failure. According to this model, when "low-level" negotiations are conducted between people with relatively little power, people are more likely to be willing to form trusting relationships and make compromises. However, the model also suggests that in "high politics" (conducted by the most powerful leaders), people are primarily motivated by "real" forces of interest, such as power, national security, and threats from perceived enemies (Steinberg, 2005).

Arab-Jewish intergroup dialogues were successfully run on a campus setting in the United States. The dialogue was designed to bring out student emotional reactions to social justice and diversity issues. Students began by discussing their own hopes and fears about participation in the dialogue. The facilitators concluded that these dialogues were similar to other intergroup dialogues currently held on other U.S. campuses (Khuri, 2004).

The Global Dialogue Institute promotes its technology of "deep dialogue/critical thinking," which combines a balance of rational and nonrational learning in educational settings. Students are asked to encounter a worldview very different from their own and to seek the truth and goodness that exists in that other worldview. The institute has brought its program into a liberal arts program for teachers in Indonesia and attempted to integrate the program into preexisting cultural models (Marion, 2002).

Dialogue in Social Work

Dialogue seems to fit well with social work, which traditionally has held the value of promoting social and economic justice. Dialogic approaches in the university and community can help promote social justice and social change across the micro-macro levels of intervention (Dessel, Rogge, & Garlington, 2006). Dialogue has applications in social work education, particularly as a method and philosophy that fosters learning about power, racism, and privilege (Rozas, 2004). One model used in social work classes incorporates the stages of creating environment, structured activities to foster understanding of group diversity, taking on "hot" topics, and social action (Rozas, 2007).

Family therapists founded the Public Conversation Projects as a way to use family therapy techniques to foster group discussions on morality. Facilitators ask participants to avoid debate, enforce ground rules for respect and sharing, and ask participants to help in developing ground rules and planning (Pearce & Littlejohn, 1997).

Community dialogue has been found to help foster self-efficacy, intercultural understanding, and alliance building. However, the direction of any social change that develops out of such dialogue is unpredictable (DeTurk, 2006). Two dialogic methods may be used in community dialogue. The collaborative behavior model does not aim to change beliefs but rather to help two opposing groups work together on some common purpose. The ideological reconciliation model does attempt to change beliefs toward some kind of resolution. The application of both models may assist in developing collaborative behaviors and ideological shifts (Pilisuk, 1997).

Community development theorists believe that the most effective social justice interventions must involve the people who are being studied and often who are least empowered. Such participation should not only involve such "token" levels of participation as informing, consulting, and placating. Citizens benefit most when they are allowed to become true partners and share in the ownership, decisions, and control of the development projects. When development is enhanced through dialogue between all participants, community members report greater levels of satisfaction (Watt, Higgins, & Kendrick, 2000).

Psychological Studies of Dialogue Process and Intergroup Prejudice

Psychologists have made contributions toward the understanding of group processes in dialogue. For example, positive intergroup change was found to have four change processes: learning about the out-group, changing behaviors, connecting emotionally, and developing new perspectives on the out-group (Pettigrew, 1998). Both cooperation and conflict are predictable developmental processes in a group, and when majority and minority subgroups are able to satisfy their needs, constructive resolution is possible (Dovidio, Saguy, & Shnabel, 2009).

Racist stereotypes still form the underlying basis of beliefs and behaviors that most Western people do not currently consider racist. This "new racism" emerges at a time when most people view racism as "bad" and has three elements: hetero-ethnicization (exaggerated cultural stereotypes), ontologization (exaggerated natural/biological traits), and infrahumanization (denial of the ability to express love and attachment) (Pettigrew, 2008). Not surprisingly, members of disadvantaged groups are most often interested in talking about power issues in dialogue. When members of the advantaged group believe that their advantage is not appropriate, then they too become more interested in discussing power (Saguy, Dovidio, & Pratto, 2008).

Social construction theory suggests that people make their own perceived social reality. Personal construct theory (Kelly, 1991) suggests that each person creates her own hierarchy of constructs, built upon a system of past experiences and beliefs. From this perspective, dialogue can help facilitate the construction of new collective constructs between individuals. Ideally, dialogue participants begin by discussing relatively nonthreatening constructs until they are able to safely share the more "core" constructs in their hierarchy of beliefs and meanings (Simpson, Large, & O'Brien, 2004).

Theories of the 1960s and 1970s stressed the removal of category boundaries as the best way to reduce prejudice between groups, whether in dialogue or through other change processes. Category boundaries define perceived differences between members of different groups; for example, the idea that "men are from Mars women are from Venus" is a category boundary (see Gray, 1992). Many theorists and practitioners thought that category boundaries were a major source of intergroup bias. Intergroup bias is the tendency to value one's in-group over an out-group. Recent studies (Deffenbacher, Park, & Correll, 2009) suggest, however, that category boundaries do not in fact necessarily lead to increased intergroup bias.

Philosophy and Dialogue

Monologue can be viewed as a "discourse of struggle and domination" as opposed to the dialogic discourse of "partnership and reciprocity," but philosophers warn that both forms of conversation can occur simultaneously and complementarily (Siemek, 2000, p. 11). Philosophers still study the contributions of the dialogues of such writers as Socrates and Plato to Western literary traditions (Blondell, 2002).

Peace and Conflict Studies and Dialogue

Conflict theorists describe four kinds of dialogue (Rothman, 1997). Adversarial dialogue is basically like debate. Human relations dialogue facilitates understanding and relationship building through the sharing of feelings, the building of trust, and the removal of stereotypes. Activist dialogue brings adversaries together to join in common action for the common good. The fourth type of dialogue is problem solving, which explores feelings and fosters understanding for the purpose of identifying and meeting shared needs.

There are at least four reasons why facilitators might not engage two groups in a dialogue. First, one or both sides might refuse to talk. Second, one side might use the dialogue as an opportunity to exert power monologue over the other side. Third, people might also seek counseling within the dialogue process. Finally, one side might still be promoting injustice (Phelps, 1996a, 1996b).

Two models have been advanced for resolving ideological differences, such as those about abortion. The collaborative behavior model strives to help participants find common ground without changing individual beliefs. The ideological reconciliation model attempts to help people modify their basic beliefs (Pilisuk, 1997).

As rhetorical critics have begun to study mutual cooperation, nonviolence, and life with diversity, they have identified elements of "nonviolent rhetoric" that can result in positive social change (Gorsevski, 1999). Nonviolent rhetoric includes the *satyagraha* of Gandhi, who felt that "nonviolent propaganda" must be part of his movement for Indian independence. Martin Luther King Jr.'s "letter from a Birmingham Jail" is also cited as an example of "nonviolent propaganda." Other nonviolent rhetoric may include marches and processions, drama and music, prayer and worship, and mass media presentations.

Intergroup dialogue programs, designed to foster mutual understanding, were found by communication researchers to foster complex thinking about diversity, a sense of self-efficacy, and communication skills development. The researchers concluded that such dialogue could promote alliance building, cross-cultural understanding, and social change but not necessarily in directions that program planners anticipated (DeTurk, 2006).

Communicative social action (which includes consensus-building activities) was found to be superior to strategic social action (which includes direct-action activities) in fostering a sense of competency in college students (Kihlstrom & Israel, 2002). Some communications professors argue that public conversations are not adequate substitutes for the policy formation required to address social problems. Other communications theorists suggest that dialogue serves the public by offering enhancement of public reason, connection of public opinion with new media, bridging between the public and private domains, and enhancement of face-to-face human interaction (Tonn, 2005).

Organizations and Dialogue

Public relations in "an age of diversity" is viewed by "symmetrical" theorists as a dialogue between "publics" and management, in which both sides speak and listen. Public relations uses planned "action strategies" to facilitate reciprocal interactions. The transactional-participatory framework has its origins in American pragmatism and incorporates not only the dialogue between the public and management but also the larger social context of the dialogue (Woodward, 2000).

Another theory of group development that can help inform dialogue comes from organizational theory (Tuckman, 1965). There are four proposed stages of small group development. The group begins with "forming," where participants are uncomfortable and cautious about sharing their differences. Then comes "storming," where differences start to emerge and conflict is out in the open. In the third stage of "norming," the members agree upon some shared values and guidelines that will help them deal with difference and conflict. In the fourth stage of "performing," the group starts to function, based on the shared values and guidelines. In a dialogue group, participants would begin listening without judging and begin sharing more honestly. Some theorists add a final stage of transforming, in which people start to understand and accept each other and form relational attachments with each other.

Reflexive dialogue emphasizes public introspection, where participants reveal their beliefs and emotions with each other, and examine the sources of those reactions (Rothman, 1996). This approach assumes that people's reactions to each other are based on emotional reactions and interpretations rather than on historical facts.

Dialogue can help transform organizational culture into healthy community. Participants learn the dialogic skills of suspending attachment to their own position, identifying their underlying assumptions, active listening, and engagement in reflection and inquiry (Gerard & Teurfs, 1995).

Appreciative inquiry has been promoted as an alternative to problem-solving approaches in organizational life. This approach focuses on what is "right" in an organization, including assets, capabilities, and possibilities. Participants are encouraged to dialogue about their positive dreams, which they then design and deliver (Cooperrider & Srivastva, 1987).

International Examples of Dialogues

Dialogue in Diversity Work

A group self-described as White, middle-class, straight women created a program of deep listening theater to discover and deal with barriers within their own coalition community, including their experiences of silence, anger, and division. Their rational approaches to "talking-it-through" seemed to be ineffective in addressing these experiences. So, they co-created a participatory learning, popular theater that used high-risk storytelling and deep listening (Butterwick & Selman, 2003).

The program began with warm-up exercises, followed by the sharing of experiences. To go deeper and be more personal, more self-revelatory, and more willing to discuss real differences, in debriefing sessions, participants and facilitators realized that they often hid their emotional reactions from others when uncomfortable. "Dangerous" views could be expressed through role-playing.

Wyatt (2004) suggests that community relations, built through dialogue, may assist women from all races and cultures to truly understand and ultimately support each other. She theorized that the tendencies of some White women to idealize and identify with African American women ultimately does not change power relationships or bring about social and economic justice and makes some African American women feel that the complexity of their own identities are made less visible. The author (Wyatt) theorizes that this largely unconscious process may originate out of a sense of lack of power and worthiness in these White women.

Health programs for Mexican Indians were improved through ideological dialogues between Indian and Western (allopathic) views (Coronado, 2005). A group of Palestinians and Jews in Israel came together in dialogues. Researchers hypothesized that dominance and control between groups would be reflected in the communication patterns of time spent speaking and distribution of controlling questions. They did find that Jewish participants used the most speaking turns and asked more cross-national controlling questions. However, cultural differences may have been an important influence in these differences (Maoz, 2001).

Health and Dialogue

In "perioperative dialogue," nurses meet with their patients for dialogue on the day before surgery, at the time of the operation, and a day after the operation. In the preoperative dialogue, the nurse co-plans the process with the patient. The intraoperative dialogue supports the operation through explanatory and supportive conversation. Finally, the postoperative dialogue has a primarily evaluative function. Nurses reported that they generally liked the experiences of both "walking together" and "creating a caring and continuing relationship" with their patients (Rudolfsson, Ringsberg, & Von Post, 2003).

Nurses who serve the frail elderly have been encouraged to use ongoing dialogue to help the frail elderly gain knowledge about their disease and aging processes. In such a process, patients learn their own coping strategies, rather than solutions imposed by the health industry. The elderly, like any oppressed group, become aware how they have made the oppressor's perspectives and truths into their own and become their own subjects, free to make choices based on their own knowing (Hage & Lorensen, 2005).

EXPERIENTIAL LEARNING 3.2

(1) Why do you think forms of dialogue have been developed all over the world?

(2) Did you belong to a debate team in high school? Would you have liked to have had a dialogue team to belong to? Why do you think most high schools do not have a dialogue team or club?

(3) Have you ever participated in a dialogue that tried to "bridge" a religious or political divide? What was it like?

(4) After reading about multidisciplinary approaches to dialogue, what similarities do you see across these disciplines regarding how dialogue is used or viewed? What differences did you notice?

INTERGROUP DIALOGUES

Intergroup dialogue addresses intergroup conflict. Intergroup conflict is often associated with sociohistorical trauma. Such conflict is often accompanied by the tendency to stereotyping, oppression, and violence directed toward members of other groups (Dovidio, 2001; Dovidio & Gaertner, 1999).

Intergroup dialogues were used to teach cultural diversity and social justice by bringing together groups of students with different social identities. Such dialogues were strongly supported by students, who especially valued learning about new viewpoints, experiences, social inequality, and impact of the social group on personal identity (Nagda et al., 1999).

The roots of intergroup dialogue in education can be traced back to Dewey's (2009) efforts in the 1930s to promote deliberative democracy in schools and Allport's (1954) contributions that promoted equal status and interdependency in the intergroup education movement of the 1940s and 1950s.

Intergroup dialogue programs are being run at a number of university settings, including the University of Utah, University of Oregon, University of Washington, University of Virginia, University of Illinois, University of Maryland, and Arizona State University (Parker, 2006).

These programs are designed to reduce intergroup conflict and prejudice and to promote improved relationships, political participation, and social change.

The sustained dialogue approach to intergroup dialogue was developed by Saunders (1999), who worked with groups of people from the USSR and United States during the cold war. He discovered that relationships comprise five key components that form over sustained periods of contact: identities, interests, power, stereotypes, and interaction patterns.

Saunders's (1999) approach has been adapted to the university setting, where students are first asked to identify a problem in their community that they want to deal with. A student facilitator training program is provided. Although the program is run by diverse student leaders, administration provides valuable support, and all students are encouraged to participate in face-to-face interactions (Parker, 2006). Students meet for 2 hours every 2 weeks during the entire academic year.

Vorauer (2006) studied the tendency of intergroup dialogue participants to evaluate themselves negatively in reaction to the impressions that members of out-groups (lower status) seem to have of them. He felt that empathy and antiracist approaches (that tend to be more overtly emotional) could result in these "evaluative concerns" for in-group members. He suggested that a more educational (cognitive) approach might be less threatening and added that although behavioral contact seemed to have benefits, such contact might also result in defensive distancing for at least some members of the in-group. On-campus intergroup dialogues have been found to become more emotionally sensitive, thoughtful, and contributing to members of society (Allimo, Kelly, & Clark, 2002).

A review of the empirical literature (Dessel & Rogge, 2008) looked at 23 studies identified on the websites of nine major national dialogue programs. A variety of study methodologies were used, both qualitative and quantitative. Most of the programs were found to use ground rules that enhanced communication, trust, and relationship. A variety of methods were used, including intellectual conversation (about such topics as prejudice and stereotyping) and emotional conversation. The researchers encourage dialogue programs to improve evaluation of their work.

In academic settings, outcome differences were observed between races. Students of color generally reported more positive feelings about conflict, less intergroup conflict, and more positive relationships and commonality with White students. Most White students reported an enhanced sense of commonality across groups, greater perspective taking, more acceptance of diversity, and more political action. Students engaged in dialogue in academic settings reported increased learning of other cultures, problem-solving skills, and awareness of social inequality and group identities. Many participants reported an enhanced feeling of hope. Often students of color had more positive reactions to the dialogues than White students.

Critical communication processes such as self-engagement, self-evaluation, alliance building, and acknowledging differences can be taught (Stephan, 2008). Empathy can be a cognitive and an emotional process and can lead to complex reactions. The complexities of empathy can be taught, and intergroup relations can be improved when students learn to include respect for the other group with their empathy (Stephan & Finlay, 1999). Four key communication processes were identified in a factor analysis, including critical self-reflection, engaging the self, understanding differences, and making alliances (Nagda, 2006).

Positive outcomes were also found in dialogues that addressed widespread interethnic conflict. Participants in dialogues in Israel, Guatemala, Panama, the Philippines, Argentina, Guatemala, and Peru reported more mutual understanding, easing of stereotypes, and increased support of social policies that promote social and economic justice. In general, both marginalized and dominant groups reported an increased sense of commonality and perspective taking across racial groups (Dessel & Rogge, 2008). Some experts remind us that oppression may create unconscious attachments to the forms of power that oppress. From this perspective, the facilitator strives to help participants create healthier attachments to nonoppressive and liberating dialogue approaches (Cho & Lewis, 2005).

The Intergroup Dialogue as Pedagogy Across the Curriculum (INTERACT) Pilot Project, funded in 2004, developed out of intergroup dialogues that were designed to help students of different social identities "listen for understanding." Faculty and student scholars across disciplines and educational levels were trained in dialogue techniques. Facilitation of dialogue was found to bring student process into the classroom, but questions emerged about the extent to which students learned content. Faculty scholars reported that their teaching effectiveness had improved, and student scholars reported increases in learning. The host institutions also developed additional dialogue activities on campus (Clark, 2005).

There is a divide between dialogue researchers and dialogue practitioners, but each group has perspectives that can benefit the other. Researchers have been found to usually have advanced degrees, are more oriented around cognitive processes than emotional processes, tend to reduce complex phenomena down to apparently measurable sections, and can offer in-depth understanding of prejudice. In contrast, practitioners were found to be action oriented, were holistic in their views of complex phenomena, were fascinated with emotional processes, were able to generate theories, and valued practice techniques over measurement (Stephan, 2006).

A four-stage model of intergroup dialogue, presented by Zuniga, Nagda, and Sevig (2002), includes forming and building relationships, exploring differences and similarities, exploring deeper topics, and developing alliances and planning. In addition, three practice principles are recommended in the model. These include the use of a social justice perspective, the balance of process and content, and a praxis of both reflection and action.

A "critical-dialogic" model uses communication processes to promote intergroup understanding, relationships, and collaboration. Students learn a multicultural (rather than "colorblind") perspective and an understanding of structural inequalities through critical thinking. They also learn to practice effective communication skills in this model as well (Sorenson, Nagda, Gurin, & Maxwell, 2009).

A combination of enlightenment approaches (that foster critical awareness of differences and inequalities) and encounter approaches (such as dialogue) may be most effective in promoting real integration of races and cultures (Nagda, Kim, & Truelove, 2004). Another model combines critical pedagogy, multicultural education, dialogic education, and experiential learning into a course for democracy and social justice. This course was found to promote mutual understanding, effective conflict skills, and sociostructural learning (Nagda, Gurin, & Lopez, 2003).

An "action research approach" to intergroup dialogue that used ongoing meetings between diverse college students was found to effectively promote multicultural goals of power sharing, full participation, and racial equality. Engagement guidelines, definitions of dialogue (vs. debate), and teaching conflict resolution methods all helped the dialogue process (Nagda & Zuniga, 2003).

EXPERIENTIAL LEARNING 3.3

(1) Is there a need for intergroup dialogue on your campus or in your community? Explain.

(2) What are the goals of intergroup dialogue? What makes intergroup dialogue work? Why might it not work?

(3) Most courses on diversity are largely theoretical. What value do you think there would be in teaching human diversity through dialogue?

(4) What other courses could be taught more effectively using dialogue in the classroom?

ECOBIOPSYCHOSOCIALSPIRITUAL DEVELOPMENT

Dialogue is an ecobiopsychosocialspiritual process, in that participants are challenged to participate and grow in the physical, emotional, cognitive, social, and spiritual dimensions of development (see Derezotes, 2000, for a description of these dimensions in professional practice).

Physical

The *physical* dimension of dialogue involves the use of the body in listening and in expressing. Intuition can be thought of as "whole-body knowing," in that people collect information about themselves and others through such sensations as a "tingle down the spine," a "gut feeling," or a "tightness in the chest." In dialogue, participants learn to "check out" such intuitions with each other (e.g., "I had a lump in my throat when you were speaking, John, and am wondering why").

Facilitators can also arrange to have nonverbal expressions in a dialogue. For example, participants could be asked to show how their week was with one physical movement. Or, a group could do a circle dance, where people hold hands and walk silently in a large circle. In an exercise, participants could be asked to notice each other's "body language."

There is evidence that dialogue can foster neurobiological development. Dialogue can therefore also be thought of as a neurological process in which the conscious mind (cerebral cortex and, to some extent, thalamus) is "training" the unconscious mind (brainstem). This training process occurs whenever humans strive to master our more "unconscious" or "lower brain" impulses to engage in such destructive behaviors as overeating, abusing drugs, and perpetuating violence toward others. When participants practice self-reflection, deep listening, empathy, genuineness, self-control, and other dialogic skills, they are essentially changing their brain structures and chemistry. Dialogue is thus conceptualized as a "homeostatic" process, in which the person detects imbalances in her life and strives to further develop such traits as self-control, self-care, and empathy for others (Damasio, 2010).

Emotional

The *emotional* dimension is also important in dialogue. Many people can experience complex and intense emotions in the dialogue process. As discussed above, trauma often generates emotionally charged memories, and people can carry long-lasting emotional reactions to trauma such as fear and anger. People also have emotional reactions to others in their dialogue groups. Such emotions can profoundly influence the way we think and act (Sayegh, Anthony, & Perrewé, 2004).

Emotional reactions from the past and about the present and future can be shared in dialogue. Participants learn how to express and listen to emotions effectively. The facilitator makes such sharing "safe" by helping people avoid "making each other's emotions wrong" and instead listen with acceptance. Such emotional sharing can help foster relation and community building.

Cognitive

Dialogue participants can learn to consciously "suspend" impulses, thoughts, and judgments they have about themselves and others. This does not mean that participants repress or deny who they are but rather expose their own thoughts, feelings, and impulses to themselves and with others in the group. In such a process, the "ground" from which such processes emerge can itself be transformed into new forms of "collective intelligence" (Eggers, 2000).

In other words, dialogue can involve mastery of thought, which is associated with increasing self-awareness, self-acceptance, and self-control. Through such mastery, the person is able to move from a state of always being in reaction to others to a state of being more proactive with others. Cognitions also can be shared in some dialogues. A facilitator might, for example, ask participants to share a category of beliefs with each other (e.g., "What is one thing that you know without a doubt is true?").

Social

Dialogue is a relationship-building process. Social development is a life-long process in which the individual gradually becomes more effective at co-creating relationships that meet her needs to give and receive love (Kail & Cavanaugh, 2004). People also become more focused on giving back to other people as they mature.

Dialogue gives participants many opportunities to work on their social skills. Often these opportunities involve practice in how to engage in difficult conversations. Some participants may have to delay gratification for extended periods of time. For example, in one dialogue on race relations, White participants were asked to just listen to the Indian people in the group during the first five sessions.

Spirituality

One could also take the position that dialogue is also associated with what Maslow (1971) called the "farther reaches of human nature." Spiritual development seems to be associated with such qualities as peace of mind, altruism, compassion, forgiveness, and love. Dialogue seems to challenge participants to gradually develop these spiritual qualities. As Martin Luther King Jr. said, "Love is the only force capable of transforming an enemy into a friend." A commitment to loving kindness is probably required in dialogue work, and such a commitment arguably has a spiritual component to it.

EXPERIENTIAL LEARNING 3.4

(1) What do you see as your current developmental strengths and limitations? Consider the physical, emotional, cognitive, social, and spiritual dimensions in your answer.

(2) Using your response to Item (1) above, now consider how you think dialogue could help you build upon your strengths and further develop in your areas of limitation.

VIGNETTE 1: WHAT IS DIALOGUE?

Dialogue is a community process of talking through differences. It involves equal commitment to self and other in a context of honesty, courage, and kindness. It is often an intense inter- and intrapersonal experience. It can include dramatic periods of anxiety and anger. Thus, a firm commitment is required for participants to continue—to "keep coming back."

How has dialogue transformed me?

Early in my experience with dialogue, I was forced to confront my antipathy toward religious people. During a dialogue session, a person of faith, reluctantly, with encouragement from the group, testified to the origins and nature of his religious faith and that he believed in the truth of his faith. I was unable to contain myself. I blurted out, "You are spiritually arrogant and ignorant."

I could see the damage I had caused. The pain was clearly evident on his face. He was a person that I liked and respected—albeit from a distance—after all he was a religious person, and in particular he was a Mormon, a religion that was dominant politically and culturally in the region where I lived.

The dialogue had occurred on a Friday and it was a long, dark weekend for me. I was ashamed for having hurt someone else, yet did not know how to resolve my conflict. I reached out to a friend who was able to offer wise and kind counsel. She helped me realize that I needed to accept my own personal experience of some faith and much doubt and that my self-judgment and confusion was being projected onto others—particularly people of much faith and little doubt. My outburst forced me to confront the pain I caused others and felt in myself.

Some months after my "dialogue moment," the person that I had directed my anger toward invited me to his church to attend his installation as leader of his congregation ("bishop of his ward" in the parlance of the Church of Jesus Christ of Latter Day Saints). I was able to attend and feel welcome and comfortable and can testify that my friendship with this man has grown and deepened over the years.

I no longer have to keep religious people at a distance—I can truly love them as friends and neighbors. I feel much more a part of my community, I no longer engage in "Mormon bashing" or allow others in my presence to do so, and I'm more comfortable continuing to explore my own spirituality. Now I am able to embrace my sense of uncertainty as a core part of my spirituality. I find wonder and reverence in all the mysteries of life.

Vignette Author: Mark Owens

Mark Owens is a licensed clinical psychologist in private practice in Salt Lake City, Utah. He has been instrumental in the development and leadership of Chamade, a nonprofit organization that began in 2003 as the Great Divide Task Force of the Utah Psychological Association. The original purpose was to address religious differences in Utah, and now the organization also addresses other differences such as race, gender, and sexual preference. The word Chamade means a drumbeat call to parley (a meeting called to settle a dispute). Dr. Owens has also been active in many other organizations in the Salt Lake area.

VIGNETTE 2: HOW HAS DIALOGUE TRANSFORMED PARTICIPANTS?

Dialogue is a rare experience for people to learn from one another and discuss issues that are challenging, difficult, and rarely discussed outside of their comfort zones. Dialogue is transformative for the individuals participating because it allows them to hear different perspectives and learn from others without judgment or ridicule. Dialogue is not about right or wrong. It is about allowing people with different levels of understanding, experience, and knowledge to learn from others. Dialogue creates space for conversations that can bring people together, but more important, it allows participants to learn more about themselves and the impact they have on others and the larger community.

Because dialogue is a skillfully crafted conversation that includes safety, respect, honesty, and integrity, it provides a unique ability to problem solve and address conflict. I believe that providing the space for people to bring their entire selves without apology—in and of itself—is transforming. This is a rare experience. I have witnessed the gift of people "agreeing to disagree" on critical issues and values that are at the very core of their identity and purpose in this life. The process of coming to these agreements *with each person's humanity remaining intact* builds unexpected relationships. That is a transformative experience that brings everyone closer to a peaceful existence.

Watching people who have a sense of hopelessness—who feel that certain groups with opposing views could never understand their needs, concerns, or values—is so very intense. I have felt the tension, seen the anger, and heard the resistance. In these situations, I have also worried about the initial lack of compassion or willingness to move. The structure and guidelines for dialogue allow openness and vulnerability to emerge. When the first person takes a risk, and the compassion and listening are clearly present, people begin to transform without even being fully aware it is happening. All of a sudden there is an unexpected relationship. Relationship changes everything. We all become more human, our needs more relevant, and our stories validated. That is transformative . . . for everyone in the space. In a well-structured dialogue, everyone comes out transformed.

Vignette Author: Debra S. Daniels

Debra S. Daniels is a licensed clinical social worker. She has spent the past 25 years working in a variety of capacities with nonprofit organizations until she began her current position at the University of Utah. Nonviolence, particularly nonviolence toward women and social justice, has been her passion and the focus of her work. She considers herself an advocate, activist, and facilitator.

Photo © Michael Schoenfeld.

REFERENCES

Allimo, C., Kelly, R., & Clark, C. (2002, Fall). Diversity initiatives in higher education: Intergroup dialogue program student outcomes and implications for campus radical climate: A case study. *Higher Education,* pp. 49–53.

Allport, G. (1954). *The nature of prejudice.* Reading, MA: Addison-Wesley.

Bartlett, L. (2005). Dialogue, knowledge, and teacher-student relations: Freirean pedagogy in theory and practice. *Comparative Education Review, 49*(3), 344–364.

Bischoff, C., & Moore, M. E. M. (2007). Cultivating a spirit for justice and peace: Teaching through oral history. *Religious Education, 102*(2), 151–171.

Blondell, R. (2002). *The play of character in Plato's dialogues.* Cambridge, UK: Cambridge University Press.

Bohm, D. (1996). *On dialogue.* London: Routledge.

Buber, M. (1958). *I and thou* (R. G. Smith, Trans.). New York: Scribners.

Burbules, N. C. (2006). Rethinking dialogue in networked spaces. *Cultural Studies Critical Methodologies, 6*(1), 107–122.

Bussey, M., & Wise, J. B. (2007). *Trauma transformed: An empowerment response.* New York: Columbia University Press.

Butterwick, S., & Selman, J. (2003). Deep listening in a feminist popular theatre project: Upsetting the position of audience in participatory education. *Adult Education Quarterly, 54*(1), 7–22.

Cho, D., & Lewis, T. (2005). The persistent life of oppression: The unconscious, power, and subjectivity. *Interchange, 36*(3), 313–329.

Chow, E. G., Leck, C., Fan, G., Joseph, J., & Lyter, D. M. (2003). Exploring critical feminist pedagogy: Infusing dialogue, participation, and experience in teaching and learning. *Teaching Sociology, 31,* 259–275.

Chufrin, G. I., & Saunders, H. H. (1993). A public peace process. *Negotiation Journal, 9*(3), 155–177.

Clark, C. (2005). Diversity initiatives in higher education: Intergroup dialogue as pedagogy across the curriculum. *Multicultural Education, 12*(3), 51–61.

Cooperrider, D., & Srivastva, S. (1987). Appreciative inquiry in organizational life. *Organizational Change and Development, 1,* 129–169.

Coronado, G. (2005). Competing health models in Mexico: An ideological dialogue between Indian and hegemonic views. *Anthropology & Medicine, 12*(2), 165–177.

Damasio, A. (2010). *Self comes to mind: Constructing the conscious mind.* New York: Pantheon.

Deffenbacher, D. M., Park, B., & Correll, J. (2009). Category boundaries can be accentuated without increasing intergroup bias. *Group Processes & Intergroup Relations, 12*(2), 175–193.

DeMare, P. (1972). *Perspectives in group psychotherapy.* New York: Allen & Unwin.

Derezotes, D. S. (2000). *Advanced generalist social work.* Thousand Oaks, CA: Sage.

Dessel, A., & Rogge, A. (2008). Evaluation of intergroup dialogue: A review of the empirical literature. *Conflict Resolution Quarterly, 26*(2), 199–238.

Dessel, A., Rogge, M. E., & Garlington, S. B. (2006). Using intergroup dialogue to promote social justice and change. *Social Work, 51*(4), 303–314.

DeTurk, S. (2006). The power of dialogue: Consequences of intergroup dialogue and their implications for agency and alliance building. *Communications Quarterly, 54*(1), 33–51.

Dewey, J. (2009). *The school and society & The child and the curriculum.* New York: CreateSpace.

Dovidio, J. (2001). On the nature of contemporary prejudice: The third wave. *Journal of Social Issues, 57*(4), 829–849.

Dovidio, J., & Gaertner, S. (1999). Reducing prejudice: Combating intergroup biases. *Current Directions in Psychological Science, 8*(4), 101–105.

Dovidio, J. F., Saguy, T., & Shnabel, N. (2009). Cooperation and conflict within groups: Bridging intragroup and intergroup processes. *Journal of Social Issues, 65*(2), 429–449.

Duerr, M., Zajonc, A., & Dana, D. (2003). Survey of transformative and spiritual dimensions of higher education. *Journal of Transformative Education, 1*(3), 177–211.

Eggers, J. (2000). Dialogue: A conversational process for arriving at shared meanings. *Corrections Today, 62*(7), 1–2.

Fay, N., Garrod, S., & Carletta, J. (2000). Group discussion as interactive dialogue or as serial monologue: The influence of group size. *Psychological Science, 7*(6), 481–485.

Freire, P. (2000). *Pedagogy of the oppressed.* New York: Continuum.

Friedman, M. S. (1983). *The confirmation of otherness, in family, community, and society.* New York: Pilgrim.

Gerard, G., & Teurfs, L. (1995). Dialogue and organizational transformation. In K. Gozdz (Ed.), *Community building* (pp. 143–153). San Francisco: New Leaders Press.

Gorsevski, E. W. (1999). Nonviolent theory on communication: The implications for theorizing a nonviolent rhetoric. *Peace and Change, 24*(4), 445–475.

Gray, J. (1992). *Men are from Mars, women are from Venus.* New York: HarperCollins.

Hage, A. M., & Lorensen, M. (2005). A philosophical analysis of the concept empowerment: The fundament of an education-programme to the frail elderly. *Nursing Philosophy, 6,* 235–246.

Hart, T. (2010). Opening the contemplative mind in the classroom. *Journal of Transformative Education, 2*(1), 28–46.

Hedeen, T. (2005). Dialogue and democracy, community and capacity: Lessons for conflict resolution education from Montessori, Dewey, and Freire. *Conflict Resolution Quarterly, 23*(2), 185–202.

Kail, R. V., & Cavanaugh, J. C. (2004). *Human development: A life-span view.* Belmont, CA: Thomson/Wadsworth.

Kelly, G. (1991). *Psychology of personal constructs.* London: Routledge.

Khuri, M. L. (2004). Facilitating Arab-Jewish intergroup dialogue in the college setting. *Race, Ethnicity, and Education, 7*(3), 1–23.

Kihlstrom, A., & Israel, J. (2002). Communicative or strategic action: An examination of fundamental issues in the theory of communicative action. *International Journal of Social Welfare, 11,* 210–218.

Lee, J. A. B. (2001). *The empowerment approach to social work practice: Building the beloved community.* New York: Columbia University Press.

Maoz, I. (2001). Participation, control, and dominance in communication between groups in conflict: Analysis of dialogues between Jews and Palestinians in Israel. *Social Justice Research, 14*(2), 189–208.

Marion, L. (2002). Developing a sustainable educational process in Indonesia: A project of the Global Dialogue Institute. *Higher Education in Europe, 27*(3), 1–14.

Maslow, A. (1971). *The farther reaches of human nature.* New York: Viking.

Nagda, B. A. (2006). Breaking barriers, crossing borders, building bridges: Communication processes in intergroup dialogues. *Journal of Social Issues, 62*(3), 553–576.

Nagda, B. A., Gurin, P., & Lopez, G. E. (2003). Transformative pedagogy for democracy and social justice. *Race, Ethnicity, and Education, 6*(2), 165–192.

Nagda, B. A., Kim, C., & Truelove, Y. (2004). Learning about difference, learning with others, learning to transgress. *Journal of Social Issues, 60*(1), 195–214.

Nagda, B. A., Spearmon, M. L., Holley, L. C., Harding, S., Balassone, M. L., Moise-Swanson, D., et al. (1999). Intergroup dialogues: An innovative approach to teaching about diversity and justice in social work programs. *Journal of Social Work Education, 35*(3), 433–449.

Nagda, B. A., & Zuniga, X. (2003). Fostering meaningful racial engagement through intergroup dialogues. *Group Processes & Intergroup Relations, 6*(1), 11–128.

Panikkar, R. (1999). *The intrareligious dialogue.* New York: Paulist Press.

Parker, P. N. (2006, March–April). Sustained dialogue: How students are changing their own racial climate. *About Campus,* pp. 17–23.

Pearce, W. B., & Littlejohn, S. W. (1997). *Moral conflict.* Thousand Oaks, CA: Sage.

Peck, M. S. (1987). *The different drum: Community making and peace.* New York: Simon & Schuster.

Pettigrew, T. F. (1998). Intergroup contact theory. *Annual Review of Psychology, 49,* 65–85.

Pettigrew, T. F. (2008). Probing the complexity of intergroup prejudice. *International Journal of Psychology, 44*(1), 40–42.

Phelps, J. (1996a, Spring). Some contemporary dialogue models. *MCS Conciliation Quarterly,* pp. 9–10.

Phelps, J. (1996b, Spring). When dialogue is NOT our hope. *MCS Conciliation Quarterly,* p. 8.

Pilisuk, M. (1997). Resolving ideological clashes through dialogue: Abortion as a case study. *Peace and Conflict: Journal of Peace Psychology, 3*(2), 135–147.

Ravenscroft, A., & Pilkington, R. M. (2000). Investigation by design: Developing dialogue models to support reasoning and conceptual change. *International Journal of Artificial Intelligence in Education, 11,* 273–298.

Rothman, J. (1996, Summer). Reflexive dialogue as transformation. *Mediation Quarterly,* pp. 345–352.

Rothman, J. (1997). *Resolving identity-based conflicts in nations, organizations and communities.* San Francisco: Jossey-Bass.

Rozas, L. W. (2004). On translating ourselves: Understanding dialogue and its role in social work education. *Smith College Studies in Social Work, 74*(2), 228–242.

Rozas, L. W. (2007). Minority fellowship program engaging dialogue in our diverse social work student body: A multilevel theoretical process. *Journal of Social Work Education, 43*(1), 5–29.

Rudolfsson, G., Ringsberg, K. C., & Von Post, I. (2003). A source of strength—nurses' perspectives of the perioperative dialogue. *Journal of Nursing Management, 11,* 250–257.

Rule, P. (2004). Dialogic spaces: Adult education projects and social engagement. *International Journal of Lifelong Education, 23*(4), 319–334.

Saguy, T., Dovidio, J. F., & Pratto, F. (2008). Beyond contact: Intergroup contact in the context of power relations. *Personality and Social Psychology Bulletin, 34*(3), 432–445.

Saunders, H. H. (1999). *A public peace process: Sustained dialogue to transform racial and ethnic conflicts.* New York: St. Martin's.

Sayegh, L., Anthony, W. P., & Perrewé, P. L. (2004.) Managerial decision-making under crisis: The role of emotion in an intuitive decision process. *Human Resource Management Review, 14*(2), 179–199.

Schelling, A. (2007, Winter). Whirling petals windblown leaves. *Tricycle,* pp. 48–55.

Siemek, M. (2000). Two models of dialogue. *Dialogue & Universalism, 10,* 11.

Simpson, B., Large, B., & O'Brien, M. (2004). Bridging differences through dialogue: A constructivist perspective. *Journal of Constructivist Psychology, 17,* 45–59.

Smock, D. R. (2002). *Interfaith dialogue and peacebuilding.* Washington, DC: U.S. Institute of Peace.

Sorenson, N., Nagda, B. A., Gurin, P., & Maxwell, K. E. (2009). Taking a "hands on" approach to diversity in higher education: A critical-dialogic model for effective intergroup interaction. *Analysis of Social Issues and Public Policies, 9*(1), 3–35.

Steinberg, G. M. (2005). Realism, politics, and culture in Middle East arms control negotiations. *International Negotiation, 10,* 487–512.

Stephan, W. G. (2006). Bridging the researcher-practitioner divide in intergroup relations. *Journal of Social Issues, 62*(3), 597–605.

Stephan, W. G. (2008). Psychological and communication processes associated with intergroup conflict resolution. *Small Group Research, 39*(28), 28–41.

Stephan, W. G., & Finlay, K. (1999). The role of empathy in improving intergroup relations. *Journal of Social Issues, 55*(4), 729–743.

Stewart, J., & Zediker, K. (2000). Dialogue as tensional ethical practice. *Southern Communication Journal, 65*(2–3), 224–242.

Tonn, M. B. (2005). Taking conversation, dialogue, and therapy public. *Rhetoric and Public Affairs, 8*(3), 405–430.

Tree, J. E. F. (1999). Listening in on monologues and dialogues. *Discourse Processes, 27*(1), 35–49.

Tuckman, B. (1965). Developmental sequence in small groups. *Psychological Bulletin, 63*(6), 384–399.

Vorauer, J. D. (2006). An information search model of evaluative concerns in intergroup interaction. *Psychological Review, 113*(4), 862–886.

Watt, S., Higgins, C., & Kendrick, A. (2000). Community participation in the development of services: A move towards community empowerment. *Community Development Journal, 53*(2), 120–132.

Wilson, J. (1996). Two Renga with Jane. http://nichirenscoffeehouse.net/dharmajim/2renga.html

Wise, J. B. (2005). *Empowerment practice with families in distress.* New York: Columbia University Press.

Woodward, W. D. (2000). Transactional philosophy as a basis for dialogue in public relations. *Journal of Public Relations Research, 12*(3), 255–275.

Wyatt, J. (2004). Toward cross-race dialogue: Identification, misrecognition, and difference in feminist multicultural community. *Signs: Journal of Women in Culture and Society, 29*(3), 879–903.

Yankelovich, D. (2001). *The magic of dialogue: Transforming conflict into cooperation.* New York: Touchstone.

Zuniga, X., Nagda, B. A., Chesler, M., & Cytron-Walker, A. (2007). *Intergroup dialogue in higher education: Meaningful learning about social justice.* San Francisco: Jossey-Bass.

Zuniga, X., Nagda, B. A., & Sevig, T. D. (2002, April). Intergroup dialogues: An educational model for cultivating engagement across differences. *Equity and Excellence in Education,* pp. 7–17.

CHAPTER 4

The Development of the Dialogue Facilitator

THE IMPORTANCE OF FACILITATOR DEVELOPMENT

Ultimately, the dialogue participants themselves are the most important contributors to success, because they do the real work of dialogue. After participants, the next most powerful predictor of dialogue outcomes is the facilitator, especially in her ability to develop effective *helping relationships*. Since dialogue is a relationship-building process, the effective dialogue facilitator is especially skilled in facilitating relationships. The dialogue facilitator uses *conscious use of self* to co-create relationships with participants. Conscious use of self is a *multidimensional* (or *ecobiopsychosocialspiritual*) skill set that develops across the life span and includes the interrelated physical, emotional, cognitive, social, and spiritual elements of development. In this chapter, these developmental processes are described.

Table 4.1 summarizes the theories of facilitator development described in the following sections.

Table 4.1   Theories of Facilitator Development

Theory	Theoretical Focus
Community of diversity	Overall movement from me to we
Psychodynamic	Integration of child, parent, observing self
Jungian	Ego complex to self
Existentialism	Moving beyond ego
Transpersonal	Flexibility in prepersonal, personal, transpersonal consciousness
Conscious use of self	Self-awareness, self-acceptance, empathy, communication skills
Multidimensional development	Physical, emotional, cognitive, social, spiritual maturity
Art and science	Integration of artistic and scientific ways of knowing

THE FACILITATOR'S ABILITY TO SHIFT FROM "ME" TO "WE"

The facilitator's intent is to help co-create a *community of diversity* in which each participant is free to experience and express both individuality and interconnection. The effective dialogue facilitator is able to consciously shift her own awareness back and forth between her individual self (the "me") and the entire dialogue group she is interconnected with (the "we"). This flexibility enables the facilitator to model the kind of consciousness that fosters dialogue and relationship building. The facilitator can develop such flexibility through her own lifelong self-development process.

Theories of lifelong development are described in our major wisdom traditions, with a common story that seems to cut across all traditions (Wilber, 2000). Essentially, the story is that a young adult develops a "me" that is increasingly independent from the influences of childhood, and then in mid-adulthood, she gradually learns to transform her primary focus from "me" toward a greater "we." This greater "we" may include a focus on the well-being of the family, local community, global community, and the ecosystems that support all life.

Wilber's (1977) language for this process is that children live primarily in "prepersonal" ("before persona") consciousness, with a "me" not yet separate from that of their family and culture. In adolescence and early adulthood, the person usually starts to create her "personal" (or "mask") consciousness, which may include identification (or attachment) with beauty, power, roles, responsibilities, and wealth. Finally, in the "transpersonal" ("beyond the mask") consciousness of later life, the person gradually "disidentifies" from personal attachments and is able to experience connection with her self and the greater whole. Disidentification can thus be thought of as a conscious shift away from the consciousness of the personal "me" to the consciousness of the transpersonal "we." Disidentification does not mean that the person necessarily has to give up her social roles, wealth, or power. Disidentification involves instead her realization that such identifications are only temporary and that she is "more" than just her persona, an integral part of a larger whole, and therefore always in relationship with the Other, whether the Other is another person, living thing, or ecosystem.

The dialogue facilitator strives to become flexible enough to proactively change her consciousness as necessary, from moment to moment. For example, in a dialogue, the facilitator might begin the group by reviewing the guidelines for dialogue that she has prepared. Acting in a responsible manner, she realizes that she is in a "personal" state of consciousness. A few minutes later, two of the participants begin to engage in an argument. The facilitator notices that she has empathic feelings toward both of them and can imagine why both feel and think the way they do. At this point, the facilitator is in a more transpersonal consciousness, in which she can observe both her own reactions as well as the reactions of others, with clarity and acceptance. Finally, at the end of the dialogue, the group shares pizza together. The facilitator laughs at a story a participant tells as they both enjoy the dinner. The facilitator is now in a prepersonal consciousness, enjoying her self with others.

The journey from me to we can also be viewed from the perspective of transactional analysis (TA) (Berne, 1961). TA theorizes three "ego states" in the human psyche that are similar to the id, ego, and superego in psychodynamic theory. The "child" state correlates with the emotional, pleasure-seeking, spontaneous, curious nature of the first decades of life. The "parent" state is the more "grown-up" consciousness associated with social roles, responsibilities, and beliefs systems. The "adult" (I prefer the term *observing self*) is the state of consciousness from which the person can watch, facilitate, and communicate interactions between the child and parent ego states.

When the facilitator is operating in the prepersonal, her child ego state is dominant over the parent and transpersonal ego states ("Prepersonal" column in Table 4.2). If the facilitator is in the personal, her parent ego state is dominant over the child and transpersonal ego states ("Personal" column). Similarly, in transpersonal consciousness, the observing self is dominant.

The more-developed facilitator can move fluidly and consciously between the prepersonal (my ability to experience child-like enjoyment), personal (my ability to present an acceptable and responsible "me" to the world), and transpersonal (my ability to disidentify from my role). The prepersonal, personal, and transpersonal are all equally essential parts of an adult human being. Each level of consciousness has a utility in everyday living. Without the prepersonal, I cannot enjoy a beautiful sunset or have my emotions. Without the personal, I cannot have the self-discipline required for love and work. Without the transpersonal, I cannot spend my entire life never feeling like I am "enough" and attempting to fill my isolation with what Trungpa (1973, 2011) calls physical, psychological, and spiritual materialism (essentially the use of roles, ideas, beliefs, etc. to try to avoid pain and stay in pleasure).

When the facilitator becomes "stuck" in one of the three levels, she is unable to respond as effectively to the changing group environment. Being "stuck" means that the facilitator is only able to relate to the world from primarily one of the three levels of consciousness.

Table 4.2   Ego States

	Prepersonal	Personal	Transpersonal
Parent	Not dominant	DOMINANT	Not dominant
Observing self	Not dominant	Not dominant	DOMINANT
Child	DOMINANT	Not dominant	Not dominant

From a Jungian perspective (Jacoby, 1990; Johnson, 1991), the "me" or "ego complex" can distort reality, become rigid, and suppress parts of the psyche that seem undesirable. These parts are then placed in the "shadow" of the psyche through such defense mechanisms as projection or stereotyping (see section on conscious use of self below). In contrast, the "self" is the ultimate director of "all-of-me," is free from ego's distortions and identifications, and is always whole. From the Jungian perspective, therefore, the process of going from me to we is analogous to the path from ego-complex to self.

The existentialists and humanists of 20th-century psychology also wrote about what we are calling the movement from me to we. Maslow (1973) included transcendence of ego in his theory of the "farther reaches of human nature." Similarly, Rollo May (1981) spoke of the transcendence of egocentrism in his "creative stage" of human development.

The facilitator's path of lifelong development can create both opportunities and dangers. As the facilitator becomes ever more developed and skilled, she is at greater risk of what we might call "facilitator materialism" that may occur when the dialogue leader forms an attachment to her own skills, knowledge, values, and self-importance. As my friend Kilo Zamora says, we do not need more charismatic leaders, because then participants have less room to be charismatic themselves. Participants do not need perfect facilitators, but facilitators who are aware of their strengths and imperfections.

Particularly in the West, with our emphasis of individuality over community, "going from me to we" thus is about valuing community more without devaluing individuality (because what is often out of balance is the "personal-level" tendency to put self over community). However, for some Westerners and in parts of the world where community is valued over individuality, the immediate work for some may be "going from we to me" (when there is lack of sensitivity to individual diversity, then the work may be about valuing individuality more without devaluing community). In either case, the developing facilitator becomes increasingly committed to the overall welfare of the local and global communities and the ecosystems that support all life, while also supporting the co-creation of *communities of diversity,* which celebrate human diversity in couples, families, groups, and larger human associations.

EXPERIENTIAL LEARNING 4.1

(1) What does the author say is the most important factor in predicting dialogue outcomes? Do you agree or disagree? Why?

(2) Can you identify with the idea of being able to go from me to we? Have you seen this process in your own life or the life of someone who you know well? What advantages and disadvantages have you experienced in the "me" and "we" positions? Explain.

(3) Which of the theories about me to we seemed most familiar to you? Explain.

RELATIONSHIP AND DIALOGUE

Relationship literally means to be in the state of relatedness, and relatedness literally means to "bring back a message" (from the Latin root *ferre*). Thus, the state of relatedness or connectedness can be thought of as listening for the message, which is also a primary goal of dialogue. In relationship, two people neither become "one," nor do they develop complete independence. Dialogic relationship is what my mentor Maurice Friedman (1983) called the "confirmation of otherness." A relationship is about the mutual respect of diversity, where both people share the principle of respectful listening and sharing and where differences are not just tolerated but even celebrated.

A relationship can be symbolized by the *mandorla,* which is an almond-shaped "8" with two overlapping circles, an ancient symbol of the overlap of heaven and earth (Johnson, 1991). If each circle represents a person, then in relationship, we seek to develop and enlarge the intersection between the two circles (see Figure 4.1). In dialogue, we seek to find that which is similar and that which is different between us. Language can also be thought of as mandorla, because the sentence makes unity out of duality. The sentence is a math equation, and the verb is an equal sign between subject and object. Perhaps that is why dialogic language can be transformative, because dialogue puts an equal sign between people.

Figure 4.1   Mandorla

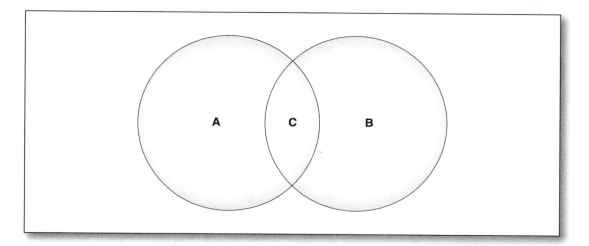

CONSCIOUS USE OF SELF IN RELATIONSHIP

In dialogue facilitation, conscious use of self involves the use of self-awareness, self-acceptance, empathy, communication skills, and other "artistic" functions to help foster effective relationships. Conscious use of self also involves the use of science in developing and using what will be described as practice-based evidence.

Relationships are difficult, in part because we humans often struggle to be good "mirrors" for each other. Instead of seeing each other accurately and mirroring back that accurate image to the other person, we usually experience and reflect distorted views of each other. My mentor, therapist Jim Magelby, often said that maybe 80% to 90% of what we see in others is actually more about our own projections and other distortions. Scientists have discovered that people unconsciously form lasting impressions of others within seconds of their first encounter with them (Gladwell, 2005). These initial and largely unconscious reactions do not so much reflect the real nature of the person being observed but often consist of what we call projections, stereotypes, or transferences. Fortunately, the facilitator can learn how to work through these "blind spots" so that she can see people more accurately.

When a person *projects* onto another person, she deals with her unconscious beliefs, feelings, and experiences by "seeing" them in other people rather than in herself. For example, a man may have sexual attractions to other men, want emotional intimacy with other men, or simply have some traditionally "feminine" characteristics such as sensitivity or compassion. If he is uncomfortable with these traits, perhaps because of the homophobia that he has learned from his family and culture, he may deny that he even has them and instead be quick to notice them in other men, even when they are not there. This kind of projection may be accompanied by negative judgments that he makes about those men he sees as homosexual or too "sissy." Obviously, he would probably have the same negative judgments about himself if he were aware of his own traits, but such awareness might still be too painful for him to make, so he continues to project.

Stereotypes (Greek root literally "solid impression") are labels that our brains seem to make about "categories" of people. Probably every person has stereotypes, and often they do become solid and lasting impressions, even when inaccurate. We can make stereotypes, for example, about women, men, people of color, White people, disabled people, abled people, old people or young people, and educated people or "uneducated" people. Since there is always wide variability within such categories, stereotypes are poor predictors of individual characteristics.

Transferences and countertransferences are other reactions that we all have toward each other. Essentially, transferences and countertransferences are two names for the same kinds of reactions; the difference is in who is having the reaction. In a dialogue, they might be experienced by the participant toward the facilitator (transference) or by the facilitator toward the participant (countertransference). Such reactions can be largely positive (idealization), largely negative (demonization), or a mixture of both positive and negative (ambivalence). Like most all interpersonal reactions, these reactions are usually combinations of past experience and current experience. For example, Sam might have a negative reaction toward Susan, partly because she somehow reminds him of his ex-wife (that part of the reaction is about his own past) and partly because she keeps on interrupting him during a conversation (that part of the reaction is about how he is reacting to her current behaviors). If he dislikes her more than likes her, then we can say the countertransference is more negative.

Students often are uncomfortable acknowledging their own countertransference reactions. Perhaps we think we should not dislike or like our clients, but the fact is that we are all human beings first and facilitators second. In fact, if we try to minimize or deny these reactions, we lose valuable information that helps us understand ourselves and others.

The dialogue facilitator works on herself, so that she can recognize, accept, and (when helpful to participants) publicly acknowledge her own projections, stereotypes, and countertransferences and thus model this process for others. She does not judge or scold others when they have these reactions but strives to assist them in becoming aware of their own reactions. The facilitator can transform these projections, stereotypes, and countertransferences from distortions of reality into allies that help inform her about the world. The main tools required in this transformation are awareness, acceptance, and hypothesis testing.

Awareness and *acceptance* work best together. This combination is a foundation of what can also be called "mindfulness," which is a process found in some of our more ancient wisdom traditions (e.g., Trungpa, 1973, 2011) and now being gradually adopted by Western psychology. Awareness without acceptance can lead to increased self-hatred and shame, whereas acceptance without awareness is a form of denial. Going back to Wilber's and Berne's models described above, mindfulness (that combination of awareness and acceptance) is the domain of transpersonal consciousness, or the observing self. The observing self and the process of mindfulness seem to be directed by processes located (at least in part) in the frontal cortex of the brain.

Mindfulness is essentially a focus in the present moment (awareness) with the intention of experiencing rather than judging (acceptance) (e.g., Tolle, 2005). The mindful facilitator is able to observe what is happening inside herself and in the world around her, from the relatively emotionally "neutral" position of the observing self. Just as a muscle grows stronger when challenged and used, the dialogue facilitator's neural circuits that direct awareness and acceptance also are gradually strengthened though mindfulness practice. Mindfulness could be said to be a fundamental "artistic" function of dialogue facilitation.

Hypothesis testing is a "scientific" function of dialogue facilitation, in which the facilitator checks out her sense of what she intuits about herself and others. In dialogue, there is opportunity to talk with the other person about one's own suspected projections, stereotypes, and countertransferences. In dialogue, people can help each check out their hypotheses or guesses about the origins of their own reactions. This kind of work, which involves emotional and cognitive sharing, can result in some of the deepest intimacy work.

MULTIDIMENSIONAL DEVELOPMENT

Participants need a facilitator who is aware of and effectively uses both her strengths and imperfections. Generally, the facilitator's strengths are also her weaknesses; for example, a sensitivity to emotions can help a facilitator assess others effectively but can also lead to a vulnerability in social situations. The dialogue facilitator brings the full range of physical, emotional, cognitive, social, and spiritual skills to the work of relationship building. These skills are associated with the interrelated dimensions of human development, as described below.

Physical Maturity

The effective facilitator uses her whole body in her assessments and interventions. Since the intuition/science process uses full-body knowing (as discussed below), the dialogue facilitator continues to develop her ability to use her whole body to inform her practice. Therefore, she is aware of and accepts all her ways of knowing, including but not limited to the following body "parts":

(1) The outer cortex of the brain (rational thought, reasoning)

(2) Intestines and stomach (gut feeling)

(3) Heart and limbic system of the brain (emotional knowing)

(4) Solar plexus (center of will, or could be called the "truth center")

(5) Spinal cord (sense of energy, electrical)

(6) Muscle tension (sensitivity to danger, other environment stressors)

The facilitator can describe her body sensations through language that empowers herself and others. For example, she may say during a dialogue, "I am noticing an increasing tension in my shoulders as we sit together today . . . does anyone else notice anything going on for them?" The technique is to notice the sensations out loud, without necessarily interpreting them. That way, other participants may also become more aware of their own bodily sensations and create and identify their own meanings for those sensations.

The facilitator is also sensitive to the body language of other people. She is able to describe such observations in ways that empower herself and others. For example, she might say, "Bill, I noticed that you started tapping your feet when Susan started talking." What do you think that your foot might have been "saying"? She also accepts her own body as well as racial diversity and the full spectrum of body types.

Emotional Maturity

The dialogue facilitator can experience and proactively express the full range of emotions. Proactive expression means that the person chooses how she is going to respond to a situation (rather than unconsciously reacts). Six "basic" emotions include the following:

(1) Sad

(2) Mad

(3) Glad

(4) Scared

(5) Excited

(6) Disgusted

She is not afraid of such "difficult" emotions as sadness and anger, when either she or other people experience and express them. Because she is comfortable with emotions, she is able to "slow down" the situation and help people experience what they are feeling and co-explore the meanings of those feelings. For example, in a dialogue, one participant (Hal) talks about his childhood and recounts how people from Culture B had been cruel to him and his family (who belong to Culture A). Immediately, a person (Willie) who identifies as being from Culture B gets angry and defensive, saying, "Well people from Culture A have been just as cruel to me!" Hal groans and rolls his eyes. The facilitator says, "Let's slow down this experience and explore what just happened. Willie, what were you just feeling?" Luckily, Willie is able and willing to do this public exploration, and he says, "I think I felt attacked." "Good," replies the facilitator. "Now Hal, how did you respond to Willie?"

Cognitive Maturity

The dialogue facilitator is capable of critical thinking. The critical thinker has these capacities:

(1) She is self-reflective—aware of and able to analyze her own beliefs, biases, and contexts.

(2) She sees the other person's context (points of view).

(3) She can establish an intellectual distance between herself and her own beliefs (particularly her cherished beliefs).

(4) She can apply logic and reasoning to situations and ideas, even those she has not yet encountered.

(5) She applies such skills as assessment, interpretation, inference, evaluation, and meta-cognition to the group process.

(6) She is aware that all people have both "good" (socially acceptable) and "bad" (not so acceptable) traits.

(7) She can tell the difference between when intellectualization is used for critical thinking and when it is used as an emotional defense.

Social Maturity

The socially mature facilitator strives to act like the person she believes will most effectively influence dialogue participants. The effective facilitator may have the following elements of social development:

(1) She is sensitive to the physical expressions, feelings, and cognitions of others.

(2) She is aware of group interactions.

(3) She is respectful of cultural diversity.

(4) She cares about the fact that other people have feelings and lives.

(5) She acts with the guidance of her own coherent value system.

Spiritual Maturity

Just like with the other dimensions of development, spiritual development is also a lifelong and ongoing process. Spiritual maturity may be associated with the following capacities:

(1) She is not afraid to experience and express her own spirituality.

(2) She honors the spirituality of others.

(3) She is respectful of religious and spiritual diversity.

ASSESSING DIALOGUE OUTCOMES: AN ARTISTIC AND SCIENTIFIC PROCESS

In this text, an inclusive approach to evidence and assessment will be presented that uses multiple ways of knowing and multiple data sources. The inclusive approach to assessment recognizes and values both practice-based evidence and evidence-based practice.

EXPERIENTIAL LEARNING 4.2

(1) Can you give examples of your own projections, stereotypes, and countertransferences?

(2) How do you deal with them? How would you like to deal with them?

(3) Do you have someone in your life with whom you can practice the "deep intimacy" of sharing these projections, stereotypes, and countertransferences honestly? What is that like for you?

(4) Consider your own multidimensional development. Can you describe where you are currently at in your physical, emotional, cognitive, social, and spiritual development?

(5) What "kinds" of people do you seem to usually dislike . . . what kinds do you like? Can you explain why?

In the past decades, many researchers have pushed for the use of so-called evidence-based treatments (EBTs) that are based on evidence-based practice (EBP) procedures, particularly when supported by research findings derived from experimental design studies and systematic reviews of such studies. Although many practitioners have adopted EBTs and EBP methods, there is still insufficient evidence that EBTs and EBP interventions, informed by published research studies, actually improve client outcomes (Anderson, Lunnen, & Ogles, 2010; Thyer, 2004).

Most of the evidence for EBTs and EBP comes from studies that compare intervention methods. However, despite the current widespread popularity of EBP, no overall significant outcome differences between methods has yet been found, especially when researcher allegiance is controlled for (Wampold, 2010). In other words, the specific methods used in the helping professions actually contribute relatively little to outcomes. Research does suggest that methods are most effective when they are consistent with helper beliefs, delivered with a sound rationale, and are acceptable to clients (Anderson et al., 2010).

Since individual models are not good predictors of outcomes, dialogue models are best thought of as a menu of alternative approaches that facilitators can choose from. Dialogue models should not be thought of as approaches that should be applied to all clients who fit a particular "type" or "problem." Since all methods are successful in at least some situations, the search for "common factors" in successful practice is a more reasonable approach to outcome research than model comparisons (Rosenzweig, 1936). As we have seen, next to client variables, therapeutic alliance is the most powerful contributor to outcomes. Effective EBP is therefore best defined as the study of common factors that are associated with positive dialogue outcomes.

In professional practice, the myth (rationale for the treatment) and ritual (the treatment based on the myth) are most effective when both client and helper believe in them (positive expectation or "placebo effect") and when client and helper agree on the tasks and goals of therapy (Wampold, 2010). Other facilitator characteristics that predict therapeutic alliance include genuineness, empathy, alliance, cohesion, therapist disclosure, and listening (Norcross, 2010).

Ultimately, the research suggests that it is the client, more than the therapist or method, who makes a therapeutic intervention work. Research suggests that positive results are enhanced when helpers build on client strengths, involvement, and desire for healing and when helpers listen to the client's suggestions and dreams (Bohart & Tallman, 2010). More than 40 years of research show that after client variables, the largest outcome variance involves therapist differences in facilitating the helping relationship, regardless of method. Ultimately, relationship works in concert with method, as well as client and helper characteristics (Norcross, 2010).

Momentum is now building in psychology for a "practice-based evidence" (PBE) approach to assessment and evaluation (Hubble, Duncan, Miller, & Wampold, 2010). In the PBE approach, the wisdom of the client herself as the primary source of evidence is valued. Client wisdom is collected through monitoring and feedback. In *monitoring,* the helper gathers progress data on how the treatment is working in a particular client-professional relationship. *Feedback* is the ongoing collection of real-time information from the client about her client's improvement. This combination of monitoring and feedback yields results superior to those using only traditional EBP methods (Hubble et al., 2010).

In this text, rather than trying to develop a "best-practice" dialogue model, the author will build on the best available outcome research evidence and emphasize the following:

(1) The development of dialogue *facilitator characteristics,* based as appropriate on PBE and EBP, that enhance the helping relationship

(2) The *full range of dialogue theories (myths) and interventions (rituals),* described and/ or evaluated in the literature (including EBP literature), that dialogue facilitators and participants can choose from

(3) *The use of participant monitoring and participant feedback (PBE)* in informing dialogue model selection, "midcourse corrections," and outcomes

In this text, the dialogue facilitator is also viewed as a *scholar practitioner,* in the sense that she uses both the artistic and scientific aspects of helping in her assessments, interventions, and evaluations. Artistic aspects include the use of intuition, empathy, genuineness (the most important relational factor), and relationship (conscious use of self). Scientific aspects include the scientific method of hypothesis generation and testing. The effective facilitator is able to integrate both art and science in her work, just as she would use both her left and right hand. Since the unconscious mind operates much quicker than the conscious mind, the facilitator may first intuit a hypothesis (artistic knowing) about what is going on with a participant or with the whole group process. She can then test her hypothesis (scientific method) by "checking it out" by asking for feedback from the group.

For example, the facilitator might feel fearful during a dialogue process. She trusts that this sensation "means something" but also recognizes that she is still unsure what her fear might be "telling her." Being capable of conscious use of self, she forms an initial hypothesis that there are others in the group who also feel scared, perhaps in reaction to one of the participants (Bill) who seems tense and upset. The facilitator checks it out by stating out loud, "I am wondering what people are feeling right now." Almost immediately, someone says, "I feel nervous!" Several others then start to talk about their feelings of fear and their anxiety. One of them asks Bill how he is, and a deeper conversation begins. The facilitator has combined both the art (conscious use of self) and the science (checking out her hypothesis) of practice.

Collaborative (or "cooperative") inquiry was developed as a research method that allows scholars to work with people rather than "on" people. Participants become co-researchers who help make decisions, collect data, and reflect on results (Heron, 1996). A guide to facilitation of "data-driven" dialogue has been developed for researchers interested in these kinds of dialogues (Wellman & Lipton, 2009). It emphasizes that all active participants are fully involved in research decisions as co-researchers. Collaborative inquiry is one approach facilitators can use to assess through dialogue and feedback.

Process evaluation is an approach to assessment outcomes that uses close monitoring of intervention activities while the dialogue is in process. Process evaluation assesses what methods and activities were planned, how they were implemented, and what outcomes occurred in the dialogue. Both positive results as well as problems are identified. Process evaluation has been found to be effective in training facilitators. These evaluations build upon the theory of the dialogue facilitator, include project staff in the assessment process, develop clear measures/criteria, and analyze results quick enough to inform the facilitation of future dialogues. In addition, process evaluations should focus on the assessment of such outcomes as empowerment process, critical thinking, and self-efficacy rather than on the standardization of curriculum (Helitzer, Yoon, Wallerstein, & Garcia-Velarde, 2000).

EXPERIENTIAL LEARNING 4.3

(1) What is the difference between PBE and EBP? Do you have any stories about how you may have used both approaches to inform your practice?

(2) The author states that relational factors are more important than techniques in predicting outcomes. What has been your experience?

(3) What is a scholar practitioner? Do you see yourself as one? Explain?

MULTIDISCIPLINARY PERSPECTIVES ON FACILITATOR DEVELOPMENT

Table 4.3 summarizes multidisciplinary literatures that can help inform facilitator development.

COUNTERTRANSFERENCE IN SOCIAL WORK

The field supervision literature suggests that the most effective social workers are capable of professional use of self, work on their own self-awareness, and strive to understand their countertransference reactions to clients (Itzhasky & Itzhasky, 1996). Self-awareness can help the social worker develop an effective therapeutic relationship. In dialogue or in any other setting, the work of relationship can be said to be the ongoing co-discovery of "where I end and where you begin," based on mutual self-exploration and trust.

Table 4.3   Multidisciplinary Facilitator Development

Discipline Area	Summary of Elements in Recent Literature
Countertransference	Awareness, assessment, intervention
Facilitator training	Common factors
Group therapy	Approaches to group work
Psychology	Transformation
Business	Leadership competencies
Participatory facilitation	Co-learning

The effective use of countertransference reactions by the social worker can help inform the therapist's assessments. Countertransference is not a problem to "solve" but a valuable source of information about other people. When the helper has a negative reaction to a client, she considers the possibility that (1) other people in the client's life also have the same reaction to him, (2) the client himself has this reaction toward himself, and (3) the client feels badly because of all this negativity.

Often, the most difficult countertransference reactions, including those that embarrass us, can provide us with the most useful clues about what our clients are experiencing and need. For example, a dialogue facilitator finds that she dislikes one of the older men. She explores her reactions to him and realizes that she does not like how he monopolizes the group conversations and considers the possibility that other people also do not like him for the same reason. She asks, "What would it be like if I irritated everyone in my life?" and realizes how lonely this man must be. She decides that she will try to help him experience his aloneness in the next dialogue.

Facilitator Training

Facilitation skills, which involve the use of personal awareness to inform practice, can be taught through educational experiences in which students share their own cognitive and emotional reactions in dialogue with instructors (Chapman, Oppenheim, Shibusawa, & Jackson, 2003). Multiple models can inform facilitator education. In the person-centered model, for example, the attitudes, presence, and other personal attributes of the facilitator are emphasized (Thomas, 2010). A technical facilitation model looks especially at the learning of facilitation skills. For example, an intergroup dialogue was effective in reducing segregation when facilitators first emphasized individual similarities, then differences, and finally helped build a shared group identity (Rodenborg & Huynh, 2006).

Group Work

Many social workers facilitate groups for participants who are "nonvoluntary." For example, people may be sent by a judge to attend a group because they were arrested for driving under the influence of alcohol or drugs. A collection of techniques for work with such groups has been developed through the McGill Domestic Violence Clinic (Thomas & Caplan, 1999). Often nonvoluntary clients need an opportunity to initially talk about why they were sent to the group and how they feel and think about the process. As in all group processes, the helping relationship is especially important in working with "nonvoluntary" clients.

Probably the most important group work theorist is Yalom (Yalom & Leszcz, 2005), who theorized a collection of "therapeutic factors" that tend to support client growth and well-being. *Group cohesion* occurs as participants feel like they belong in the group and experience support and acceptance. *Universality* is the recognition by group members that they share similar feelings, thoughts, and behaviors, which can help them accept traits that they currently struggle with. Group members can offer *hope* and *information* and the *modeling of behaviors* to each other. *Altruism* occurs when group members reach out to help each other. Groups offer opportunities to *rework traumatic family experiences* and experience greater *self-understanding* and *interpersonal learning. Catharsis* can occur when emotions are expressed and the person experiences relief and *personal growth. Existential factors* are in part about taking responsibility for one's own decisions and about making meaning out of suffering.

Yalom also stressed the importance of the development of group facilitator characteristics, including self-awareness, use of transference, and self-disclosure. He believed that the group facilitator's development is crucial to her success as a facilitator. Yalom found that as the therapist learns to be more authentic and shows who she "really" is, the group becomes more helpful to participants.

Many psychodynamically oriented group therapists have moved to group therapy modalities. In such group work, therapists have increasingly stressed the importance of relationship in positive group outcomes. Important relational factors include the use of humor, countertransference, noninterpretive reactions, and spontaneity by group facilitators (Wright, 2000). Object relations and self-psychology theorists also emphasize the importance of interpersonal relations in group psychotherapy (Schermer, 2000).

One specialty form of group work is family therapy. According to constructionist and systemic family therapy theory, the family therapist actively engages and participates within a family system (rather than acts upon that system). The therapist's relationship with the family is emphasized more than therapy techniques, such as systemic positioning and influencing (Real, 1990).

Although there is little agreement in the literature on the definition of *facilitator,* most agree that facilitators help manage group tasks, form helping relationships, and perform group maintenance. A survey of 63 expert practitioners identified a list of facilitator competencies. These included (in order of identified importance, beginning with the most important) active listening, skillful questioning, monitoring of group dynamics, paraphrasing of content simulation of insights and creativity, and focusing on feelings and body language (Kolb & Rothwell, 2002). Similar findings came from another large sample of facilitators, with the addition of such competencies as keeping group focus, completing follow-up, clarifying group purpose and ground rules, handling disruptive members, and using methods appropriate to group characteristics (Kolb, Jin, & Song, 2008b).

Facilitators of problem-solving groups were found to use the following general competencies: understanding group context, group management skills, interpersonal skills, task process skills, and other personal characteristics. Some specific competencies included time management, problem-solving skills, objectivity, verbal and nonverbal communication, establishing trust, and openness to learning (Nelson & McFadzean, 1998). Six competencies are provided in the facilitator competency model: participation in professional growth, collaborative relationship building, creation of participatory environment, use of multiple sensory approaches, guidance of group journey, and commitment to a "life of integrity" (Pierce, Cheesebrow, & Braun, 2000).

Some group facilitators point out that professional group facilitators draw from different values and skills than other managers, trainers, and consultants, who may only occasionally use facilitative techniques. The International Association of Facilitators (IAF) has developed a list of key values and roles for facilitators. The role of the facilitator, for example, is viewed as a process guide who is neutral in any decision-making process and respects group process and autonomy. Although all significant, the relative importance of relationship building over results, facilitator values, and the meaning of consensus making was unclear (Hunter & Thorpe, 2005).

A list of facilitator competencies developed from 20 experienced practitioners included the following: listens actively, creates an atmosphere of interaction and discussion, uses nonverbal language effectively, encourages group ownership and involvement in issues, uses humor effectively, handles disruptive behavior effectively, stimulates insights and creativity, uses questions skillfully, and monitors group dynamics (Kolb, Jin, & Song, 2008a).

Experts disagree on the validity and value of existing leadership competency models. On one hand, such models may glamorize "great leaders" instead of focusing more on the unique competencies that bring "great results" in each unique group context. On the other hand, a comprehensive model of effectiveness, which includes desired competencies, may help inform beginning facilitators (Hollenbeck, McCall, & Silzer, 2006).

Psychology

According to leadership psychologists, the interaction between a leader and followers can be transactional or transforming. Transactional leadership happens when the leader and participant engage in psychological, economic, or political exchanges with each other. The goal is mutual benefit rather than a lasting relationship or social change. In transforming leadership, the facilitator and participants foster higher levels of moral vision and motivation in each other. The facilitator inspires participants to look beyond their individual interests toward the greater good (the "we") of the group and community. Researchers have found that positive outcomes seem to be related to the degree to which participants and leaders share a similar view of the leader's transactional style. Stylistic characteristics may include consistency, commitment, and clarity of expectations (Whittington, Coker, Goodwin, Ickes, & Murray, 2009).

Business

Facilitative leadership draws from the collective wisdom of the group, rather than wisdom from the top down. Organizational managers have increasingly adopted facilitative leadership methods. These methods work best when there are clearly defined roles and structures, leaders have appropriate skills and values, and efforts are supported by top management. Facilitators are encouraged to schedule multiple meetings, provide key facts, allow feelings to be expressed, use humor and self-disclosure, and confront inappropriate behaviors (Hensey, 1999).

More than 350 business managers and 1,400 employees were surveyed about perceived leadership competencies. The highest performing managers had significantly higher "emotional competence." Such traits as self-confidence, achievement orientation, initiative, change catalyst, and influence were identified by all groups. There were gender differences, with the highest scored female managers seen as having adaptability and service orientation and the men seen as being a change catalyst (Cavallo & Brienza, 2010). Similarly, four major forms of emotional intelligence were found by researchers to contribute to effective leadership. These forms include emotional assessment and expression, use of emotion to enhance decision making, knowledge about emotions, and emotional management (George, 2000).

"Emotional intelligence" has been found to contribute to performance and leadership. To facilitate emotionally intelligent behaviors, leaders are taught to identify their deepest values and ideals, see their current state of being accurate, decide on a method of change and maintenance, and ask for help from those who can assist (Goleman, Boyatzis, & McKee, 2001).

Participatory Facilitation

Participatory facilitation is about more than methods and techniques. In this "transformative" or "growth-centered" approach, facilitators and participants become co-learners, share group power, engage in critical self-reflection, and strive to be transparent about group process. Such facilitation has been found to build reciprocal trust in the relationships between participants and facilitators, as well as individual experiences of self-actualization and spiritual development (Hanson & Hanson, 2001).

EXPERIENTIAL LEARNING 4.4

(1) After reading summaries of literature from various disciplines, what similarities and differences do you see?

(2) What do you believe is most important in the development of a dialogue facilitator? Explain.

AUTHOR'S DIALOGUE WITH THE READER

I notice my own strong feelings about the topic of this chapter. My experience of the academic work of professional helping (social work, psychology, psychiatry, etc.) is that the *methods* of practice are still valued more than *relational factors,* despite the overwhelming evidence that relationship is more important than method in predicting outcomes.

I believe that this devaluing of relational factors probably diminishes facilitator effectiveness. When, as Carl Jung would say, any important part of myself is devalued (in this case, relational factors are the devalued or "inferior" function and method the "superior" function), then the devalued function becomes part of my unconscious "shadow" and influences me in ways I am not aware of. As a facilitator, to the extent that I am not aware of my feelings of anger or fear, for example, they will be expressed in the group in ways that are counterproductive.

I worry that beginning group facilitators are still being asked to look for the best model, rather than being encouraged to develop their own ability to co-create helping relationships. I know in my own experience in dialogue that such artistic factors as genuineness, empathy, supportiveness, appropriate self-disclosure, respect, and commitment tend to foster the kinds of trusting relationships that are the foundation of cooperation and peaceful conflict resolution. In contrast, methods seem to take a secondary role; without effective relationships, the best "state-of-the-art" approaches do not make a difference.

VIGNETTE 1: EFFECTIVE DIALOGUE FACILITATOR

I believe an effective facilitator must be aware of her or his

(1) passion—what energizes the individual to facilitate these conversations?

(2) awareness—what are the triggers/triggering points that would cause the facilitator to react and respond while remaining in dialogue mode?

(3) skills—the necessary tools to provide knowledgeable resources and coaching to a participant or co-facilitator in a dialogue setting; and

(4) knowledge—a comprehensive understanding of the theoretical frameworks and models that are used in educating participants.

It is often said that it is hard to hate someone whose story you know. The semistructured dialogue process helps participants to engage in activities of listening, sharing, and offering feedback to one another. These stories and experiences allow for individuals to share their lived experiences and hear perspectives that are different from their own. Through this dialogue experience, participants are able to critically examine their own misconceptions and perceptions, as well as question the misinformation about members of dominant and dominated groups. Most of all, I believe the dialogue process has no arrival dates but assumes that each participant is "doing his or her best" to behave in multiculturally productive ways. Finally, each participant has an obligation to actively combat the myths and stereotypes by challenging the idea and not the person while holding one another responsible for repeating incorrect information or offensive behavior after she or he has learned otherwise.

Photo © Michael Schoenfeld.

Vignette Author: Wazir Jefferson

Wazir Jefferson is an African American male from Poughkeepsie, New York. Consciousness and equality have always been at the forefront of his being. As both a teacher and a learner, he believes it is important to recognize the "intent" and "impact" of words. He graduated from Temple University in 2003 with a bachelor's degree in Business Administrations in Legal Studies and Human Resources; The George Washington University in 2005 with an MA in Education and Human Development in Human & Organizational Studies; and the University of Utah in 2012 with a PhD in Education with a Higher Education emphasis.

VIGNETTE 2: A DIALOGUE

To me, dialogue means conversation—a type of conversation between two or more parties where all ideas are intended to be constructive. The parties' thoughts, beliefs, and experiences are free to be shared. Questions are welcomed, and clarification of various viewpoints is encouraged. In a healthy dialogue situation, there is an inherent ability to listen to others while feeling safe to share your own experience. I have found it can be difficult at times for individuals to participate in dialogue, especially if the issues are emotionally charged or sensitive.

It is helpful in some situations to encourage an individual to separate the person from the message, if she or he finds the message inflammatory. We need to help others understand that our thoughts, beliefs, and feelings are often a culmination of our experiences from birth to the present. During our journey, we form schemas about how the world operates. When I hear a point of view that may be difficult for me to understand, I step outside of my own experience and attempt to hear the information from their perspective. I strongly believe for cultural healing to take place, it is imperative to have dialogue, and this allows us to garner a greater respect and understanding for each other.

Good dialogue facilitators have "done their own work," meaning they have thought about and gained insight into their own experiences and biases. They have respect for all humans and work to understand why each individual may see the world the way he or she does. Strong facilitators have found peace with their ethnicity, social class, gender, ability, age, and sexual orientation. They are able to tolerate difficult emotions and manage their own transference. It can be helpful for the facilitators to know ahead of time general areas that they may find emotionally challenging. Possessing good communication skills and the ability to operate from an assertive communication standpoint is critical. The dialogue facilitator should be able to keep dialogue goals in mind and work to ensure a safe environment for sharing. A safe environment does not mean that people cannot be passionate about their own viewpoint, but it does mean that participants will not be placed in harm's way as a result of transparency.

Vignette Author: Shauntele Curry-Smid

Shauntele Curry-Smid, MSW, LCSW, is a contract therapist and consultant for the Ute Tribe, is the Clinical Director at the Urban Indian Center of Salt Lake, and teaches as an adjunct instructor at the University of Utah, Graduate School of Social Work Program. She is an enrolled member of the Pyramid Lake Paiute Tribe. She can be contacted at Shauntelecurry@gmail.com.

REFERENCES

Anderson, T., Lunnen, K. M., & Ogles, B. M. (2010). Putting models and techniques in context. In B. L. Duncan, S. D. Miller, B. E. Wampold, & M. A. Hubble (Eds.), *The heart and soul of change: Delivering what works in therapy* (2nd ed., pp. 143–166). Washington, DC: American Psychological Association.

Berne, E. (1961). *Transactional analysis in psychotherapy.* New York: Random House.

Bohart, A. C., & Tallman, K. (2010). Clients: The neglected common factor in psychotherapy. In B. L. Duncan, S. D. Miller, B. E. Wampold, & M. A. Hubble (Eds.), *The heart and soul of change: Delivering what works in therapy* (2nd ed., pp. 83–112). Washington, DC: American Psychological Association.

Cavallo, K., & Brienza, D. (2010). Emotional competence and leadership excellence at Johnson & Johnson: The emotional intelligence and leadership study. http://www.branchenbuch.ch/portrait/files/raw/00012340-leadershipstudie.pdf

Chapman, M. V., Oppenheim, S., Shibusawa, T., & Jackson, H. M. (2003). What we bring to practice: Teaching students about professional use of self. *Journal of Teaching in Social Work, 23*(3/4), 3–14.

Friedman, M. (1983). *The confirmation of otherness in family, community, and society.* New York: Pilgrim Press.

George, J. M. (2000). Emotions and leadership: The role of emotional intelligence. *Human Relations, 53,* 1027–1054.

Gladwell, M. (2005). *Blink: The power of thinking without thinking.* New York: Little, Brown.

Goleman, D., Boyatzis, R., & McKee, A. (2001, December). Primal leadership: The hidden driver of great performance. *Harvard Business Review/Breakthrough Leadership,* pp. 43–51.

Hanson, L., & Hanson, C. (2001). Transforming participatory facilitation: Reflections from practice. *PLA Notes, 41,* 29–32.

Helitzer, D., Yoon, S., Wallerstein, N., & Garcia-Velarde, L. D. (2000). The role of process evaluation in the training of facilitators for an adolescent health education program. *Journal of School Health, 70*(4), 141–147.

Hensey, M. (1999, May/June). The how and why of facilitative leadership. *Journal of Management in Engineering,* pp. 43–46.

Heron, J. (1996). *Cooperative inquiry: Research into the human condition.* London: Sage.

Hollenbeck, G. P., McCall, M. W., & Silzer, R. F. (2006). Leadership competency models. *The Leadership Quarterly, 17,* 398–413.

Hubble, M. A., Duncan, B. L., Miller, S. D., & Wampold, B. E. (2010). What works and what does not: The empirical foundations for the common factors. In B. L. Duncan, S. D. Miller, B. E. Wampold, & M. A. Hubble (Eds.), *The heart and soul of change: Delivering what works in therapy* (2nd ed., pp. 23–46). Washington, DC: American Psychological Association.

Hunter, D., & Thorpe, S. (2005). Facilitator values and ethics. In S. Schuman (Ed.), *The IAF handbook of group facilitation* (pp. 545–562). San Francisco: Jossey-Bass.

Itzhasky, H., & Itzhasky, T. (1996). The therapy-supervisor dialectic. *Clinical Social Work Journal, 24*(1), 77–87.

Jacoby, M. (1990). *Individuation and narcissism: The psychology of the self in Jung and Kohut* (Myron Gubitz, Trans.). London: Routledge.

Johnson, R. A. (1991). *Owning your own shadow: Understanding the dark side of the psyche.* New York: HarperOne.

Kolb, J. A., Jin, S., & Song, J. H. (2008a). Developing a framework of facilitator competencies: Lessons from the field. In T. J. Chermack & J. Storberg-Walker (Eds.), *2008 conference proceedings of the Academy of Human Resource Development* (pp. 336–343). Bowling Green, OH: The Academy of Human Resource Development.

Kolb, J. A., Jin, S., & Song, J. H. (2008b). A model of small group facilitator competencies. *Performance Improvement Quarterly, 21*(2), 119–133.

Kolb, J. A., & Rothwell, W. J. (2002). Competencies of small group facilitators: What practitioners view as important. *Journal of European Industrial Training, 26*(2–4), 200–203.

Maslow, A. (1973). *The farther reaches of human nature.* New York: Viking.

May, R. (1981). *Freedom and destiny.* New York: W. W. Norton.

Nelson, T., & McFadzean, E. (1998). Facilitating problem-solving groups: Facilitator competencies. *Leadership and Organizational Development Journal, 19*(2), 72–82.

Norcross, J. C. (2010). The therapeutic relationship. In B. L. Duncan, S. D. Miller, B. E. Wampold, & M. A. Hubble (Eds.), *The heart and soul of change: Delivering what works in therapy* (2nd ed., pp. 113–142). Washington, DC: American Psychological Association.

Pierce, V., Cheesebrow, D., & Braun, L. M. (2000). Facilitator competencies. *Group Facilitation: A Research and Applications Journal, 2*(2), 24–31.

Real, T. (1990). The therapeutic use of self in constructionist/systemic theory. *Family Process, 29,* 255–272.

Rodenborg, N., & Huynh, N. (2006). On overcoming segregation: Social work and intergroup dialogue. *Social Work With Groups, 29*(1), 27–44.

Rosenzweig, S. (1936). Some implicit common factors in diverse methods of psychotherapy. *American Journal of Orthopsychiatry, 6,* 412–415.

Schermer, V. L. (2000). Contributions of object relations theory and self psychology theory to relational psychology and group psychology. *International Journal of Group Psychotherapy, 50*(2), 199–212.

Thomas, G. (2010). Facilitate first thyself: The person-centered dimension of facilitator education. *Journal of Experiential Education, 31*(2), 168–188.

Thomas, H., & Caplan, T. (1999). Spinning the group process wheel: Effective facilitation techniques for motivating involuntary client groups. *Social Work With Groups, 21*(4), 3–21.

Thyer, B. A. (2004). What is evidence-based practice? *Brief Treatment and Crisis Intervention, 4,* 167–176.

Tolle, E. (2005). *The power of now.* New York: Hodder and Stoughton.

Trungpa, C. (1973). *Cutting through spiritual materialism.* Boston: Shambhala.

Trungpa, C. (2011). *Work, sex, money: Real life on the path of mindfulness.* Boston: Shambhala.

Wampold, B. E. (2010). The research evidence for common factors models: A historically situated perspective. In Duncon, B. L., Miller, S. D., Wampold, B. E. & Hubble, M. A. (Eds.). *The heart and soul of change: Delivering what works in therapy.* (2nd ed., pp. 49–82). Washington, D.C.: American Psychological Association.

Wellman, B., & Lipton, L. (2009). *Data-driven dialogue: A facilitator's guide to collaborative inquiry.* Sherman, CT: Mira Via, LLC. (Study guide developed by Peggy Olson.)

Whittington, J. L., Coker, R. H., Goodwin, V. L., Ickes, W., & Murray, B. (2009). Transactional leadership revisited: Self-other agreement and its consequences. *Journal of Applied Social Psychology, 39*(8), 1860–1886.

Wilber, K. (1977). *The spectrum of consciousness.* Wheaton, IL: Quest.

Wilber, K. (2000). *A theory of everything: An integral vision for business, politics, science, and spirituality.* Boston: Shambhala.

Wright, F. (2000). The use of self in group leadership: A relational perspective. *International Journal of Group Psychotherapy, 50*(2), 181–198.

Yalom, I., & Leszcz, M. (2005). *The theory and practice of group psychotherapy* (5th ed.). New York: Basic Books.

CHAPTER 5

Basic Dialogue Phases, Tasks, and Issues

INTRODUCTION AND ORIENTATION

Basic phases, tasks, and issues of the dialogue process are described in this chapter. These phases, tasks, and issues are common to all the dialogues described in this book and are summarized in Tables 5.1 and 5.2. Three phases are described: engagement and assessment, relationship and community-building work, and evaluation and follow-up. Each phase has its own set of tasks. In the last section of the chapter, five additional dialogue issues are discussed.

Table 5.1 Basic Phases and Tasks

Phases of Dialogue Process	Cooperative Group Tasks
Engagement and assessment	Identifying need Inviting participants Setting goals Making a commitment Ground rules
Relationship and community-building work	Creating space Opening up Managing difficult conversations Acting-processing-acting Bigger and smaller Checking in, checking out
Evaluation and follow-up	Social action Renegotiating Referring Re-searching

Table 5.2   Additional Dialogue Issues

Dialogue issues	Participants are supervisors
	Dialogue training groups
	Co-facilitation
	Structure
	Dealing with challenging participants
	Mistakes
	Debriefing

In Section II (Chapters 6–10), theory, research, and methods in selected dialogue models are described. The methods informed by these models can be used throughout all three phases of dialogue, particularly in the relationship work phase. Key foci in the dialogue phases are provided for each dialogue model in Table 5.3. The "inclusive" model in the bottom row is included to emphasize that the skilled dialogue facilitator is able to use any and all of these models in the ever-changing dialogic situation. Such flexibility (also called integrative, multimodal, or inclusive approach) has been strongly linked to successful helping outcomes (Beutler, Consoli, & Lane, 2005; Brooks-Harris, 2008; Lambert, 1986; Lazarus, 1992, 2005). This inclusive model is used in each chapter in Section III, in all five dialogue application areas.

In Section III (Chapters 11–15), the phases and models are applied to five dialogue practice areas. The basic focus of each of these areas is summarized in Table 5.4. As indicated

Table 5.3   Foci of Dialogue Models

Dialogue Model	Focus
Psychodynamic Chapter 6	Transformation of the past to create a new here and now
Cognitive-behavioral Chapter 7	Transformation of awareness and expression of thoughts and behaviors
Experiential-humanistic Chapter 8	Transformation of awareness and expression of emotions
Transpersonal Chapter 9	Transformation of awareness and expression of spirituality
Biological and ecological Chapter 10	Transformation of relationship with the body and the environment
Inclusive (applied in Chapters 11–15)	Flexible use of any model as the dialogue situation changes

above, an "inclusive" approach is used in all of these chapters, which includes methods drawn from all the dialogue models described in the text.

Table 5.4 Foci of Dialogue Practice Areas

Dialogue Practice Areas	Focus
Bridging divides Chapter 11	Bridge the ideological differences that divide us through relationships
Diversity and social justice work Chapter 12	Build relationships that reduce discrimination, economic inequality, and social injustice
Community building across the life span Chapter 13	Build community-building relationship skills with children, youth, adults, and the elderly
Peace, reconciliation, and conflict resolution Chapter 14	Build relationships that form a basis for resolving conflicts, fostering reconciliation, and developing deep peace
Community therapy Chapter 15	Foster well-being through relationships and community-building dialogue

ENGAGEMENT AND ASSESSMENT

Identifying Need

This text presents dialogue as an approach that can be used to help transform sociohistorical trauma. As described in Chapter 2, such trauma can "show up" in many different kinds of individual and community symptoms. People can engage in dialogue in response to these symptoms, not to necessarily "cure" the symptoms but to respond to the underlying roots of the symptoms, so that both the individual and community can be transformed.

Every community has *divides,* which are areas of human diversity that are burdened with a history of sociohistorical trauma and where there are wide spaces of misunderstanding between groups (see Chapter 11). Such history can result in many individual symptoms (see Chapter 1) as well as difficulties in relationships and communities. For example, in the local high schools in my community, most adolescents still sit at lunch tables segregated by such differences as race, culture, socioeconomic status, and sexual orientation.

In most communities, divides commonly occur across such elements of diversity as gender, religion, political ideology, sexual orientation, race, and culture. A divide in the community can show up in tensions and even open conflicts and can also be symbolized in informal and formal communications. For example, when racist and sexist graffiti showed up on the restroom walls on one campus, some members of that community saw this as a symptom of divides of race and sexual orientation.

In response to such symptoms, the dialogue facilitator can hold an open public forum at which people can speak about the concerns they have. At a forum, the facilitator can present information on what a dialogue is, answer questions, and perhaps arrange a follow-up meeting for people who might want to volunteer to help plan and/or attend the dialogue. Such forums should be local and community-friendly. For example, I participated in an effort to bring a more diverse population of people to a particular community clinic. One night, we held an open dialogue, at a community center in a neighborhood that was heavily represented by a race of people who had not yet participated in clinic events. We offered a light dinner and had a good turnout, and some of the people attending eventually became members of the dialogue group we formed.

Sometimes a community crisis draws attention to a divide. In one community, for example, a young man who identified as gay was physically attacked by several other men who identified as straight. When such "hate crimes" occur, many people in the community may pay more attention to divides and may be willing to participate in dialogues for transformation.

Inviting Participants

The facilitator and planning committee can make a list of dialogue participants. If there are not enough participants, or if the committee wants to open the dialogue up to the community, the dialogue can be advertised. In the engagement and assessment phase of my dialogue training group, for example, I first met with my co-facilitator. We identified the need and made a list of potential future dialogue leaders who we would want to invite to the first group. As co-facilitators, we were careful to balance out invitations so that equal numbers of each race were represented in the list. In addition, after the group was full, we decided that we would only admit new members if we could keep that balance.

Setting Goals

Dialogue can be used to help prevent future trauma and/or to respond to past trauma. Often these goals are motivated by the individual and community symptoms that have become uncomfortable or even unbearable. For example, when individuals have any of the symptoms typically associated with posttraumatic stress disorder (PTSD), they tend to become motivated by their pain and may want to join a dialogue group that is focused on trauma. If a family or community has symptoms of multigenerational sociohistorical trauma, such as depression, violence, and substance abuse, then members might want to participate in a dialogue that gives them opportunities to address their stories. For example, I have had many American Indians in my community volunteer to participate in our campus dialogues on historical trauma, and they often share that they notice many symptoms of sociohistorical trauma in their families and communities.

Commitment

As described in Chapter 3, dialogue is an ongoing process that is rarely completed in one session. Trust between members may take time to develop, over many sessions. A commitment to the group over time can add to the chances of transformation for participants. The facilitator can ask members to attend regularly for a particular number of weeks or sessions, for example, perhaps 12 weeks or 10 meetings. Although occasional absences are understandable, patterns of absence are usually not acceptable, and facilitators may meet separately with such members and perhaps need to eventually counsel them out of group.

Ground Rules

The group may need some kind of ground rules to function effectively as a dialogue group. A list of typical ground rules is presented in Chapter 3. The facilitator knows that ground rules are most important when working with groups that are lower functioning, such as children or developmentally immature teens and adults. Whenever possible, ground rules tend to be most effective when participants co-invent them themselves, because then they are more likely to "buy in" to the rules. The facilitator can also model ground rule behavior.

EXPERIENTIAL LEARNING 5.1

(1) What might (or did) make you want to join a dialogue group? What kinds of hopes and fears did you first have?

(2) What might (or did) the facilitator do that helped you deal effectively with your hopes and fears?

(3) What factors help you trust other people in a group meeting? What factors get in the way? What control (if any) do you have over these factors?

RELATIONSHIP AND COMMUNITY-BUILDING WORK

There are many reasons to do relationship and community-building work. The five chapter headings in Section III suggest five major practice areas that might present as reasons for dialogue. These areas are not exclusive and are often overlapping. For example, all five practice areas could be applied in working with interstate conflicts around water rights.

Creating Space

Often, when I ask, participants tell me that the most important function of the facilitator is to create a "space" for people to work in. What does this mean? The creation of space involves a combination of intention, trust, confidence, modeling, transparency, letting go, and public learning.

Intention means to hold the anticipation that the process and outcome of a dialogue will result in the highest good. In other words, when I enter into a dialogue, I act on faith that things will turn out "good enough" for everyone in the group. I hope that people will all get something out of the experience, although their individual outcomes will always vary. *Trust* here means that I have faith that the people in the group come with "good" intentions to grow and help others grow as well. I also believe that they have "good" intentions toward me, in that they want me to be successful in facilitating the dialogue for them.

I also enter the dialogue with *confidence* in myself, that I will be able to facilitate the conversation. Instead of lecturing or preaching, I *model* dialogic behavior. I want to show participants what dialogue is by being respectful and by really listening to people. That does not mean that I am afraid to be assertive when necessary. For example, if one participant makes a verbal attack on another participant, I will talk about the behavior and remind the group that such behavior is not allowed under the guidelines.

I am also willing to be *transparent,* which means that when I think it will help my group, I will share my own feelings, thoughts, and histories. Clients, clinical researchers, and theorists increasingly have agreed for decades on the usefulness of self-disclosure by professional helpers, particularly when such transparency is done with the clear intention to help the client (Bridges, 2001; Greenspan, 1986; Kessler & Waehler, 2005; Lambert, 1991; Lazarus, 1994; Petersen, 2002).

I am also able to *let go* of expectations that my ego may have of myself and of the group. For example, I do not expect that the dialogue will be "perfect" (whatever that might mean to my ego). I can accept when things go "wrong" or become intense, that the most difficult conversations often bring the opportunities for learning and growth that everyone most needs.

Finally, *public learning* is my favorite definition of teaching and facilitation. In other words, I think teachers and facilitators are most effective when they are willing to learn in front of other people. Public learning means that I strive to be open, conscious, and present in the here-and-now moment to learn and grow. I am OK with not knowing what to do next and to co-discover with the group what we need to do in the moment. I am willing to be "transparent" about this process in front of the group.

Opening Up

Often, but not always, dialogue groups struggle at first to open up with each other. As discussed in Chapters 7 and 8, people often hide their true thoughts and feelings in their public and even in their close interpersonal worlds. Therefore, the facilitator strives to help create the conditions that will help people speak more honestly, directly, and from the heart.

Often the facilitator can help start the process by doing a warm-up activity. One dialogue group I have been involved in for over 7 years still loves to do a warm-up every time we meet. We take turns coming up with ideas that might be fun, novel, and thought-provoking. Some examples of these ideas include (a) everyone talks about what they would eat for lunch if they could eat anything, (b) we go around the circle and talk about what it is like to be in the middle of winter, and (c) participants explain a time period and location that they would choose to live in if they could go anywhere back in time.

The facilitator can help others participate by modeling participation herself. One time, for example, I sat in a group that had planned to do a funeral exercise with the oldest member of the group (see Chapter 9). We spent almost an hour of the 2-hour session talking about the exercise, making jokes, and philosophizing, but no one seemed ready to actually start the exercise. I finally decided to try modeling the behavior I wanted, so I looked at the person whose life we were celebrating and spoke to her directly. I started by saying something like, "I notice that I feel nervous beginning this exercise . . . perhaps I am afraid to become vulnerable or to look foolish if I show you my feelings . . . so I want to just try to start talking about what I would say if this was your real funeral." After I finished speaking, another participant immediately began sharing, and the process began.

The facilitator can also talk about why authenticity can result in transformation. We know that many people are more likely to try activities if professionals *briefly* explain to them the reasons for the activities (see, e.g., Duncan, Miller, Wampold, & Hubble, 2009). The facilitator is also most effective when rewarding positive behaviors than when punishing negative ones, so whenever possible, the facilitator gives special attention to participants who are authentic sharers and reverent listeners.

Managing Difficult Conversations

Ironically, as soon as the facilitator is successful in supporting authentic conversation, she is confronted with a new challenge, which is how to now manage the difficult conversations that usually arise out of authenticity. A difficult conversation occurs when two or more participants are in some kind of conflict with each other, and defensiveness or anger or other intense emotions start to surface. As discussed in earlier chapters, dialogue ends and monologue begins when the Other is silenced through violence or the threat of violence. The facilitator must help the group identify what happened in the group and then assist the group in "moving" through the difficulty back to dialogue. Some techniques that might be useful in this process involve direct processing of what is happening.

The facilitator can turn to the group and ask, "What just happened?" or (less directly) "What are people feeling in their bodies right now?" Often, someone in the group is able and willing to respond, perhaps saying, "I feel uncomfortable" or "I am scared after what Jimmy said."

The facilitator can then turn to the participant who became defensive or angry and ask, "What just happened for you, Jimmy?" Jimmy might respond at first with more defensive or angry words, but the facilitator is gently persistent, and says, "Jimmy, what *emotion* did you have, mad, sad, glad, scared, or excited?" (see Chapter 8). Often, Jimmy can say, "Well I think I felt scared." This is a breakthrough, and the facilitator says, "Good job, Jimmy . . . now do you know why you were scared?" I have noticed that often people are the most frightening to others when they themselves are frightened. A transformation can occur when a person can just own her fear directly (name it) rather than acting it out (through defensive or aggressive behavior).

I like to say that when you move the *a* (the *a* could stand for increased "awareness" as well as "attachment") in the word *scared,* you get the word *sacred.* In other words, when we apply nonjudgmental awareness to our fear, we usually learn about what we are currently holding sacred or are attached to. For example, if I notice I am scared in a group and realize that I am afraid of being hurt, then I have uncovered how I am currently especially attached to being accepted. This is of course neither "good" nor "bad," but is just where I am at in the present moment (see Chapter 9).

Action-Processing-Action

Dialogue work goes in repeating cycles of acting-processing-acting-processing. The acting part of the cycle is when the group engages in some kind of activity, such as going around the circle in a check-in, doing a circle dance, or sharing memories of a certain event. The processing part of the cycle happens when the group talks about talking (sometimes also called *meta-communicating*). When the group processes, it dialogues about what the acting part of the cycle was like. The facilitator might say, for example, after an activity, "What was it like doing that conversation?" Processing gives the dialogue group an opportunity to go more deeply into their experience. I almost always give the dialogue group an opportunity to process after every activity we do.

Bigger and Smaller

Sometimes a dialogue group needs to be divided into smaller groups for part of the meeting. The facilitator can move the group back and forth between large and small group sizes, as the need shifts. For example, one time I was asked to facilitate a dialogue with a group of immigrants from a particular country. Expecting maybe 15 people, I was confronted with a room full of almost 100 people in the school cafeteria. Only about two thirds of them could speak English well enough to carry on a conversation. Luckily, 8 church volunteers had come with the participants to help with transportation. We divided the group into 8 subgroups of about 14 people (each group was to be facilitated by 1 of the "emergency volunteers" from the church). I gave simple instructions: "Will each small group go around the circle, introducing themselves, and then take turns telling a story about how they became a refugee?" The evening went surprisingly well. We eventually came back to the large group and, during the last 20 minutes, processed what happened in the small groups.

Checking In and Checking Out

Checking in and checking out is a nice way to begin and end a group, as well as to foster relationship and community. The check-in is usually a time-limited go-around-the-circle activity when participants have the opportunity to talk about where they are at or what their life has been like since the last dialogue. Usually the agreement is that everyone just listens to the check-ins until everyone is done. The facilitator can be the timekeeper and let people know if they go over their time limit.

The check-out is an opportunity for participants to talk about where they are at, near the end of the dialogue, before everyone leaves. The check-out also has to be time limited. Sometimes I ask people to just do a one-word check-out if we only have a few minutes. Usually the check-out seems to pull things together and gives everyone a chance to reflect on themselves and each other.

EVALUATION AND FOLLOW-UP

Following Up With Social Action

Sometimes dialogue groups decide that they want to be involved in some kind of social actions or projects outside of the group (see Section III). For example, my men's

EXPERIENTIAL LEARNING 5.2

(1) Do you like checking in and out of a group? Explain.

(2) Is it harder for you to speak out in a group or to remain silent? Explain.

(3) Do you relate to the idea of "holding space"? What does it mean to you?

dialogue group occasionally agrees to meet to do presentations or dialogues in front of community audiences. Also, my dialogue training group has regularly responded to "diversity emergencies" in the community, as well as provided campus program diversity trainings. These events are usually not attended by everyone in the group. Some want to volunteer, while others may be busy or not ready to participate. The dialogue group always does a follow-up conversation about how the event went and what we each learned about ourselves.

Renegotiating

What is the length of the group? Is it ongoing or time limited? These are decisions that usually involve both participants and the facilitator. Most participants in dialogue are voluntary members, and as such, they will want input into such factors as the nature of the commitment to the group, the date and time, and length of the sessions. These decisions are made at the beginning of the group and are often renegotiated during the dialogues or at the end of the commitment. Thus, the group might decide, after a 10-week dialogue series, to recommit for another 5 weeks, for example.

Referring

Some participants may want additional formal or informal supports, especially if the dialogue group is actually ending. The facilitator can assist with this and can also encourage other group members for ideas and help. For example, one man wanted to find a more local dialogue group to continue in, after the men's group ended. It turned out that there was no men's group in his small town, so he started one himself, with the support of the group.

Re-searching

Each dialogue group should have some kind of assessment. I like to ask for some kind of feedback at the end of every session, even if all that happens is a one-word check-out. There sometimes also may be a need for more formal evaluation at the end of a dialogue series. Table 5.5 offers a list of questions that the facilitator might consider using for monitoring (ongoing procedure to measure ongoing dialogue process) or evaluation (performed after the program is done to measure more long-term and overall results). These questions may work best if asked in the order given.

Table 5.5   Questions for Monitoring and Evaluation

(1) What did you like and dislike about the dialogue(s)?

(2) What did the facilitator(s) do that helped or hindered the dialogue(s)?

(3) What recommendation would you make to us about future dialogues?

(4) What activities did you like the best? Why?

(5) What activities did you like the least? Why?

(6) Is there anything else you would like to comment on?

ADDITIONAL DIALOGUE ISSUES

Participants Are Supervisors

My participants are my supervisors. They teach me what to do by the way they react to the exercises and processing in the group. They provide a stream of feedback that informs the "midcourse corrections" that I must constantly make during the course of a dialogue. I try to observe, for example, the extent to which people feel safe, feel engaged, and feel connected and then try to respond in ways that might help the process. If I am not sure what is going on, I might ask the group a question, for example, "What are people feeling right now?" or "How is this process working right now?"

Dialogue Training Groups

My favorite method for training future dialogue facilitators is what we have called the dialogue training group (DTG). Our DTG meets once a month for a 2-hour session, and we ask members for a yearlong commitment. During the training each month, we start with a brief check-in and then launch into dialogues about the divides and diversity issues in our own lives. The participants learn about dialogue both by participating and by taking turns leading the group in exercises. We have developed enough mutual trust to be able to give each other direct feedback about the ways we participate and lead. This group is one of the most intense experiences I have every month, and I enjoy the learning that takes place. As a co-facilitator (see section below) and participant, I learn as much about myself as the participants learn about themselves.

The DTG both responds to campus/community diversity emergencies as well as provides trainings for interested programs and departments. A small subgroup of us will go out and do these events and then come back to the large group for debriefing and evaluation. For example, I asked the DTG to meet in front of a large Master of Social Work (MSW) class (with 80 students). We organized the room so that the DTG was in a small circle inside a larger half circle of the students. We conducted a dialogue in front of them, starting off with the question, "What are some issues of racial and cultural diversity that you face in your daily life today?" After a 45-minute session, I asked my class to join in the dialogue and provided some empty seats in the small circle for people to come in and make a statement or ask a question. About 15 students came in and out of circle to participate. A later class evaluation indicated that most students found this "fish bowl" exercise to be extremely valuable.

Co-facilitation

Co-facilitation of a group presents both potential benefits and challenges. When co-facilitating, the leaders can take turns observing group members and leading exercises, so that fewer things get unnoticed in the process (four eyes are better than two). In addition, the best co-facilitators probably are two people with different traits who can work in a complementary manner.

One of my favorite co-facilitators is a woman who is of a different race and sexual orientation than me. She is also more extroverted than I am and has different coping mechanisms than I do. In other words, our differences complement each other. We are able to meet independently from time to time to talk about the dialogues, plan, and support each other's growth.

Structure

Structure includes the planned exercises that the facilitator asks participants to do. In general, the facilitator strives to find the balance between too much and not enough structure. Too much structure can be oppressive and reduce growth. Not enough structure can result in an experience that does not feel safe, which can also reduce growth. As is the case with ground rules, increased structure is also most important when working with groups that are lower functioning, such as children or developmentally immature teens and adults.

The participants will show me what level of structure they need, by how well they can participate in dialogue. Often a dialogue group will need the most structure in the first meetings, so I will bring an exercise for them to do for those sessions. Eventually, I hope that the group will become more self-directed. They may let me know that they are ready to set the agenda themselves when they take over the group, refuse to do the exercise I brought, or become openly rebellious.

Dealing With Challenging Participants

Some participants are very quiet, and some are rarely quiet. On one hand, the facilitator wants people to feel comfortable being themselves in the dialogue. On the other hand, the facilitator also wants people to have transformations of their sociohistorical trauma. I also want everyone in the group to be able to have opportunities to participate. So when clients are very quiet or very verbal, I might ask them to reflect on what they are feeling and thinking and to consider sharing that with the group. If the client absolutely refuses to talk, I have to honor that request.

Over many years of facilitation, there have only been a few times that I have had to deal with serious aggressive or threatening behaviors, but these moments have been memorable.

I have learned that I have a responsibility as the facilitator to immediately respond to aggressive or threatening behaviors, because if I remain silent, I am giving permission for such behavior and the group becomes unsafe for all members. As discussed in Chapter 2, violence is a monologue, because it silences and ignores the other. If one participant is silenced, in a way we all are silenced.

What are some techniques for dealing with these behaviors? I first want to stop the behavior, perhaps by referring to the ground rules, and then to follow up with some processing about what happened, so that the difficulty can become another learning experience. If the aggressive participant is willing and able to control his behavior and tune in to the impact of his behavior on others, then I am willing to continue working with him. If the behaviors continue, I have counseled some participants out of the group.

Mistakes

Facilitator mistakes are unavoidable, and often what seem at first to be mistakes may ultimately turn out not to be. I would much rather see my students take some risks to facilitate transformation than to be so careful that they do not stand in the facilitator role and say what they actually think.

When I make a mistake, I know I can usually change direction. I try to stay open to the feedback I get from the participants and forgive myself for my imperfections so I can move on. For example, in one dialogue, a participant said that I had said something "stupid." I sensed that she was angry and asked her how she was feeling. She said, "Nothing," and I confronted her, suggesting that I believed she actually was angry at me. This argument went on for a while, and then I realized that I was not being helpful to the woman and that, whether or not she was angry, *I* was feeling hurt and angry at her. I backed off and focused on other people in the room.

Debriefing

Finally, following a dialogue, both participants and facilitators often require a "debriefing" conversation. The purpose of debriefing is to give people a chance to relax and process frankly what the dialogue was like for them, within their own "safe group." For example, in one dialogue on "American Indian Historical Trauma," I invited a group of Navajo and Ute Indians to my dialogue models class. I knew all the visitors quite well except for one woman, who happened to come when her friends invited her at the last minute. I found out later that this new woman had never processed much about her own historical trauma before. The dialogue was finished about 30 minutes before class was over, and I went to another room with only the Indian guests for a debriefing session, leaving the class with my teaching assistants, who debriefed with them at the same time. The new woman cried during the debriefing, and we listened to her talk about all the memories and feelings the dialogue had brought up for her. We also talked about what worked and did not work in the dialogue.

I try to do debriefings like this whenever I can, particularly with subgroups that seem to be especially vulnerable. My dialogue training group also does debriefings after we do public dialogues or trainings. In such settings, we can safely discuss and evaluate our own co-facilitation and give each other helpful feedback and support.

EXPERIENTIAL LEARNING 5.3

(1) What do you think about the idea that the participant is the supervisor?

(2) Can you relate to the idea of a dialogue training group being an effective learning space for yourself? Why or why not?

(3) As a beginning facilitator, would you rather work with a co-facilitator or alone? Explain.

(4) How would you feel if a participant threatened someone else in a group you were facilitating? What would you do?

(5) How much structure do you like to have as a participant? Does this influence how much structure you like to impose on others when you facilitate?

VIGNETTE: WHAT IS DIALOGUE?

Where do you sit when you want to talk? I mean *talk,* not just chit-chat. Oh, but wait, do you actually sit when you want to talk? Or do you walk or simply stand, leaning against something maybe? I sit, I definitively sit! It is the same when I see a beautiful painting that attracts me or an amazing landscape; I sit to contemplate. It matters to me, something of the stillness, of the resting place. And then, silence happens all around and the contemplation becomes meditation somehow. When I talk, I mean *talk,* it is like that: I contemplate and meditate. And in these moments, I see sky and openness; I feel comfort, safety, too, and the building of an intimacy of words and stares. Dialogue is about talking for me, no way around that. It is deeply connected to the Word, the ability to speak, to produce meaning, sounds that mean. Yes, of course, language is broader than just words: body language, postures, gestures, eyes, and smiles. And yet, it goes together; a subtitle for the words. In my life, I spent so many late evenings and early mornings just talking; it is part of who I am—I have been shaped and transformed through countless dialogues. Sometimes difficult, sometimes passionate, other times quiet and profound: a whole spectrum of emotions and feelings inhabit them. Impossible to put it under one definition; dialogue seems to be an ongoing experience, a living thing that lasts and lasts and is making me every time a little bit different than the time before that. *Recollection* may be a good word to describe it; it indicates a mix of memories and regrouping; a gathering of oneself in order to go forward. Dialogue has this effect: It reminds me of who I am and opens doors to go through; it lets me revisit the past and, at the same time, projects me into the future. In short, dialogue corresponds to the present time, to be present to myself.

Vignette Author: Muriel Schmid

Muriel Schmid is originally from Switzerland, where she earned her PhD in Protestant Theology; while studying theology, she also pursued the ordination track in the Swiss Reformed Church and worked as a minister for several years. Her recent research interest focuses on religion and peacemaking; she conducted fieldwork in Palestine/Israel and has developed projects on interfaith dialogue.

Source: Photo courtesy of Adelaide Ryder.

REFERENCES

Beutler, L. E., Consoli, A. J., & Lane, G. (2005). Systematic treatment selection and prescriptive psychotherapy: An integrative eclectic approach. In J. C. Norcross & M. R. Goldfried (Eds.), *Handbook of psychotherapy integration* (2nd ed., pp. 121–143). New York: Oxford University Press.

Bridges, N. A. (2001). Therapist's self-disclosure: Expanding the comfort zone. *Psychotherapy, 38,* 21–30.

Brooks-Harris, J. E. (2008). *Integrative multitheoretical psychotherapy.* Boston: Houghton-Mifflin.

Duncan, B. L., Miller, S. D., Wampold, B. E., & Hubble, M. A. (2009). *The heart and soul of change: Delivering what works in therapy* (2nd ed.). Washington, DC: American Psychological Association.

Greenspan, M. (1986). Should therapists be personal? Self-disclosure and therapeutic distance in feminist therapy. In D. Howard (Ed.), *The dynamics of feminist therapy* (pp. 5–17). New York: Haworth.

Kessler, L. E., & Waehler, C. A. (2005). Ethical issues in professional practice: Addressing multiple relationships between clients and therapists in lesbian, gay, bisexual, and transgender communities. *Professional Psychology: Research and Practice, 36,* 66–72.

Lambert, M. J. (1986). Some implications of psychotherapy outcome research for eclectic psychotherapy. *Journal of Integrative & Eclectic Psychotherapy, 5*(1), 16–45.

Lambert, M. J. (1991). Introduction to psychotherapy research. In L. E. Beutler & M. Cargo (Eds.), *Psychotherapy research: An international review of programmatic studies* (pp. 1–11). Washington, DC: American Psychological Association.

Lazarus, A. A. (1992). Multimodal therapy: Technical eclecticism with minimal integration. In J. C. Norcross & M. R. Goldfried (Eds.), *Handbook of psychotherapy integration* (pp. 231–263). New York: Basic Books.

Lazarus, A. A. (1994). How certain boundaries and ethics diminish therapeutic effectiveness. *Ethics and Behavior, 4,* 255–261.

Lazarus, A. A. (2005). Multimodal therapy. In J. C. Norcross & M. R. Goldfried (Eds.), *Handbook of psychotherapy integration* (2nd ed., pp. 105–120). New York: Oxford University Press.

Petersen, C. (2002). More than a mirror: The ethics of therapist self-disclosure. *Psychotherapy: Theory, Research, Practice, Training, 19*(1), 21–31.

Dialogue Models

INTRODUCTION TO SECTION II

All professional helpers are dialogue facilitators. The social worker who does family therapy, the grade school teacher who helps her children learn about social science, and the nurse practitioner who helps the elderly cope with chronic disease are all playing the role of dialogue facilitators.

In each chapter in Section II, a dialogue model drawn from one of the multiple theories that inform the ecobiopsychosocialspiritual elements is described. Chapter 6 presents a first force dialogue model, based on psychodynamic theory. The main insight of psychodynamic psychology is that the past can have a significant but often unconscious influence on the present. In this chapter, methods of making these unconscious dynamics more conscious are described and applied to individual, couple, family, and group dialogue situations. Chapter 7 offers a cognitive-behavioral (trying out new ways of thinking and acting) approach to dialogue. Experiential dialogue (speaking from the heart) is examined in Chapter 8 and transpersonal dialogue (owning the shadow) in Chapter 9. Additional chapters follow.

Psychodynamic Dialogue

Telling Our Stories

Psychodynamic dialogue is, most of all, about telling our stories. When people are in difficult conversations, talking about issues that strongly divide us, the exercise of storytelling can help further the relationship-building process. Most people enjoy talking about themselves and will willingly tell stories about their past experiences. The sharing of such stories can help shift focus from ideological differences about such subjects as religion and politics. As we better understand other people, especially "where they are coming from," we seem to often become more willing to try to understand their ideologies, beliefs, and feelings.

Psychodynamic dialogue can also help participants better understand and accept themselves. As I explore my own personal story, I start to gain insight into why I currently feel, think, and act the ways I do. These insights do not by themselves help me change my feelings, thoughts, and behaviors, but insight can help inform and sustain my decision to make such changes. As described in the next section, such insight can help inform my relationship building with others.

A GENERAL PSYCHODYNAMIC APPROACH TO DIALOGUE

There are three stages of psychodynamic work in dialogue.

(1) Telling my stories: What happened?

Each participant has stories to tell about her own life and the lives of her family, community, and ancestors. The facilitator invites stories from participants and trusts that they will share the best stories they currently are ready to share. The work of the rest of the dialogue circle is to listen to the story with respect and compassion. The facilitator does not interpret the stories or try to give them meaning but simply models listening.

For example, I invited a group of American Indians I had previously worked with into one of my dialogue classes. The purpose of the dialogues was to talk about sociohistorical trauma as their lands were invaded in the 18th and 19th centuries. In the first dialogue, our visitors chose to sit in a small circle inside the larger circle of students. I asked the students to just listen as our visitors shared stories. Some of the stories were ones that had been told to the speakers by their own parents or grandparents, many about forced resettlement to reservations and boarding schools. Other stories were about micro-aggressions that had occurred a few days or weeks ago, perhaps in grocery stores and fast-food restaurants. After the stories were told, the students had a chance to respond with comments and questions. Later, I met with the Indian group and gave them a chance to "debrief" about what their experience in the class was like. Although everyone was glad they had participated, the conversation had for some opened up old wounds, and we talked about the difficult emotions that had come up for the participants.

(2) Developing insight into my relational dynamics: How does the past affect my current relationships?

"Relational dynamics" are the ways my own psychology interacts with my relationships. As will be described further in the review below, psychodynamic work can help people gain insight into these relational dynamics and gradually transform them.

Often, participants can begin this work by noticing the stereotypes or other relational dynamics they carry from their past, perhaps about a particular group of people. When I use stereotypes to attack or to protect myself, I go out of relationship with the Other. When stereotypes are owned (shared) in a dialogue, with the intent to move toward transformation of historical trauma, relationship building can occur. In the psychodynamic language, stereotypes might be called transferences or countertransferences, depending on whether the client or professional helper holds them.

In a dialogue on sexuality and disabilities, for example, I asked participants to share their stereotypes about children and youth with disabilities and about their parents. The group was composed of parents of disabled children, multidisciplinary professionals who work with these parents, and multidisciplinary students. The students and faculty were initially reluctant to share, so I asked if they could first talk about what made this a difficult conversation. One faculty person said that she was embarrassed, especially as a medical professional, to admit that she has feelings and thoughts that could be viewed by her peers as stereotypes. This comment broke the ice, and others also agreed that they felt uncomfortable publicly admitting they had stereotypes, although we all agreed that it is "normal" to have them. Gradually, the group members began sharing stereotypes that we have regarding the sexuality of people with disabilities. These included that people with disabilities do not have sex, that they don't think about sex, and that they cannot have satisfying marriage-type relationships as adults.

(3) Using that insight to working on where "I end" and "you begin" in our dialogue: To what degree are the reactions that I am having about you actually about me?

Each of us has some reaction to every person we meet and relate with. Usually this reaction is actually a complex collection of feelings and thoughts (or relational dynamics) that is at least partly rooted in our own past histories in this practice, and participants learn to take ownership of their interpersonal reactions and other internal dynamics.

In a dialogue series on bridging the gender divide, I asked participants to share their judgments about another person of the opposite gender in the room. This is, of course, an emotionally challenging exercise for most people, perhaps because we are afraid to hear how others judge us (and perhaps even more because we are afraid to admit publicly that we have similar judgments of others).

As we all took turns sharing our judgments, we discovered that, when judgments are shared with loving intent, healing and transformation become possible. As people shared their judgments, they often also shared insight into the historical origins of the trauma, because probably most of our judgments originate from our own sociohistorical trauma. For example, my judgment about men being bullies might have come from my childhood experiences with a bullying father. We also discussed how we usually hide our judgments from ourselves and others, which keeps us from ever "checking out" whether those judgments are still based on reality.

WHAT IS THE PSYCHODYNAMIC APPROACH?

The goal of psychodynamic psychology is to help the person gain insight into her past so that she can get her needs better met in the present. Psychodynamic interventions help people explore the internal dynamics of their psyche, or soul. These dynamics are viewed, at least in part, as a reflection of the person's history and are understood as the often unconscious motivations behind that person's present behaviors (Frederickson, 1999; Freud, 1962; Jones, 1981). Thus, in psychodynamic work, the client uncovers her internal conflicts and develops insight into herself by making her unconscious more conscious.

Psychodynamic psychology, originating in late 19th-century Europe, was the "First Force" of modern Western psychology (Maslow, 1971). Although no longer the most popular approach to practice, psychodynamic theory is the oldest, most developed, and theoretically richest of the "Four Forces" of modern psychology. Psychodynamic interventions especially target cognitive and social development. The exploration into the past is largely a *cognitive* function, in which the person increases her insight into how her personal history still affects her life. Like interventions from many other models, psychodynamic interventions work best when the person understands why he is doing the work, is motivated enough to face sometimes painful material, and has sufficient intelligence to develop insight into his internal dynamics (Lambert, 2003).

The person also "works through" these insights, making changes in the way he relates *socially* in the two key areas of life, love and work. The person's love life begins at birth with her relationship with her earliest caretakers. Freud (1950) believed that this story of love is the most revealing story in any person's life. The person's work life begins, for the most part, in preschool or grade school and continues through adulthood. Most psychoanalytic therapists hope that their clients will learn how to improve their ability to love and work with a sense of happiness and satisfaction (Cogan, 2007).

SCIENTIFIC EVIDENCE FOR PSYCHODYNAMIC APPROACHES

Several key concepts of psychodynamic theory have received some verification from science (Hunt, 1993). There is increasing evidence, for example, supporting the existence of the unconscious. Indeed, some scientists have concluded that most self-regulation of human behavior occurs on the unconscious level (Bargh & Chartrand, 1999). Recent advances in neurobiology may now help scientists link specific unconscious processes to specific brain circuits. The unconscious processes that have been linked to brain circuit activity include the person's ability to keep a stable equilibrium (homeostasis), to influence reactions to the environment (modulation), and to understand and respond to social cues (processing). These unconscious processes are now thought to happen in a number of brain regions, including subcortical structures in the basal forebrain, hypothalamus, and brainstem, as well as the amygdala, orbitofrontal cortex, and higher association cortices (Viamontes & Beitman, 2007).

Psychodynamic methods have also been shown to be effective in helping people. Studies based on client reports, measurable treatment outcomes, and long-term measurements have all shown evidence of varying degrees of client improvement (Cogan, 2007). A meta-analysis of studies of psychodynamic therapy showed evidence of positive long-term changes in client well-being (Leichsenring & Leibing, 2003). Psychodynamic interventions also have been shown to be effective with adolescents and young adults (Barusch & Fearon, 2002) and in both individual and group settings (Guseva, Iovlev, & Shchelkova, 2002).

PSYCHODYNAMIC STORY 6.1

I can imagine I am a 40-year-old man, married, with two children. For the past 10 years, my wife constantly nagged at me and never seemed to be happy with anything I did. I often retreated into my alcohol as I found myself staying away from home as much as possible. My son and daughter became teens and seemed to no longer stay at home very much, and now they only talk with me when they need money. I became a partner in my law firm several years ago, and my income almost doubled. But after all my hard work, including making a name for myself in corporate law, I felt less and less life satisfaction. After all my hard work, there was less and less love expressed and felt in my home.

After my law partners confronted me about my drinking, I agreed to get some professional help. I did not realize until I did some work with a psychodynamic therapist that much of my present life is related to my past. My social worker helped me see that I had married a woman who was in many ways like my own mother, who also seemed to be constantly unhappy with me. I had forgotten how my mother nagged my father and how my father used alcohol as an escape. I also realized that I had unconsciously re-created my father's work experience. My dad was a physician, but he frequently seemed unhappy with his job. He would complain about his patients and his own fatigue but continued to work long hours away from home.

Maybe the most important thing I have learned is that I do not need to blame my parents or myself anymore. After I realized what happened in my past, I was angry at my parents for a while, but my social worker helped me forgive them when I was ready. I have also learned to forgive myself as well. I am not sure if I changed or if my family changed, but my wife and I are getting along with each other a little better now, and my kids sometimes talk with me about other things besides wanting money. I am also mentoring the younger lawyers at the firm, which gives me more job satisfaction than I had before.

EXPERIENTIAL LEARNING 6.1

(1) Can you see relationships between your life today and your past life experiences? Do you think that increased insight into these relationships could help you increase your life satisfaction? Explain.

(2) Does insight into the past automatically change a person in the present? Explain.

(3) Do you think that forgiveness should be the ultimate goal of psychodynamic work? Why or why not?

Psychodynamic Dialogue

The purpose of the psychodynamic dialogue model, like all dialogue models presented in this book, is the transformation of sociohistorical trauma. Built upon the core ideas of psychodynamic theory, this approach uses stories about the past to help transform trauma. People also learn to dialogue with the different "parts" of themselves.

Although all are interrelated, dialogue models can be separated into two broad types, internal and collective, which will both be presented in this chapter.

Internal dialogue is dialogue between different "parts" or "voices" of the self. From a psychodynamic perspective, these different voices all have an origin in the person's past history.

The purpose of internal dialogue is to help the person understand the nature and origins of all of her voices so that she can make effective decisions that support her highest good. The self-understanding and self-acceptance that can come from internal dialogue can enable the person to engage in deeper collective dialogue with the other.

Collective dialogue is dialogue between the person and the other, which may be "another" person, another living thing, or a part ("ecopart") of the ecosystem that supports all life. In psychodynamic collective dialogue, participants share stories about the past and insights about their own personal dynamics. Collective dialogue also may help develop relationships across religious, economic, political, and ecological divides.

The Role of the Facilitator in Psychodynamic Dialogue

Like all dialogue models, psychodynamic dialogue does not necessarily require a facilitator. However, a facilitator frequently is able to assist participants in their own self-analysis and deep conversation with the other. The psychodynamically oriented facilitator actively helps participants explore their past stories, uncover their unconscious internal dynamics, and work through these insights so that they can get their current needs better met.

The facilitator *sets the tone*. She may begin the dialogue session by briefly asking each participant to talk about his intent for the group. This discussion is done because, as mentioned above, clients use psychodynamic techniques more successfully when they understand and support the purpose of the work. The facilitator may begin the dialogue by asking the entire group, a subgroup, or an individual participant to begin sharing.

The psychodynamic facilitator often acts as a *catalyst*. The facilitator may at times ask participants to tell stories that are about painful and uncomfortable issues. The purpose of such direction is to help the participants engage in more meaningful topics that are closer to the roots of their own internal dynamics. If the discussion of the group seems superficial and rather intellectual, the facilitator might suggest a change of subject or focus.

Although the facilitator listens deeply and does not interrupt, she may also *ask questions* that are designed to help the participant further explore his own psyche. Often the goal of these questions is to help the participant shift her focus away from the limitations of the other and instead toward her own self-awareness and self-acceptance. For example, if a participant says, "A lot of women like to nag men," the facilitator might ask, "It sounds like that might have happened to you. Could you tell us more about that and how it may have affected you?"

The facilitator may offer *interpretations* at times. The facilitator knows that these interpretations may not be accurate or helpful, so instead of stating her perceptions as if they are facts, she usually checks them out with the client. For example, when a participant repeatedly gets angry at others in the group, the facilitator might offer the interpretation, "Bill, I wonder when you get angry like that whether you are still feeling angry at your father."

The facilitator also sets *boundaries*. The facilitator helps participants notice when someone "makes someone else wrong," makes threats, or acts in other abusive ways. If such statements are ignored by the facilitator, then the dialogue space may become too unsafe for dialogue to continue. For example, a participant might say, "Anyone who is a Christian is just not using his head." The facilitator can respond to this by asking, "How did other people in the group feel when Mary said that?" After several people tell Mary that they felt attacked by her, the facilitator might focus on Mary again and say, "Mary, I wonder if you could talk with us a little about why you made a comment like that . . . maybe you could talk about what made you feel the way you do toward Christians."

The facilitator is *patient*. She understands that dialogue typically brings small changes, rather than dramatic ones. She accepts these small changes because she realizes that human beings can grow only as fast as they are ready to. For example, at the start of a dialogue, a participant may feel a strong dislike for another participant. By the end of the dialogue, the participant may still not like the other person, but she may understand him just a little more. Such a change may eventually lead to other more significant shifts over time, such as increased self-awareness and a more loving attitude toward self and others.

The facilitator is able to be fully *present* with the participants. She is aware of her own internal dynamics, but she is not distracted by them. Since she largely accepts herself, she does not bring a "false self" to her leadership style but rather leads the group with personal integrity and wholeness. Her ability to be present models the same way of being for participants in the dialogue group.

The ultimate goal of the facilitator is to help people learn to dialogue (be in relationship) without a facilitator. In psychodynamic terms, the facilitator hopes to gradually become an *introject* or, in other words, to become a part of the participant's own psyche. When the participant introjects the facilitator, she has an "inner facilitator" growing inside of herself who can eventually do all of the functions that the "real" facilitator did. Thus, gradually, the person conducts more and more of her daily interactions as dialogue, with, for example, her family, her employer, and her neighbors.

Internal Dialogue: An Ego State Model

Internal dialogue is dialogue between the voices inside the person. There are many possible ways to think about these voices inside all of us. One psychodynamic theory, transactional analysis, categorizes the voices of the human psyche into three easily understood "ego states" (see Berne, 1964; see also Chapter 1). As illustrated in Table 6.1, the "child" ego state represents the childlike or more selfish "part" of the self, and the parent represents the parental or more authoritarian "part." The third ego state, the observer, can be thought of as the facilitator of the ongoing dialogue between the child and parent. These three ego states—child, observing self, and parent—are based on Freud's (1962) theory of the id, ego, and superego.

According to psychodynamic theory, all three ego states gradually become more developed, balanced, and accessible in the maturing adult. All three states have utility. Typically, the child ego state wants to experience pleasure and avoid suffering. The parent ego state (which, according to psychodynamic theory, is the "introject" of the person's early caregivers) often wants the child to be more disciplined, to delay gratification, and to conform to familial and cultural expectations. The observing self is capable of listening to both the child and the parent and can help make decisions that balance both perspectives. There is scientific evidence that these ego states actually are reflected in our brain structures (Kline, 1981).

An example of an ego state dialogue is shown in Dialogue 6.1. In this illustration, Bill creates an internal space or "container" for the dialogue inside himself. His own "inner child" wants to go to college at a location that seems like fun. His "parent" wants the child to put a good education ahead of pleasure. His "observing self" wants each ego state to have both a "voice" and an "ear" so that the child and parent can develop decisions based on mutual understanding and respect.

The facilitator can help a person conduct her own internal dialogue. One way to do this is to use a technique called "empty chairs" drawn from experiential psychology (see Chapter 13). The facilitator sets up three empty chairs, each of which represents the "position" of one of the ego states: child, parent, and observing self. The facilitator has the other person move from chair to chair and speak as if she is the ego state represented by that

Table 6.1 Ego States Engaged in Internal Dialogue

Ego States	Child	Observing Self	Parent
Ego state voices	What I want and do not want What I feel and think What I will do and will not do	The observer and dialogue facilitator	What I should and should not think What I should and should not want What I should and should not do

Dialogue 6.1: Child and Parent Ego States

Bill is conflicted about what college he will go to after he graduates from high school. Since he is taking a dialogue class in school, he decides to dialogue his conflict. He sits down in a comfortable chair by himself. Part of the dialogue goes like this:

Bill's observer: OK. I want the child to start first.

Bill's child: Well, I think it would be fun to go to the West Coast. I could find an apartment by the beach. I hear they have some great parties.

Bill's parent: No! You are not going to school to party; you are going to school to get an education so you can have an occupation and so you can be a provider of a family some day.

Bill's observer: I want to ask the parent to be more respectful to the child here. Dialogue is about listening, not persuading or intimidating. This is a dialogue, not a debate.

Bill's parent: OK. Let me say it like this. I am worried that if I go to the West Coast, I might not learn anything, and then I will be sorry later. The most important thing to me is not fun but a good education.

Bill's observer: Thank you, parent; I like the way you said that. Now, is a common interest emerging here?

Bill's child: Well, I want to have fun, but I also see it's no fun being a loser my whole life.

Bill's parent: And I acknowledge that a little fun is not so bad; maybe I can focus on my studies best when I also get some good recreation in my life.

Bill's observer: Maybe there *is* a compromise emerging where you both could win.

chair position. Thus, the same dialogue illustrated in Dialogue 6.1 could be conducted by a person alone or with a facilitator. Often a facilitator is also particularly helpful if a person feels "stuck" in a particular child-parent conflict, perhaps because one of the ego states has been dominating the other two. The facilitator can help the person first find all the various voices and then hear each respectfully.

EXPERIENTIAL LEARNING 6.2

(1) Can you relate to the idea that you have three ego states? If so, do they sometimes seem in conflict with each other, even "at war"?

(2) What do you think about the idea that a person can engage in internal dialogue? Have you ever conducted an internal dialogue?

(3) Describe a conflict or "divide" that currently exists between your own inner child and parent. Try conducting a dialogue about the conflict and see if you can develop greater understanding and even a decision.

(4) With another person, take turns facilitating an internal dialogue with each other.

Internal Dialogue: Working Through Transference and Projections

One of the goals of dialogue is an increased mutual understanding. Our own psyches can, however, become obstacles to deep understanding of self and others. Internal dialogue can help the person transform these obstacles into pathways toward greater understanding. Psychologists suggest that people decide what they think and feel about another person in less than a minute (Demarais & White, 2004). Often such first impressions are at least partly inaccurate because they are distorted by past experiences in the person's life (transference) and/or by uncomfortable reactions that the person can have when encountering the other (projection).

Past experiences can easily color current perception. In psychodynamic theory, an individual has a *transference* toward another person when he "transfers" the memory of how he felt in a past experience onto the current situation. For example, a woman might encounter a man who reminds her in some way of her former verbally abusive husband. The woman might assume that the man is also verbally abusive and react accordingly, perhaps by keeping her distance from him and acting defensively. If the woman is not aware and accepting of this transference, she may never see who this man really is. However, if the woman can be aware of and accept her transference reaction, then she can understand what "part" her own personal life history plays in creating her uncomfortable reaction to this man. She can choose to not react defensively and to keep her heart and mind open until she has more information about who he is. She can also use the transference reaction as a clue, a potential source of information about herself and the other. If, for example, she knows that he reminds her of her father, she now has a specific issue that she can further investigate. As shown in Dialogue 6.2, the person can dialogue with her transference until she understands and accepts the reaction.

Transference reactions are thus historical reactions that, if we pay attention to them, can remind us of our past experiences and give us clues to what is happening around us now. No matter how "healthy" he is, there is always a transference reaction inside of an individual to each person he meets. Transference is thus at the same time a source of information about the past, a "voice" inside the person, and a part of that person's internal dialogue.

Dialogue 6.2: Transference

Tiffany is a real estate agent in a small town. She has a new client, Sam, who wants to buy a house. Tiffany notices right away that she does not like Sam and is unsure why. She decides to have an internal dialogue with her transference reaction. Tiffany has the following internal conversation with her transference.

Tiffany: What is my transference reaction?

Transference: I do not like Sam.

Tiffany: What do I not like about him?

Transference: I don't trust him. He seems to be devious.

Tiffany: Who does he remind me of?

Transference: Hmmmm. . . . He is actually a little bit like my father, very articulate and charming, but also manipulative and sneaky! That's it!

Tiffany: Good job, but now the real work begins. I need to keep an open mind. Just because he reminds me of my dad does not mean he is necessarily like him. However, it is also possible that he reminds me of my dad *because* he is at least a little bit like him. I will have to figure this out.

EXPERIENTIAL LEARNING 6.3

(1) Think of a person you have recently met.

(2) Allow yourself to have an internal dialogue regarding the transference you have experienced with that person. Remember that you always have some kind of transference in every situation, and it can be positive and/or negative, powerful or subtle.

(3) What clues does the transference you identified give you about who the other person is and who you are? How can you find out more about the truth?

Psychodynamic theory also suggests that a person may not see the other accurately because she has an uncomfortable reaction in the presence of the other and *projects* the reaction experience onto the other person rather than owning it herself. An individual usually projects a characteristic upon another person when he has that same characteristic himself but is not yet aware and accepting of it. For example, in Dialogue 6.3, Peter sees his boss as arrogant. His friend Jane challenges him to do an internal dialogue about this perception, and Peter quickly realizes that he may be projecting characteristics that he does like about himself onto his boss.

Dialogue 6.3: Projection

Peter: My boss is so arrogant! He thinks he is smarter than everyone else!

Jane: Would you like to dialogue that statement with me?

Peter: Well, OK, but go easy on me.

Jane: Of course, that is part of the agreement when you dialogue. So pretend that what you see in your boss may be true of him but is certainly true of yourself.

Peter: That is a bit painful to do, but OK, I want to get through this thing I have with my boss. So maybe I am arrogant and think I am smarter than everyone else too.

Jane: Yes maybe you are like that, Peter, and that is OK because most people I know probably are at least a little like that too.

EXPERIENTIAL LEARNING 6.4

(1) Think of someone you do not like. What characteristics does this person have that are annoying to you?

(2) Engage in an internal dialogue with your perceptions of the other person. Consider the possibility that you have the same characteristics that the other seems to have.

(3) If you do discover that you own the same characteristics, experiment with the idea that it is "OK" to have them.

Collective Dialogue With Couples

Collective dialogue can be used with any couple (or any two people), at any stage in their relationship, to facilitate relationship building in their lives. The two participants and facilitator begin the dialogue with a shared intent that the work will lead to increased reverent understanding of each other. Like all psychodynamic dialogue, the focus is on working through past experiences and uncovering unconscious dynamics.

The psychodynamically oriented facilitator often notices that couples struggle when difficult material is shared. Often one of the hardest things for a person to hear from his partner is that he has somehow hurt her. When a person hears this, he may suddenly feel attacked and bad about himself, and then he may react defensively. Ironically, he may hurt his partner even more when he tries to protect himself by using such *defense mechanisms* as minimization, denial, and blame. The inability to tolerate any negative feedback from a partner is often a reflection of the person's vulnerability to having his *shame* (or sense of inferiority) activated by any suggestion that he is not perfect.

The dialogue facilitator knows that there is no human experience that cannot be talked about. When a participant feels attacked, has an internal shame reaction, and reacts with minimization, denial, and blame, the facilitator can ask that participant to talk about those experiences (see Dialogue 6.4). As in any other dialogue situation, the facilitator does not engage in dialogue if there is evidence that one partner will be at risk for violence during or following the dialogue session.

The psychodynamic dialogue facilitator may assess the content of the couple's current conflicts to help her determine what past issues might be explored (see Dialogue 6.4). When one partner is sharing, the facilitator asks the other person to listen as deeply as he can until the other is finished. Couples can engage in dialogue in a single dyad. They can also do couple dialogue in front of a group attended by other couples, family members, or other participants.

Dialogue 6.4: Couple

Mary and Bill have lived together for 5 years. They state that they are still committed to each other but that they are also very tired of the frequent fights they seem to have. The fights are often about Bill's jealousy. Bill states that Mary is too flirtatious with other men. Mary thinks that Bill is much too controlling. The following is a segment of a dialogue they engaged in:

Facilitator: I want to ask you both to tell some stories about your past. Bill, let's start with you. Can you tell us a story about trust in a relationship in your past?

Bill: When I was a boy, my mother kept promising us that she would stop doing meth. I would trust her when I was younger, but later on I knew she was just lying to us. I could always tell when she was using by how she acted. I knew I could not trust her.

Mary: So is that why you are such a "control freak"?

Bill: You know, I get tired of you calling me a control freak. I really don't think I try to control you at all. Maybe you are just paranoid.

Facilitator: Bill, what just happened inside of you?

Bill: Well, I felt attacked when she said I am a control freak.

Facilitator: Yes, and then what did you feel and do?

Bill: Then I felt what you told us last week is shame, and I denied that it was my problem and made it her problem.

Facilitator: Good, and Mary do you have a response?

Mary: I was angry and that's why I called him a control freak. After Bill talked about his feelings, I started to feel less angry at him.

Facilitator: Can you say that directly to Bill instead of to me?

Mary: Bill, after you talked about your feelings, I started to feel less angry at you. I am sorry I attacked you.

EXPERIENTIAL LEARNING 6.5

(1) Engage yourself in a couple dialogue, either with a facilitator or without one. If you are not in a romantic relationship, you can engage in dialogue with a friend or other person. Notice what happens inside yourself as you and your partner share stories.

(2) Do you think storytelling can promote relationship building? Can exploration of the unconscious also promote relationship and community? If so, why?

(3) It has been said that the shortest distance between a person and the truth is in a story. What do you think about that statement?

Collective Dialogue With Families

Family psychodynamic dialogue engages family members in relationship-building work. The dialogue often is about parent-child conflict. When there are parent-child conflicts, the family can talk about the life experiences that may have led up to those conflicts. Children may benefit from hearing stories about their parents' own childhood experiences, for example. Or children might learn that all their siblings feel as jealous as they do. Psychodynamic family dialogue can also be facilitated across multiple generations, with a child, her mother, and her grandmother, for example.

In families that have been constantly argumentative, ineffective at communication, or even verbally abusive, the dialogue facilitator may need to model how to listen effectively so that the other family members can also begin to listen to each other (see Dialogue 6.5).

The facilitator does not engage in dialogue if there is evidence that any family member will be at risk for violence during or following the dialogue session.

Dialogue 6.5: Family Dialogue

Marsha asks a facilitator to help her family start a dialogue. After living as a single parent for 5 years, she recently began a relationship with Rebecca. Marsha's oldest child, Ted, just turned 16 and does not like Rebecca. Marsha's other child, Sharon, who is 14, seems quiet and withdrawn.

Dialogue facilitator: What if we take turns with this talking stick and each tell a story about something that happened that makes living in this family difficult today.

Ted: I can do that. I remember you coming to pick me up at school with Rebecca, holding her hand. The next day everybody at West High was giving me shit about how my mother was a lesbian.

Dialogue facilitator: That sounds painful.

Ted: Yeah it was.

Dialogue facilitator: Who wants the talking stick next?

Rebecca: I have a story to tell too. I have loved your mother very much. (She looks at Ted.) When I moved in with her, it was because I thought I could make her life better. I have wanted to make your life and the life of your sister better also. I have felt very sad that your life has become harder.

EXPERIENTIAL LEARNING 6.6

(1) Set up a role-play, using the scenario in Dialogue 6.5. In groups of four, participants can each pick one of the four characters in the dialogue. Continue the dialogue.

(2) Share the experience of playing out the role-play with each other. What did each person think and feel? Did the characters move toward relationship?

(3) Continue the dialogue and switch roles until each person has experienced all four roles.

(4) Do you think that this kind of role switching (or "role reversal") can increase empathy and understanding between individuals, family members, or even representatives of nations?

(5) Imagine what might happen if you could have a dialogue with your own family of origin or your current family. What do you think would happen?

Collective Dialogue With Institutions

Psychodynamic dialogue can help foster relationships between members of an institution, such as a school, church, or business. Through small group dialogue, for example, individual members may be able to better understand and accept themselves and others in their organization. The dialogue process may also help members co-create an institution that is more effective in supporting relationship and community.

When people develop relationships with each other, they feel better and are more generative. There is evidence that when relationships improve in institutional settings, productivity also improves (McCann, 2007; Tavistock Institute of Human Relations, 1999). For example, collegial relationships between faculty at university settings are associated with faculty productivity (Katula & Doody, 1990; Wheelan & Tilin, 1999). Similar findings in the private business sector suggest that employees are also more productive when their relationships with each other are positive (Gennard, & Judge, 2002).

From a psychodynamic perspective, institutional dialogue is about the sharing of stories and internal dialogues. The *stories* are the personal experiences of participants who are members of the institution. The stories are told so that all the voices of the members can be heard. Participants may also discuss how these past experiences continue to influence how they think, feel, and act in the institution (see Dialogue 6.6).

Dialogue 6.6: Institutional Stories

At the XYZ Church, a member recently revealed that he is a gay man. There is a divide in the church about whether homosexuality is a sin, and many members have very strong opinions about the subject. Ten members have gathered to have a dialogue about the issue of homosexuality. The dialogue facilitator asks them to begin the first dialogue by telling stories. Each member is asked to tell a story about a personal experience in the church. A limit of 10 minutes is set for each person to talk.

The first speaker is a man who talks about how his parents brought him to the church when he was a little boy. He adds that he was taught by his parents that God thinks that homosexuality is a sin.

The second speaker is an older woman. She tells the group that her older brother, now deceased, was also gay and that she loved him very much.

By the end of the dialogue, the members agree that, although no one has changed their position about homosexuality and sin, they all have a better understanding of and enhanced respect for each other. The members agree to form a committee that will continue to explore ways that the church can both honor its traditions and also respond in a humane way to sexual minorities. In addition, the members like the dialogue meetings so much that they decide to continue them and open the dialogue to other controversial topics and issues that divide the church membership.

Transparent internal dialogues occur when participants share personal self-explorations with the larger group. When people share these internal dialogues, they give others insight into the often complex conflicts that exist inside their own psyches (see Dialogue 6.7). Such insights can enhance compassion and cooperation between members.

Dialogue 6.7: Sharing Internal Dialogue

In the university, the College of Human Relations has had a history of unresolved conflict between faculty. The conflict or divide is between a group of older male faculty and a group of younger female faculty. The two groups hardly speak with each other.

The faculty agree to join in a dialogue with a facilitator. There are about a half dozen participants from each side of the divide.

The facilitator explains what internal dialogue is and asks for a volunteer to start the dialogue.

One of the women starts the conversation. She explains that she wanted to have collegial relationships with both the men and the women but that she was told by one of the women that if she did that, she would suffer politically and would not get support for tenure. She explains that she was torn and unsure what to do.

One of the men states that he felt very hurt by how some of the women treated him. He said that he felt stereotyped as sexist, even though he actually was sympathetic to the situation of many of the women.

Not all of the members share these kinds of internal dialogues, but most of the members do participate. By the end of the first session, several of the faculty state that they thought the work had helped them understand the "other side" of the divide and asked that another dialogue be done at the next month's faculty meeting.

The meetings continue, once a month, over a period of 2 years. At the end of that time, the dean announces that college productivity has increased by over 33%. Perhaps even more important, she states, is the fact that faculty job satisfaction has increased by about 50%.

EXPERIENTIAL LEARNING 6.7

(1) Think of an institution you belong to, perhaps your school, church, or place of employment. Identify a "divide" that seems to separate the members of your institution.

(2) What would need to happen if members in the group "bridged" this divide? Would opinions need to change before the bridging could occur?

(3) What kind of dialogue might help your institution bridge this divide?

(4) Try role-playing such a divide with a group of people or with your class. Have half the class pick one "side" of the divide. After doing the role-play for a while, then have people switch sides and role-play the other side of the divide.

Collective Dialogue With Cultures

Psychodynamic dialogue can also be used both within and between cultures. The purpose of such dialogue is to foster relationships by helping participants share the experiences, thoughts, feelings, and other internal dynamics that are associated with historical trauma. In this section, a small group psychodynamic model is described.

Most cultures have collectively experienced historical trauma or significant suffering in their past. Such trauma, if left unhealed, can continue to affect the well-being of individuals over entire lifetimes (Herman, 1992). Psychodynamic theory suggests that past trauma can also affect entire cultures as well, across individual and even multiple generations (Reik, 1957).

Trauma can be shared by a family, culture, or nation when there is a collectively held history of suffering. For example, Native Americans in the United States share a common history of suffering during the first centuries of European colonialization. Such trauma can be transmitted from one generation to the next (Brave Heart & DeBruyn, 1998). The healing work requires understanding of the traumatic events and the elimination of self-destructive and other violent behaviors (Apprey, 1999). The sharing of stories can help heal historical trauma, especially when the facilitators and participants are culturally sensitive (Tully, 1999). Similarly, in psychodynamic dialogue, participants share stories to transform historical trauma.

Like any of the other models of psychodynamic dialogue described in this chapter, collective dialogue is as much an art as a science. There is no one format or procedure that will work with every population. However, some methods can be forwarded. Since the work may become emotionally uncomfortable at times, collective dialogue works best when participants are committed to the dialogue process.

From a psychodynamic perspective, collective dialogue between cultures is simultaneously both internal and collective:

The dialogue is an *internal* process because each participant is responsible for doing her own self-analysis. Some participants may chose to be "transparent" about their self-analysis and may share what they find with the group. For example, a man might say in front of a group that he has discovered that he is racist. Others may be reluctant to share their discoveries, particularly if they represent uncomfortable or "shadow" material. Such sharing of these internal discoveries often helps confirm and support the *diverse* experiences, thoughts, and feelings that always exist in any group.

The dialogue is also *collective* because participants also may talk about the *shared* experiences, thoughts, and emotions associated with their culture's historical trauma. For example, if a woman tells the group that she believes that her entire culture still is in shock from experiencing genocide, then other participants will probably respond by agreeing or disagreeing with the woman's statement. The facilitator's goal is not necessarily to help the group reach 100% consensus about what happened, but the facilitator does want to help the group notice when some collective wisdom seems to be emerging about the truth of their collective history.

Community-building theory helps inform all models of cross-cultural dialogue. As Peck (1998) has suggested, when people first gather together in a group, they tend to co-create a "pseudo-community" in which they essentially pretend to be similar. Often when the first real differences appear and disagreements start to emerge, the group moves into a state of "chaos," which may feel quite scary to members. "True community" only emerges when the individuals in the group are willing to be authentic with each other and to take responsibility for the welfare of the group as a whole. Such group process can be seen in any size group, for example, in a couple, a family, or a community of 25 people.

Not all groups go through these stages, particularly when there is longstanding historical trauma, and the group process may seem full of hostility and chaos from the start. Thus, the facilitator may find a dialogue group to be initially "stuck" in either the first (pseudo-community) or second (chaotic) stage of community process. The facilitator knows that if the dialogue community stays frozen in either stage, the dialogue may not facilitate relationship building. The pseudo-community stage could be said to represent one extreme way of relating in which people are still afraid to risk discovering their differences. The chaotic stage represents the opposite extreme, in which people are afraid to find their mutuality. With groups that begin with pseudo-community, the facilitator often has to first help the group move into more honest sharing (chaos) and then help them to move out of chaos into "true community." With groups that begin in a chaotic state, the facilitator does not try to help participants move into pseudo-community but does assist them to "own" their mutual hostility, projections, and transferences and thereby move toward true community.

From the psychodynamic perspective, the process of healing collective historical trauma involves not only the mutual sharing of painful stories but also the mutual acceptance of those stories. When a dialogue participant accepts the story of the other, she does not necessarily agree that the story represents *capital "T" truth*. However, she does affirm that the story represents the personal *"little t" truth* of the other person. The dialogue facilitator can help promote such mutual acceptance by modeling and creating a core elder group. The facilitator and elder group both can model self-disclosure and deep listening, as well as put positive social pressure on younger or newer participants.

The psychodynamically oriented facilitator listens deeply to participants and watches for opportunities to help them uncover their past experiences and internal dynamics. She is often quite active herself in asking guiding questions and offering interpretations. The facilitator allows members to ask questions of each other because they can often facilitate deeper understanding. The facilitator, however, usually discourages other members from making interpretations because member interpretations are often associated with transferences, projections, and other defensive behaviors (see Dialogue 6.8).

Dialogue 6.8: Collective Dialogue

The social worker is asked to facilitate a dialogue between Native Americans and European Americans. The group's intent is to work on issues of historical trauma. The worker has everyone sit in a circle and then introduce themselves and say what they would do if they had 3 months off and a little extra money. All group members participate in this "warm-up." Then the facilitator asks the Native people if they would start the dialogue. She asks, "What do you want to say today about what it is like for you to be a Native person here today?"

One of the men says, "I want to welcome you all to my land." He goes on to talk about the name of his family and tribe. He talks about some of the values that he was taught as a child, including the importance of spirituality in daily life.

A Native woman speaks next. She tells the group how angry she still is at "White people," not only because of what happened historically to her people but also because of the racism she has experienced growing up on the reservation and then moving to an urban area.

Some of the European Americans respond, talking about how they feel guilty but don't know what to do. One of the men says he would like to be friends with a Native person but often feels rejected.

A Native man replies, "The most important thing you can do for me is to love yourself."

Another Native woman says that ending racism is more important to her than creating new friends.

One of the European Americans says that she felt judged and attacked by some of the Native speakers. She says, "I do not feel guilty. I never did anything to Native people, and this is my land too now."

One of the Native women responds, "I do not need you to feel guilty for me. However, I want to say that I never forget that I am an Indian when I walk down the streets of this city. I do not think you think about your race like that because you were born White. You have a privilege that I have never had."

The conversation continues like this for several dialogue sessions. The facilitator notices that people are starting to hang out after the sessions and talk. New relationships are starting to form.

EXPERIENTIAL LEARNING 6.8

(1) Think of a group of people that you do not like or are angry at. They could belong to a particular religion, culture, race, or country. Imagine what would have to happen for your hurt and anger to start to heal. Describe that process.

(2) Review Dialogue 6.8. What happened in this dialogue segment? Why do you think people might be "hanging out" after the meetings and starting to form friendships?

(3) Imagine that you belong to a group of people who had collectively hurt another group, perhaps through oppression, colonization, or war. What do you think would have to happen before your sense of guilt healed? Describe that process.

The Psychodynamically Oriented Dialogue Facilitator's Self Work

Since the psychodynamically oriented facilitator seeks to help participants see their own internal dynamics, she needs to continue to do her own inner work as well. The facilitator examines her own transferences (in the literature, these therapist reactions are called coun- tertransferences) and her own projections (which we could call "counterprojections") so that they do not interfere in her ability to see others accurately. She also knows that quality of the helping relationship she has with other dialogue participants is more important than which specific dialogue methods she uses (see Lambert, 2003). Because relationship is so important, the facilitator seeks to improve her ability to be present with the other, show that she cares, create a safe space, and lead with a balance of confidence and humility.

REFERENCES

Apprey, M. (1999). Reinventing the self in the face of received transgenerational hatred in the African American community. *Journal of Applied Psychoanalytic Studies, 1*(2), 131–143.

Bargh, J. A., & Chartrand, T. L. (1999). The unbearable automaticity of being. *American Psychologist, 54*(7), 462–479.

Barusch, G., & Fearon, P. (2002). The evaluation of mental health outcome at a community-based psychodynamic psychotherapy service for young people: A 12-month follow-up based on self-report data. *Psychology and Psychotherapy: Theory, Research, and Practice, 75,* 261–278.

Berne, E. (1964). *Games people play: The psychology of human relations.* New York: Grove.

Brave Heart, M. Y. H., & DeBruyn, L. M. (1998). The American Indian holocaust: Healing historical unresolved grief. *American Indian & Alaska Native Mental Health Research, 8*(2), 60–82.

Cogan, R. (2007). Therapeutic aims and outcomes of psychoanalysis. *Psychoanalytic Psychology, 24*(2), 193–207.

Demarais, A., & White, V. (2004). *First impressions: What you don't know about how others see you.* New York: Bantam.

Frederickson, J. (1999). *Psychodynamic psychotherapy: Learning to listen from multiple perspectives.* London: Taylor & Francis Group.

Freud, S. (1950). *Civilization and its discontents.* Garden City, NY: DoubleDay Anchor.

Freud, S. (1962). *The ego and the id.* New York: W. W. Norton.

Gennard, J., & Judge, G. (2002). *Employee relations.* London: CIPD Publishing.

Guseva, O. V., Iovlev, B. V., & Shchelkova, O. I. (2002). Combined (individual and group) psychodynamic psychotherapy in the rehabilitation of schizophrenic patients. *International Journal of Mental Health, 31*(2), 61–67.

Herman, J. (1992). *Trauma and recovery: The aftermath of violence—from domestic abuse to political terror.* New York: Basic Books.

Hunt, M. (1993). *The history of psychology.* New York: Anchor/Random House.

Jones, E. (1981). *The life and work of Sigmund Freud.* New York: Basic Books.

Katula, R. A., & Doody, A. (1990). The collegiality model: An alternative for evaluating faculty productivity. *ACA Bulletin, 74,* 74–82.

Kline, P. (1981). *Fact and fantasy in Freudian theory* (2nd ed.). London: Matthew and Company.

Lambert, M. J. (2003). *Bergin and Garfield's handbook of psychotherapy and behavior change* (5th ed.). New York: John Wiley.

Leichsenring, F., & Leibing, E. (2003). The effectiveness of psychodynamic therapy and cognitive behavior therapy in the treatment of personality disorders: A meta-analysis. *American Journal of Psychiatry, 160,* 1223–1232.

Maslow, A. (1971). *The farther reaches of human nature.* New York: Viking.

McCann, V. (2007). *Human relations: Art & science.* New York: Hamilton/Prentice Hall.

Peck, M. S. (1998). *The different drum: Community making and peace.* New York: Touchstone Simon & Schuster.

Reik, T. (1957). *Myth and guilt.* New York: George Braziller.

Tavistock Institute of Human Relations, University of Michigan Research Center for Group Dynamics. (1999). *Human relations.* New York: Plenum.

Tully, M. A. (1999). Lifting our voices: African American cultural responses to trauma and loss. In K. Nader, N. Dubrow, & B. H. Stamm (Eds.), *Honoring differences: Cultural issues in the treatment of trauma and loss* (pp. 23–48). Philadelphia: Brunner/Mazel.

Viamontes, G. I., & Beitman, B. D. (2007). Mapping the unconscious in the brain. *Psychiatric Annals, 37*(4), 243–256.

Wheelan, S., & Tilin, F. (1999). The relationship between faculty group development and school productivity. *Small Group Research, 30*(1), 59–81.

Cognitive-Behavioral Dialogue

Exploring Attitudes and Behaviors

In this chapter, theories and interventions associated with cognitive-behavioral dialogue are presented. As is true of any methods described in the text, the methods (rituals) described below can be used in concert with methods drawn from other models described in other chapters.

TWO "KINDS" OF COGNITIVE CONVERSATION

People can engage in either relatively safe conversation or in conversation that is relatively more courageous. Both kinds of conversation can be useful in the process of transforming historical trauma.

Everyday conversation usually includes the sharing of relatively "safe" attitudes that are likely to be accepted by others. Such conversation may help us initially connect with other people, so that deeper connection may follow. For example, we might say, "Nice morning, isn't it?" or "Too bad that the football team lost last night." Such sharing of attitudes is often called "talking from the head." When I speak from my head, I am sharing cognitions (or mental information processing) about my world. For example, in school, teachers usually engage children in conversations about such topics as math, science, spelling, and history. When people gather with friends or family, it is common for the conversation to be about such topics as the weather, news, current movies, or even politics. Similarly, much of the conversation we observe or participate in through media technologies, including the Internet, cell phones, and television, is also relatively safe cognitive conversation.

Most of us seem to feel most comfortable when we are "in our heads," as opposed to being in other parts of our body. Such intellectual conversation feels safe probably because it is the most common style of conversation. In typical social interactions, we usually feel much less comfortable when we speak from "below the neck," as when we share emotions "from the heart" or reveal a "gut feeling" or talk about a "shiver down the spine."

Although we usually like to believe that our cognitions are individual and original, probably many if not most of our ideas are associated with what social scientists now call memes. Memes (from the Greek root meaning "imitation") are concepts that work as the "building blocks" of our minds and of our shared culture (Dawkins, 1989). Memes can be "contagious" and easily transmitted between people (Brodie, 1996). It is usually relatively safe to share our currently popular memes with other people, such as popular fashions, catchphrases, and common political theories. As will be further described below, safe conversation can help people begin the relationship-building process, especially at the beginning of a dialogue. When dialogue participants come together to talk about difficult topics, such as historical trauma or community divides, safe conversation might help people initially become more at ease, as they prepare to take on much more challenging topics.

Cognitive conversation is more courageous when people uncover and share the underlying attitudes we have about ourselves, each other, and world. In such conversations, we not only engage in "critical thinking" about conventional memes but also explore cognitions that may be viewed as unusual, politically incorrect, or even "crazy" by others. For example, although most people probably have some racist, sexist, or ageist beliefs, today we often tend to hide them from ourselves and others. Or, as discussed in Chapter 5, people often have projections that they "put" on other people but rarely openly admit. In cognitive dialogue, participants might agree to share such stereotypes and projections. This kind of exploration usually feels relatively unsafe, but when done with the intent of building relationships, we might call this kind of exploration a more "courageous sharing" of attitudes.

In contrast with psychodynamic work, such sharing is done with the primary goal of here-and-now shifts in thinking and acting, rather than the goal of insights into the past origins of our beliefs and actions. However, as is emphasized throughout the text, both models can work together in the same dialogue, both insight and cognitive-behavioral change.

What is the purpose of engaging in such "courageous conversation"? We currently live in an era where many people are cautious to admit that they are prejudiced about people who are different from them. On one hand, perhaps this caution is inevitable, as we collectively work toward creating communities that are safe for diversity and want to appear to be accepting of diversity. On the other hand, such caution can make it more difficult for people to truly transform their trauma, since real transformation requires that we take an honest look at who we are, what we feel, and what we think.

When participants share difficult material about themselves, they can also deepen their cognitive intimacy, which is a form of relationship building. There are at least five interrelated forms of intimacy in relationships. Physical intimacy includes the sharing of both sexual and nonsexual body interactions. Emotional intimacy is the sharing of feelings. In social intimacy, people share their families, communities, and other social affiliations with each other. Spiritual intimacy is the sharing of spiritual experiences. Cognitive intimacy involves the sharing of cognitions.

Cognitive-behavioral theory suggests that our attitudes about ourselves and our worlds influence our emotions and behaviors. As we saw in previous chapters, many of my negative attitudes about myself and others are associated with my sociohistorical trauma. As I mature, I hope to become more aware of these attitudes, so I can better accept and temper them. I hope to live less in reaction to other people, because when I am less in control of my responses to others, I may be more likely to act in ways that hurt them and myself. I hope to become more proactive and able to make the conscious choice to respond in ways that will help empower myself and others. By working on discovering, expressing, and accepting the attitudes we all have about ourselves and each other, dialogue participants can help each other transform trauma and be more effective community builders. The intent in sharing unhelpful attitudes in a dialogue is to ultimately transform them into more helpful attitudes.

For example, most people I know have at least some sexist attitudes. We might still hold stereotypes about men, such as that all men are incapable of making coffee, are unable to express vulnerability appropriately, or are obsessed with sex and violence. We also may hold stereotypes about women, such as that they all should enjoy housework, their emotions are always unpredictable and extreme, and they can never make strong leaders. In a dialogue group, participants could agree to own their own sexism by sharing their sexist attitudes with each other. The underlying agreement in such a group might be that everyone is committed to creating a safe place to explore these attitudes, so that transformation can occur. Safety means simply that people do not make each other wrong in the group but do protect each other's right to confidentiality. Safety does not mean that everyone has to agree, but we agree to disagree with respect.

In such a conversation, for example, Richard might say, "Jane, when you were crying I noticed what has to be an old attitude come up . . . something about how girls and women cry when they want to get their way . . . I think I learned that from my dad. I wonder what were you were actually thinking?" Jane might reply "Yes, thanks for telling me that. . . . I was thinking I was offended by this conversation, and became angry, but you know I learned as a girl to not show anger because it is unladylike . . . I think my father and mother especially taught me that."

Old attitudes can transform. The brain can change itself and has more neuroplasticity, or ability to change, than scientists thought even a few decades ago. Neurogenesis (neuron growth) can be stimulated by a variety of activities, including exercise, attention, mental activity, and talk therapy (Begley, 2007). As I become more aware of my cognitions and learn how to talk about them, I gradually can have more choices in how I might think about myself and the world.

BEHAVIORS

Just like attitudes can seem relatively safe or unsafe, behaviors can also seem more or less safe. Dialogue can be a place where we simply act out old behaviors that have become habitual in our lives. Ideally, dialogue groups can be spaces where we notice (or "own") the tendency for old and destructive behaviors to rise up and gradually develop new behavioral options that may serve us better. The group tries to notice together when destructive or other unhelpful behaviors start to emerge and work together to name and challenge them so the old patterns can be transformed.

For example, many people have automatic reactions to being in uncomfortable social situations that they often learned in childhood, in reaction to traumatic events. Many people withdraw and become quiet. Others may talk even more. These patterns may become so automatic and habitual that some people's behavioral options get very limited. Just like a bicycle with only one gear or a washing machine with only one speed, a person with only one social behavior is less able to deal with a variety of situations effectively. Most behavioral patterns will usually be noticed over time by other dialogue participants, and each person always has the option of working on his or her patterns by talking about them and perhaps trying new behaviors.

Sometimes we also develop personal defense systems that also become reactive and habitual, such as defensiveness and anger. For example, Mary might react to something Fred says by becoming defensive: "Fred, you have no right to criticize me. Look how screwed up you are!" Debra, who is sitting next to Mary, puts her hand on Mary's and says, "How are you reacting, Mary?" Mary stops and at first frowns at Debra, too, but then smiles a little: "I am becoming defensive." Debra adds, "And is that how you want to act?" Mary responds, "No, let me start over" and she turns towards Fred. "Fred," she says, "when you told me that you were angry with me, I had some negative thoughts about myself and you in response . . . and then I did get defensive." Mary was able to look at her attitudes and behaviors and how they do seem to often interact together. This is why they are now put together under the theoretical label of *CBT* (cognitive-behavioral therapy).

Another common pattern that seems to inhibit many of us, for example, is the tendency to avoid telling others how much we love them. I have repeatedly heard people talk about how hard it is for them to express love. Such themes may come after someone dies, when the survivors express love and also their regret about having been cautious about expressing such attitudes while their loved one was still alive. I therefore often ask participants to consider whether they feel love toward someone else and challenge them to express their love in the here-and-now moment, directly to the Other.

EXPERIENTIAL LEARNING 7.1

(1) What percentage of all your conversations involve mostly "talking from the head"? What percentage of your conversations with the people you are closest to involve talking from the head? How would you like to change this percentage, if at all, in a year from now? Why? How would you make this change?

(2) Describe a more "courageous" conversation you were involved in this year. What was it like for you? What was the outcome?

(3) Describe a behavioral pattern you seem to have in difficult social situations. Do you think you learned this behavior or was born with that behavior? How would you like to modify this pattern, if at all? Why? How would you do that?

What Is the Cognitive-Behavioral Approach?

Cognitive-behavioral therapy (CBT) is the most studied and popular approach to counseling and therapy today. CBT is attractive to many professional helpers in part probably because it is widely supported by researchers, it can be used in short-term approaches, and demands for accountability can be met with built-in measurements of behavioral change. CBT is now routinely used in concert with psychopharmocology with many "mental health" issues, including attention-deficit hyperactivity disorder, adult depression, and obsessive compulsive symptoms. However, there is still insufficient evidence that CBT is in fact superior overall to other methods and that clients will necessarily respond well to the authority role that the CBT therapist often takes with the client (Thomlison & Thomlison, 2011).

In Chapter 5, psychodynamic psychology was referred to as "first force" psychology. CBT, or "second force" psychology, has its own core assumptions, including that "problem behaviors" can be changed, cognitions influence behaviors and feelings, and a systematic approach is required to change behaviors (Thomlison & Thomlison, 2011). CBT theory also assumes that people have access to their thoughts and that people can intentionally modify responses to life difficulties (Dobson & Dobson, 2009).

Three waves of CBT have been identified over the past century, and techniques drawn from all three waves can be used in dialogue. The first CBT wave had its origins in the behavior modification approaches of the early 20th century and elaborated upon such approaches as classical conditioning and systematic desensitization in the 1950s and 1960s.

The second wave followed with the cognitive therapies of the 1970s and 1980s. Such techniques as operant conditioning and the replacement of irrational thoughts were developed. For example, A. T. Beck (1976) thought that we can use our own awareness to deal with our life difficulties and that disorders in thinking are common in most mental health diagnoses.

The overall goal of current, "third-wave" CBT is to move mental focus from negative to more positive experience, act more effectively, and develop greater acceptance of and mindfulness in the world (Moran, 2008). The "third-wave" approaches include dialectical behavioral therapy, mindfulness-based cognitive therapy, acceptance therapy, and commitment therapy. These approaches emphasize engagement with the client, analysis of dysfunctional patterns, and substitution and maintenance of healthier patterns of thinking and acting (Sperry, 2006).

Dialectical behavioral therapy (DBT) was first developed as a treatment for borderline personality disorder (BPD). DBT focuses on improving the client's regulation of affect, hopefully resulting in reduction of self-harming behaviors, negative mood swings, and angry interpersonal reactions. Researchers have found that DBT therapy with females diagnosed with BPD was associated with decreased reactivity in the posterior cingulate and in other limbic and cortical regions (regions that may be associated with regulation of the interaction of emotion and memory) (Schnell & Herpertz, 2006).

The acceptance and commitment therapy (ACT) approach asks the client to live more in the here and now, accept what is, identify her own values, and act according to her own values (Wilson & Dufrene, 2010). Mindfulness is defined by some practitioners as awareness of present experience with acceptance (Germer, Siegel, & Fulton, 2005).

Motivational interviewing (MI; Miller & Rollnick, 2002) is a way of being with new clients that has become popularized over the past decade. MI is a collaborative approach to beginning therapeutic relationships that emphasizes client autonomy and the building upon existing client strengths and resources. Today, MI is often used by adherents of CBT approaches.

These most popular third-wave CBT therapies share a set of basic approaches to dealing with difficult emotions (McKay, Fanning, & Ona, 2011). The approaches include building upon basic values, development of nonjudgmental awareness, detachment from negative thoughts, awareness of alternative ways of viewing a situation, use of soothing activities, experimentation with new behaviors, and development of communication skills. These approaches will be adopted to dialogue in examples offered later in this chapter.

CBT group work often focuses on teaching interpersonal skills, such as assertiveness (Rose, 2004). Community behavioral practice uses some of the same techniques in individual CBT, such as modeling, contingency management, and feedback, to help people cope with community violence or natural disasters (Mattaini, 1993).

As alluded to above, CBT also tends to use "vertical" helping relationships (as defined by Satir, 1983), in which the facilitator takes on a higher level of authority (such as that of the traditional physician) than that of the participant. For example, CBT approaches may be used in dialogue to help participants look at the beliefs that they hold, especially the beliefs they have about each other. The facilitator usually takes the lead in helping participants look at these beliefs. CBT may also be used to encourage new behaviors, especially behaviors that are effective in the dialogic process (like listening). Again, the facilitator usually takes the lead in teaching, encouraging, and rewarding such new behaviors.

Scientific Study of CBT

CBT approaches continue to be the most popular and most frequently tested interventions. Although CBT is frequently described in the scientific and popular literatures as being the most effective paradigm of practice, researchers continue to find that theoretically different approaches generally have very similar outcomes (Stiles, Barkham, Twigg, Mellor-Clark, & Cooper, 2006). Again, although meta-analyses of CBT support its "efficacy for many disorders," there is little evidence forwarded that CBT is superior to other approaches (Butler, Chapman, Forman, & Beck, 2006). Most studies do not actually compare CBT with other psychotherapies, and meta-analyses of comparisons that have been made show that the efficacy of different approaches is essentially equivalent (Wampold et al., 1997). Meta-analyses of therapies for depression, for example, show that all "bona fide" treatments (including CBT treatments) are equally efficacious (Wampold, Minami, Baskin, & Tierney, 2000).

Many studies have found changes in selected outcomes following CBT. In one literature review (Thomlison & Thomlison, 2011), the authors found varying levels of empirical evidence that CBT is associated with symptom reduction in 21 problem areas, including addictions, depression, posttraumatic stress, and stress management. A meta-analysis of CBT for bulimia, for example, showed evidence of positive treatment outcomes (Lewandowski, Gebing, Anthony, & O'Brien, 1997).

Group CBT has been used successfully with various populations. Group approaches were found to be the most cost-effective CBT interventions for social phobia (Gould, Buckminster, Pollack, Otto, & Yap, 1997). Cognitive-behavioral group therapy (CBGT) has been repeatedly shown to help reduce symptoms of social phobia (Hope, Heimberg, & Bruch, 1995; Mortberg, Karlson, Fyring, & Sundin, 2006). CBGT was also reported to be helpful to many people hospitalized in psychiatric settings (Veltro et al., 2006). However, group therapy treatments do not appear to be overall more effective than individual therapy (McRoberts, Burlingame, & Hoag, 1998).

Of special interest to dialogue facilitators, 20 years of research into the efficacy of CBT treatment of anger has shown generally positive results. A total of 1,640 people in 50 studies showed an average improvement of 76% over "untreated subjects" (Beck & Fernandez, 1998). In comparison, relatively little is known about the efficacy of other treatments for anger.

CBT approaches are frequently viewed as evidence-based treatments associated with evidence-based research methods and the scientific-practitioner model. However, a practice-based evidence (PBE) approach is more likely to adequately inform practitioners, given the lack of evidence that models predict outcomes, the strong evidence that relationships are the most significant common factors, and the demonstrated usefulness of monitoring and feedback (see Chapter 4). Thus, for example, Persons (2008) recommends a "case formulation" approach to CBT that replaces evidence-based practice with the use of progress monitoring of each individualized treatment plan (progress monitoring being one of the elements of PBE).

There is evidence that at least some CBT strategies used to build and correct therapeutic relationships may actually undermine the quality of these relationships. CBT therapists often were found to try to convince clients that their beliefs were irrational or distorted, which typically was unhelpful. Some experts recommend using an integrative CBT approach that shares values and techniques used in client-centered therapy (Castonguay et al., 2004).

Studies suggest that cognitions are indeed interrelated with emotions and thoughts, although the causal relationships are probably multidirectional and complex. For example, men who show angry and controlling behaviors often seem to also have beliefs in their own entitlement, ownership, control, and public image (Bancroft, 2002). Most of our fears about the world have been shown to be irrational (emotional), and research indicates little association between perceived risk and actual risk (Gardner, 2008). In addition, happiness seems to be contagious, although the causal factors seem complex. We do know that you are 15% more likely to be happy if your friend is happy, 10% more likely if your friend's friend is happy, and 5.6% more likely if a friend of the friend of your friend is happy (Park, 2008). Relational factors have also been shown to be more powerful than environmental factors, weather, employment, and sporting results in predicting happiness, although the causal factors also remain relatively unknown.

Some CBT approaches use treatment manuals. Studies suggest that the use of such manuals by experienced therapists seems to make little difference in outcomes, although manuals may be more helpful to beginning therapists (Crits-Christoph et al., 1991).

When seen as one of the many valuable tools available to practitioners, CBT approaches remain useful. It is hard to imagine, for example, not using a smile or nod of the head to reinforce the new thinking or behaviors that the helper sees in the client. The movement toward integrating CBT methods with other approaches, as seen in MI, DBT, and ACT, is a hopeful trend as well.

CBT Dialogue

The purpose of the CBT dialogue model, like all dialogue models presented in this book, is the transformation of sociohistorical trauma. Built upon the core ideas of CBT theory, this model uses organized cognitive and behavioral group activities to help transform trauma.

Beginning Dialogue With an Intellectual "Warm-up"

As introduced above, sometimes participants need to begin dialogue with safe intellectual discussion (or "talking from the head"). The wise facilitator may at times allow this conversation and even promote it because she realizes that people are not yet ready to engage in more courageous dialogue. The purpose of the warm-up exercise, then, is to *gradually begin the process of relationship building*. Descriptions of some of my favorite warm-up exercises follow. I have used these with people from all walks of life, ages, genders, and cultures. The facilitator asks people to say their name and then answer the same question.

CBT STORY 7.1

I can imagine that I have developed PTSD symptoms, perhaps in response to the trauma I experienced in my home country. Before I moved to the USA, my family lived in a small town in the countryside that was attacked by another tribe. Many people were injured and killed, including family members. I waited for years in a refugee camp before I was allowed to immigrate to the USA.

Now, although I am safe, I still react to many life situations with extreme fear and worry. I would like to forget about what happened but I cannot. I have trouble sleeping, and when I do sleep, I still have nightmares where I see people I care about being killed.

One of the things that has helped me is the work I did with a social worker at the neighborhood center. She was kind enough to talk with me after our dialogue group, and she told me that she had heard my stories and had another group I could join that might help.

The group was called a transformation group. I was with other refugees, from all over the world. One thing we had in common was that we had all had trauma caused by other people. We did this exercise where we all looked at some of the attitudes that we had about ourselves and the world. Mine was that you can't trust anyone and that I must be a bad person to have had all these bad things happen to me. Many of the other people had similar ones; it made me think I am not so crazy. I started thinking maybe there are some people I can trust, at least a little bit.

EXPERIENTIAL LEARNING 7.2

(1) Do you experience that your cognitions (beliefs, thoughts) influence the way you feel and act? Or do you experience your emotions influencing your cognitions and your behaviors leading to your thoughts? Or do these influences go both ways?

(2) Why do you think CBT has emerged as the most popular therapy approach in the 20th century and now in the first decade of the 21st century?

(3) How do you think and feel about CBT? Why?

(4) CBT facilitators are often more directive than facilitators using other models. Would this fit with your personal style? Why or why not?

(1) Food Fantasies

Most people like to eat. The facilitator can ask participants to say what they would like to eat for lunch, if they could eat anything they would like, for example. This fantasy can be paired with a location; for example, the question could be, "Where would you like to eat breakfast tomorrow if you could go anywhere in the world?"

(2) Vacation Fantasies

The facilitator can ask participants to imagine where they would go, if they had some time to recreate. The fantasy can include a large travel budget.

(3) Money Fantasies

This one is about what each person would do with a sum of money. For example, what would you do with $10,000 if you had to spend it on yourself or on your family?

(4) Vocation Fantasies

The facilitator asks each person, "What would you do for a living, if you could do any vocation in the world very well (besides the one you currently are in or are preparing to enter)?"

(5) Attraction Fantasies

The facilitator could ask, "What famous person is the most beautiful or handsome person to you?"

(6) Political Fantasy

What would you do first if you were made the political leader of the community, city, state, or country in which you live?

(7) Famous Person Fantasy

If you could spend a day with any living (or not living) famous person, who would it be, and why?

Work With Values

One way to foster relationships through CBT is to facilitate a conversation about values. Values are always in a hierarchy, which means that we value things in some kind of order of importance. Participants can be asked to go around the circle and respond to questions such as the following:

(1) What are your three most important values?

(2) What value is most important to you?

(3) Which of the following do you value the most: your beliefs, relationships, property, or career?

(4) Have you ever gone through a value change when you reordered your values? Explain.

(5) Are you currently going through a value change? If so, describe.

In this dialogue, the task of the group is just to listen, not to analyze or judge. Participants may ask each other questions, for the purpose of fostering deeper understanding.

Development of Nonjudgmental Awareness Through Detachment From Negative Thoughts

In this more advanced exercise, participants practice listening without judgment (forming opinions, "making something good or bad"). Such an exercise could also be viewed as practice in a form of mindfulness. Each participant will be asked to comment on some topic, such as, "What is the most difficult thing about having your gender, race, or age?"

As people go around the circle, the facilitator asks participants to notice their reactions to the comments. The facilitator helps participants notice that, although they may not want to make judgments, there usually are judgments inside of us about other people and what they say and do. The facilitator then asks participants to own their judgments out loud. For example, Marcy might say, "Jack, when you said that it is hard to be a man because you are often sexually frustrated, I noticed that I judged you in my mind to be narcissistic and selfish." When people are able to do this kind of activity with the intent to understand and accept each other more, there is often an increase in trust and an experience of greater intimacy.

Awareness of Alternative Views

One of the key goals of diversity work is to help people see their world in expanding ways, including imagining how the world might look to another person. One of my friends, who happens to be a clergyman in town, says that if his parishioners could only learn one thing, he would wish that they would learn how to see the world from someone else's viewpoint. In this advanced exercise, participants are asked to attempt to see the world through the mind of another person. During a moment in the dialogue, when someone is communicating something important that others may be struggling to hear, the facilitator stops the conversation and asks the group to imagine what the world looks like to the speaker.

For example, in a mixed-race group, a participant is talking about racial "microaggressions" she experiences every day and about how much privilege White men have in the world. A White man in the group starts to get defensive and says, "I never had any privilege. I had to work hard for everything I got!" At this point, the facilitator can ask the man to imagine how the situation might look to the woman, and he asks the woman to imagine how the situation might look to the man. Both participants are also asked to "check out" what they say with the other person. Since the woman and man have both done some inner work and developed some mutual trust in the group, they are able to respond.

The man says, "My guess is that you have personally experienced many of these microaggressions and have become increasingly unhappy with the White males who are often the perpetrators. I also suppose that you are experiencing me as being defensive and unable to hear your pain without reacting. And that, like most White men you know, I am not aware of my privilege. Is that pretty much true?"

She says, "Thank you, yes."

Then the woman responds, "And I imagine that you have worked hard in your life and you think that I do not appreciate that. And you probably also see me as wanting to blame you for all of my suffering, rather than take any responsibility for my life situation . . . am I close?"

"Yes," he responds.

Development of Communication Skills

Verbal communication involves both speaking and listening. Facilitators can model and teach effective speaking and listening skill sets and have participants practice these skills.

One skill set uses reflective listening. Although this technique has been used by experiential therapists to help people become empathic with the emotions of others (see Chapter 8), reflective listening can be used to simply restate the cognitive content of the other, to help both people clarify what cognitions were said and heard. The participant listens to another person and then paraphrases back what she just heard. When someone does reflective listening, she can effectively "check out" if what she thought she just heard was also what the other person meant to say.

Another skill set involves the ability to distinguish and choose between passive, assertive, and aggressive styles of communication. The facilitator can use a chart, such as the one in Figure 7.1, to help participants distinguish between the three styles of communicating. Often, examples are especially helpful. The facilitator might ask people to give examples of how someone might show anger passively (one person says "by withdrawal" and another says "by pouting silently"). When the facilitator asks how people might show anger aggressively, the examples given might include "by yelling" or "by calling people names" or "by making threats." Finally, an example of assertive anger might be "by simply stating that I am angry and explaining why."

Figure 7.1   Defining Assertive Communication

	Passive	Assertive	Aggressive
Who gets put down	Myself	No one	The other
Who gets put up	The other	Both self and other	Myself

EXPERIENTIAL LEARNING 7.3

(1) Suggest some additional warm-up exercise topics.

(2) Practice reflective listening with a partner. Pick an interesting topic. Take turns speaking and listening.

(3) Practice assertive communication. Break up into small groups of four to six people. Pick a real situation that one of the people in the group has recently had, in which he or she experienced conflict with another person. Then go around the circle and take turns role-playing how someone might communicate in this conflict in aggressive, assertive, and passive ways. Help each other if necessary.

(Continued)

(Continued)

(4) Go around your entire class or group and take turns sharing each person's top two or three values.

(5) In a small group, go around the circle and take turns letting each other know what judgments each person has had about others in the group. Start with the intent to simply understand, and avoid making judgments about each others' judgments.

(6) Practice awareness of alternative views. In a small group of six to eight people, first go around the group and take turns sharing how each person thinks about any controversial issue (e.g., a current political issue, a recent news event, a conflict that had arisen in the class). Then go around the circle one more time, and take turns focusing on the views of each person. When it is Jack's turn, for example, everyone else in the circle tries to describe what they thought was Jack's view of the controversial issue. Jack's task is to listen and then clarify if the feedback was correct or not.

Behavioral Experiments

Dialogue participants can engage in behavioral experiments that may encourage personal growth and enhance relationships. The facilitator can offer any number of suggestions for the group, when she thinks that they might enhance the relationship-building activities of the group. The facilitator can plan an experiment for her group but must always be prepared to "throw it away" if the plan does not fit the group's process and try something new. A list of some suggested behavioral experiments follows, beginning with the ones that most people find the easiest and then moving to those that are increasingly difficult for most people. All of these experiments involve some degree of personal "risk" and also offer potential transformation and growth. Growth is usually not possible without some risk.

(1) Have people choose the person who seems most similar to them. Then, go around the circle and each "first person" explains who that person (the "second person") is and why he or she thinks that the person is similar. (The facilitator can then ask each "second person" to respond to the assumptions that the first person made about him or her . . . perhaps they are true and perhaps not.) During this initial round of conversations, the rest of the group listens. After the round is done, the group can talk about what it was like to have this experience ("meta-communicate").

(2) Have people each choose the person in the group that seems most different from them. Then, go around the circle and each first person explains who that "second person" is and why he or she thinks that the person is different. (The facilitator can then ask each "second person" to respond to the assumptions that the first person made about him or her . . . perhaps they are true and perhaps not.) Again, during these conversations, no one in the group (including the facilitator) is allowed to speak. After the exercise is done, the group can talk about what it was like to have this experience ("meta-communicate").

(3) Have people pick the person they think would dislike them the most. Then have the first and second persons share, as explained above, and the rest of the group follow the same rules.

(4) In this one, each participant (Person A) picks someone in the group (Person B) who especially reminds her of someone from her family of origin (Person C). Then each person ("A") in turn describes this transference and explains what the similarity is between the person in the past ("C") and the person in the group ("B"). Finally, each Person B responds by explaining to what degree she actually does have the same transferred characteristic that Person C had. This exercise can be further intensified by asking that the transference needs to be positive (the easier task) or negative (usually the more difficult task).

All of these exercises can help participants further their journeys of self-discovery and enhance their relationships with each other.

EXPERIENTIAL LEARNING 7.4

Try out the behavioral methods described above in small or large groups.

REFERENCES

Bancroft, L. (2002). *Why does he do that? Inside the minds of angry and controlling men.* New York: Berkeley Books.

Beck, A. T. (1976). *Cognitive therapy and the emotional disorders.* New York: Penguin.

Beck, R., & Fernandez, E. (1998). Cognitive-behavioral therapy in the treatment of anger: A meta-analysis. *Cognitive Therapy and Research, 22*(1), 63–74.

Begley, S. (2007). *Train your mind, change your brain.* New York: Ballantine.

Brodie, R. (1996). *Virus of the mind: The new science of the meme.* Carlsbad, CA: Hay House.

Butler, A. C., Chapman, J. E., Forman, E. M., & Beck, A. T. (2006). The empirical status of cognitive-behavioral therapy: A review of meta-analyses. *Clinical Psychology Review, 26,* 17–31.

Castonguay, L. G., Schut, A. J., Aikins, D. E., Constantino, M. J., Laurenceau, J., Bologh, L., & Burns, D. D. (2004). Integrative cognitive therapy for depression: A preliminary investigation. *Journal of Psychotherapy Integration, 14*(1), 4–20.

Crits-Christoph, P., Baranackie, K., Kurcias, J. S., Beck, A. T., Carroll, K., Perry, K., et al. (1991). Meta-analysis of therapist effects in psychotherapy outcomes studies. *Psychotherapy Research, 1*(2), 81–91.

Dawkins, R. (1989). *The selfish gene.* Oxford, UK: Oxford University Press.

Dobson, D., & Dobson, K. S. (2009). *Evidence-based practice of cognitive-behavioral therapy.* New York: Guilford.

Gardner, D. (2008). *The science of fear: Why we fear the things we shouldn't and put ourselves in greater danger.* New York: Dutton/Penguin.

Germer, C. K., Siegel, R. D., & Fulton, P. R. (2005). *Mindfulness and psychotherapy.* New York: Guilford.

Gould, R. A., Buckminster, S., Pollack, M. H., Otto, M. W., & Yap, L. (1997). Cognitive-behavioral and pharmacological treatment for social phobia: A meta-analysis. *Clinical Psychology: Science and Practice, 4*(4), 291–299.

Hope, D. A., Heimberg, R. G., & Bruch, M. A. (1995). Dismantling cognitive-behavioral group therapy for social phobia. *Behavioral Research and Therapy, 33*(6), 637–650.

Lewandowski, L. M., Gebing, T. A., Anthony, J. L., & O'Brien, W. H. (1997). Meta-analysis of cognitive-behavioral treatment studies for bulimia. *Clinical Psychology Review, 17*(7), 703–718.

Mattaini, M. A. (1993). Behavioral analysis and community practice: A review. *Research on Social Work Practice, 3,* 420–447.

McKay, M., Fanning, P., & Ona, P. Z. (2011). *Mind and emotions: A universal treatment for emotional disorders.* Oakland, CA: New Harbinger.

McRoberts, C., Burlingame, G. M., & Hoag, M. J. (1998). Comparative efficacy of individual and group psychotherapy: A meta-analytic perspective. *Group Dynamics: Theory, Research, and Practice, 2*(2), 101–117.

Miller, W. R., & Rollnick, S. (2002). *Motivational interviewing: Preparing people for change.* New York: Guilford.

Moran, D. J. (2008, Winter). The three waves of behavioral therapy: Course corrections or navigation errors? *The Behavioral Therapist,* pp. 147–157.

Mortberg, E., Karlson, A., Fyring, C., & Sundin, O. (2006). Intensive cognitive-behavioral group treatment (CBGT) of social phobia: A randomized controlled study. *Anxiety Disorders, 20,* 646–660.

Park, A. (2008, December 22). The happiness effect. *Time,* pp. 40, 42.

Persons, J. B. (2008). *The case formulation approach to cognitive-behavioral therapy.* New York: Guilford.

Rose, S. D. (2004). Cognitive-behavioral group work. In C. Garvin, L. M. Gutierrez, & M. J. Galinsky (Eds.), *Handbook of social work with groups* (pp. 11–136). New York: Guilford.

Satir, V. (1983). *Conjoint family therapy.* Palo Alto, CA: Science and Behavior Books.

Schnell, K., & Herpertz, S. C. (2006). Effects of dialectical-behavioral-therapy on the neural correlates of affective hyperarousal in borderline personality disorder. *Journal of Psychiatric Research, 41,* 837–847.

Sperry, L. (2006). *Cognitive behavioral therapy of DSM-IV-TR personality disorders.* New York: Routledge.

Stiles, W. B., Barkham, M., Twigg, E., Mellor-Clark, J., & Cooper, M. (2006). Effectiveness of cognitive-behavioral, person-centered and psychodynamic therapies as practiced in UK National Health Service settings. *Psychological Medicine, 36,* 555–566.

Thomlison, R. J., & Thomlison, B. (2011). Cognitive behavior theory and social work treatment. In F. J. Turner (Ed.), *Social work treatment: Interlocking theoretical approaches* (pp. 77–102). Oxford, UK: Oxford University Press.

Veltro, F., Falloon, I., Vendittelli, N., Oricchio, I., Scinto, A., Gigantesco, A., et al. (2006). Effectiveness of cognitive-behavioral group therapy for inpatients. *Clinical Practice & Epidemiology in Mental Health, 2*(16), 1–9.

Wampold, B. E., Minami, T., Baskin, T. W., & Tierney, S. C. (2000). A meta-(re)analysis of the effects of cognitive therapy versus 'other therapies' for depression. *Journal of Affective Disorders, 68,* 159–165.

Wampold, B. E., Mondin, G. W., Moody, M., Stich, F., Bensen, K., & Hyun-nie, A. (1997). A meta-analysis of outcome studies comparing bona-fide psychotherapies: Empirically, "all must have prizes." *Psychological Bulletin, 122*(3), 203–215.

Wilson, K. G., & Dufrene, T. (2010). *Things might go terribly wrong: A guide to life liberated from anxiety.* Oakland, CA: New Harbinger.

CHAPTER 8

Experiential-Humanistic Dialogue

Talking From the Heart

In this chapter, dialogic interventions and research associated with experiential-humanistic (EH) theory are presented. These methods can be used in concert with methods drawn from all other models described in other chapters.

WHAT DOES IT MEAN TO TALK FROM THE HEART?

When I speak from the heart, I share my emotions as honestly as I can and with the intent of loving kindness toward others. In other words, I share my emotions with you in the hope that my words and expressions ultimately will support the highest good for everyone (even if I do not really know what the highest good might ultimately be). In such conversation, it is possible for us to talk about any emotion, even difficult emotions such as anger and hurt, in a conscious and caring manner. The basic technique, described in the chapter, is for the speaker to own and express her emotions in a direct, assertive manner, without blaming herself or anyone else. The listener notices the emotions coming from the speaker, notices his emotional reactions, and expresses those reactions when the speaker is finished.

HOW ARE COGNITIONS, EMOTIONS, AND FEELINGS DIFFERENT AND RELATED?

Cognitions (Latin root is "to know" or "to recognize") involves processes such as remembering, knowing, and judging used in such mental functions as understanding, solving problems, processing language, or making plans (e.g., Stanovich, 2009). Although many scientists call these cognitions "higher level processes," and although they may indeed be largely processed in the upper (cortex) parts of the brain, I prefer to not refer to them in this way, because then emotional processes are viewed as "lower level" and tend to be devalued in comparison.

What are emotions (Latin and French roots suggest "to move out" or "to motivate") and feelings (Greek and Latin roots suggest "to touch")? A search of the literature reveals an ongoing lack of consensus on the definitions of emotions and feelings (e.g., Lewis, Haviland-Jones, & Barrett, 2008; Pettinelli, 2011). For the purpose of clarity in this discussion, some working definitions and distinctions can be offered.

In this text, feelings are considered sensations that can occur anywhere in the body and seem to be processed faster than emotions are processed by our brains. Emotions are reactions to our feelings that also involve our ego, or sense of self. They are slower acting probably because emotions have a frontal cortex, or cognitive component. Emotions usually put us into "motion" (or action). Basic emotions include sad, mad, glad, scared, excited, and disgust. Another useful distinction is that a feeling is primary sensory data input and emotion is the process the brain uses to compute the value of that input (LeDoux, 2002).

WHAT COMES FIRST, EMOTIONS OR THOUGHTS?

Although, as we saw in Chapter 6, many cognitive theorists (e.g., Lazarus, 1982) consider affect to be postcognitive (meaning that emotions follow thoughts). However, experiential theorists (e.g., Schneider, Bugental, & Pierson, 2001) tend to view emotions as primary to cognitions (thoughts follow emotions). From the experiential-humanistic perspective, emotions are essential to our humanness, and people can become more aware, accepting, and skilled at expressing emotions. I prefer to think of emotions and cognitions as overlapping processes that are always in interaction with each other in our brains and bodies, and that work on one will affect the other. Thus, emotional work will also affect my cognitions, and cognitive work will also affect my emotions.

EXPERIENTIAL LEARNING 8.1

(1) What does it mean to you to "speak from the heart"? In Experiential Learning 6.1, you were asked to consider what percentage of all your conversations involves mostly "talking from the head." How much of the time do you speak from the heart in your interactions with others?

(2) Why do you not speak from the heart all the time? What gets in the way? Would you like to have more conversations from the heart and, if so, why?

(3) Does it seem to you that your emotions come before your thoughts, your thoughts come before your emotions, or some combination of both? Explain.

EXPERIENTIAL-HUMANISTIC THEORY AND RESEARCH

EH therapy is based on several assumptions about human nature and the process of change. One assumption is that people have free will and have a basic drive toward growth and self-actualization. As people grow, they become more whole and integrate their often-conflicting emotions and thoughts into a coherent self. In addition, here-and-now self-awareness is seen as supporting healthy decision making. People are also viewed as able to support each other's growth in the group process.

Another assumption in EH theory is that the helping relationship is fundamental in therapeutic change. Emphasis is put on the genuineness, warmth, and empathy of the professional helper in these relationships (Rogers, 1951). Meta-analyses over the past decades consistently indicate in fact that the working alliance is predictive of positive therapy outcomes (Horvath & Symonds, 1991; Martin, Garske, & Davis, 2000). Subjective well-being of the person has been found to be positively related to such attitudes as democracy, postmaterialistic values, and tolerance of diversity (Diener & Tov, 2007). Humanistic approaches have been found to be effective in work with sex offender groups (Bauman & Kopp, 2006) and with substance abuse (and alcohol) group therapy (Koehn, 2007). In EH group work, the facilitator uses the client for supervision, acknowledges errors, uses feelings as data, and works in the here and now (Yalom, 2002).

EH approaches can work effectively with both high-functioning and less-abled people (Page, Weiss, & Lietaer, 2002). Humanistic group treatment was found overall to be superior to cognitive-behavioral treatment groups with children (Schechtman & Pastor, 2005). The value of the therapeutic factors of group treatment is cited in outcomes studies of EH group work, including normalization, mutual support, and group cohesion (Bauman & Kopp, 2006; Koehn, 2007). Social work students reported that they witnessed the humanity and experiential world of people with mental illness diagnoses through structured in-class dialogues with EH methods (Shor & Sykes, 2002).

In EH, the client's own goals are honored by the helper. The client is seen as the supervisor of the therapist, and the therapist asks for input from the client to set goals, choose interventions, and evaluate outcomes. The therapist's role is to create a "safe space" where the client can work. Such a space encourages clients to engage in true dialogue; when people experience "attachment security," they are more likely to respond to others with compassion and altruism (Mikulincer & Shaver, 2005).

EXPERIENTIAL LEARNING 8.2

(1) Do you believe that people have a basic desire to grow? Is that true of you?

(2) What do you think about the idea that the helping relationship is fundamental in therapeutic change? Has that been true in your life, when people have helped you?

(3) How important is it for the facilitator to honor the goals of the participants in a dialogue group?

PSYCHODRAMA

Psychodrama is a technique used by many EH therapists. In psychodrama, the client uses dramatic techniques to express "parts" of herself or aspects of other people. These techniques can be both verbal and nonverbal. EH theory suggests that psychodrama involves genuine encounter in the here and now, which is necessary for therapeutic change (Tauvon, 2010). With interpsychic psychodrama, the clients play out situations they have encountered in their lives with other people. Clients can use role-plays, nonverbal expressions, and other expressions. For example, a dialogue group would dramatize the experience of a participant who sat on a plane next to someone who was very different from her.

With intrapsychic psychodrama, the client is "on stage." The goal of intrapsychic psychodrama is usually to help the client "heal" herself, which usually means to become more whole through the expression of all parts of the self. This process of "wholing" is often focused on reclaiming underdeveloped or denied (or "shadow") aspects of self. Hopefully, the shadow is further healed or transformed as the client expresses that shadow (Johnson, 1993). For example, the child, observing self, and parent ego states (as introduced in Chapters 4 and 6) might be played out in a psychodrama alone in front of a therapist or in a group therapy circle. The therapist could set out three chairs and help the client speak from the "child chair," the "parent chair," and the "observing self" chair about some issue. The client would focus on "reclaiming" the underdeveloped ego state that he has most lost contact with.

Psychodrama shares key components with Gestalt therapy, which was one of the first EH models. In Gestalt therapy, the client is also often asked to play out "parts" of herself or the "voices" of herself and another person (Perls, 1969). For many Gestalt therapists, the dialogical relationship is a foundation for the work, in which genuine contact occurs between the self and the other (Polster & Polster, 1973). Gestalt therapists might encourage a client to notice and express an underdeveloped ego state, which Perls (1969) would call the "underdog," and learn to stand up to the "top dog" ego state that has bullied the underdog. Often, Perls worked with clients who had an overdeveloped superego, who bossed around the underdeveloped inner child (see EH Story 8.1 below, in which Brian was working with a "top dog" superego).

EH STORY 8.1

Early in the semester, Brian, a young, self-identified White straight man, says that he finds his diversity class very difficult and is not sure he wants to continue attending. He says he is confused about what he feels. Deborah, the facilitator in the diversity dialogue group, wants to help Brian express some of his shadow parts. She asks Brian for permission to do this work with him in front of the group and he agrees. She sets out three chairs in the middle of the circle and asks Brian to sit in the first chair, which she calls "the child."

Brian is able to sit in the chair and play the child role.

He says, "I am sick of being the 'bad guy' in the dialogue, everyone attacks me, I feel guilty about being a straight White male after every group, and then I am angry all week later on!"

When he sits in the "parent chair," he says to his now-empty child chair, "What is wrong with you? Stop complaining! You should show everyone how mature you are, and how you are not a racist! You sound like a child!"

Deborah sits in the child chair and responds, "But I am a child!" Brian does not know what to say, so Deborah asks Brian to pick three people from the group to help him play his child, parent, and observing self. Three people are chosen and they are instructed to stand behind the chair they are assigned to and speak out when they think they have something to add to the voice of the position their chair represents.

As the dialogue continues, Mary, who now stands behind the child chair, says, "I AM a child and I have the right to feel hurt and guilty and mad."

John, who now stands behind the parent chair, says, "I am worried that everyone thinks I am a racist!"

Deborah asks Brian to sit in the observing self chair. Brian then says, "OK. I am going to try to find a common and sane ground somewhere between my child and parent. . . . So . . . I do have feelings of hurt, guilt, and anger. . . . In fact, I even have feelings that could be called racist that I think I learned long ago. And all of these feelings are OK. I am not bad to have them. I do want to control these feelings, though, not because I want people to like me (although I want that too). I want to control my feelings because I want to treat people with kindness and respect . . . it makes me feel good, it is the right thing to do, I believe."

The dialogue class claps at the end of this. Willie, standing behind Brian (who is still in the "observing self" chair), adds, "As the observing self, I love both my child (my emotional self) and my parent (my responsible self). And when I love myself, I feel more empowered to love others, in all of their humanness." The class claps again.

The "founder" of psychodrama, Moreno (1985), held that spontaneity, creativity, and mutual trust in good intentions were the foundations of his approach, in which people explore truth through dramatic action. Moreno felt that the facilitator-director has three roles: a producer of dramatic action, a therapist, and an analyst who interprets the group responses.

Psychodrama has been used to promote a variety of health promotion and prevention programs. Student performers, for example, successfully created and presented a drama on body image and social pressures. This process was viewed as an "interactive performance practice" that encourages critical understanding, empowers participants, and stimulates transformation (Howard, 2004). Collective drama was found to foster relationship building in an antiviolence psychodrama done by adolescents. From the feminist perspective of the program designers, such relationality is associated with nonhierarchical, participatory, and social action–oriented programs (Community Education Team, 1999).

Psychodrama has been scientifically evaluated. A meta-analysis of studies showed that psychodramatic approaches are at least as effective as other group therapy approaches. The techniques of role reversal and doubling (where a participant adds a voice to a role) were found to be particularly effective (Kipper & Ritchie, 2003). Psychodramatic techniques may also be able to help people deal with grief and addiction-related loss and trauma (Dayton, 2005). There is increasing theory and evidence that supports the use of psychodrama in treating trauma (Kipper, 1998). Psychodramatic and cognitive-behavioral therapy (CBT) techniques have both been found to be effective in various group settings and, when combined, may even be more effective (Zaratas & Gokcakan, 2009).

Psychodrama has been used successfully with a variety of diverse populations, including a school-based teen sexuality program in Zaria, Nigeria (Kafewo, 2008). In this program, the teens identified their own issues, chose one issue for a 10- to 15-minute performance, and included audience participation in the desired drama outcomes. A similar program was used successfully in Canada (Ponzetti, Selman, Munro, Esmail, & Adams, 2009). A psychodramatic program with Latino adolescents in the United States successfully reduced oppositional behavior, family conflicts, and depression (Smokowski & Bacallao, 2009).

THE NEUROLOGY OF EMOTIONS

Although science is just beginning to understand some of the complex biological mechanisms involved in emotion, some findings can be reported. Neurologists believe that, although the limbic brain is involved in emotion, there are many other complex interactions in emotional processing. For example, in some emotional reactions, the central nucleus of the amygdala activates the paraventricular central nucleus of the hypothalamus (PVN). The PVN releases corticotropin-releasing factor (CRF) into the pituitary gland (PIT). The PIT then releases adrenocorticotropic hormone (ACTH) into the bloodstream, which then travels to the adrenal cortex. The adrenal cortex releases cortisol into the bloodstream, which circulates into the entire body. The amygdala normally excites the PVN. In contrast, the hippocampus normally inhibits the PVN (LeDoux, 2002). Some scientists believe that we will eventually find that emotions involve even much more complexity than described in the proceeding series of events.

As discussed in Chapter 1, humans can store memories as emotional reactions that may seem mysterious and irrational when they suddenly surface. When we experience such emotional memories (such as a panic reaction to a loud noise), we may not know that this reaction is related to some event that happened in our past. Emotional arousal organizes and coordinates brain activity, so that working memory receives greater inputs during emotionally intense moments. In such arousal, there may be a weakened ability to form explicit memories and regulate fear by thinking and reasoning (LeDoux, 2002).

Research that demonstrates how females and males process emotion differently also helps reveal the neurochemical roots of our emotional worlds. The female and male brains process emotions under the influence of hormones that interact with neural networks and other bodily functions. The neurology of emotion in women is especially influenced by estrogen, which regulates such functions as aggressive seduction and the desire to cuddle and emotionally relate. Progesterone is the female brain's "chill pill." Testosterone, surprisingly, does influence the female brain, helping women to be assertive, focused, and even aggressive when necessary. Oxytocin influences women to find pleasure in helping and serves as a feel-good chemical. Cortisol can be associated with feelings of stress and sensitivity. Vasopressin can bring subtle aggressive male energies. DHEA is the "mother hormone" that is strong in youth and then wanes (Brizendine, 2006).

In contrast, the male brain is especially influenced by testosterone, which is associated with aggression and the need for power and influence. Vasopressin moderates aggression and seems associated with gallantry and monogamy. While Müllerian inhibiting substance (MIS) seems to influence strong tough, fearless emotions, oxytocin tends to be associated with empathy, trust, relationships, romance, and fathering. Prolactin is the "Mr. Mom," which seems to be associated with sympathy for the mother, paternal behavior, and lower sex drive. Finally, cortisol is "the gladiator" that will fight when threatened (Brizendine, 2010).

Neurological research, including the studies of gender differences cited above, suggest that there are probably many individual differences in the biochemical processes of emotional and cognitive processing, across not only gender but many other elements of *neurodiversity* as well. The concept of neurodiversity suggests not only that each person has a unique brain but that the dialogue facilitator needs to respect such diversity as much as any other element of human diversity. Principles of neurodiversity that can inform dialogue may include the following: (a) Brains have continuums of competence across different spectrums, such as emotional, cognitive, mechanical, and social intelligence; (b) our neurological competence is often defined by our cultural values; and (c) labels such as "disabled" and "gifted" depend largely on where and when a person is born (Armstrong, 2010).

EH TECHNIQUES FOR DIALOGUE: USING "REAL PLAYS" TO EXPERIENCE AND EXPRESS EMOTION

EH dialogue can enhance participant learning. Research shows that learning by doing is a very effective, perhaps overall the most effective, teaching strategy (Itin, 1999). EH dialogue challenges participants to notice and express their here-and-now experiences, with an emphasis on emotional experience. EH methods also can make theories derived from other methods become alive. Participants, for example, can act out past experiences that they uncovered in psychodynamic dialogue sessions or behaviors identified through CBT dialogue sessions. In most EH dialogue techniques, the whole group can participate by adding their voices to the conversation and/or by listening.

In all of the techniques described below, the facilitator can set up a role-play, in which people play out a real or hypothetical situation. I prefer to use *real plays* whenever possible, where participants play out the actual life situations that they find themselves in.

Simple Sharing of Sensations and Emotions

In this technique, the facilitator asks participants to share what they are feeling during any moment in the dialogue. Such sharing can be verbal and/or nonverbal (e.g., through art, music, movement). This technique can contribute to the group process, especially when done right after another technique has been used.

For example, a facilitator asked participants to share stories about historical trauma that they had heard passed down from family and other community members. Then she asked participants to go around the circle and share, one at a time, what they felt during the storytelling. A number of responses were heard, including, "I was both relieved and scared," "I felt angry," and "I was scared." As in any dialogue exercise, participants had the right to pass if they were not yet comfortable sharing. Also, the facilitator asked participants to follow her own lead and only listen to each other, without offering analysis, judgments, suggestions, or other responses.

Listening With Presence: Genuineness, Empathy, and Warmth in Dialogue

Listening is the most important "intervention" in dialogue, and effective listening is a core component of EH therapy. Although most people probably think that it is easy to be present with another person, I have learned that real presence is a relatively rare and valuable gift that, with practice, I can learn to give to you, or you to me. Presence can be thought of as the practice of listening with genuineness, empathy, and warmth. These three elements were called the core conditions of the helping relationship by Rogers (1951), and a review of a half century of outcome research since then confirms that genuineness, warmth, and empathy do indeed help foster the therapeutic relationships (Patterson, 2000).

Genuineness is being "real" with the other, instead of just playing roles or acting defensively, detached, or incongruently with one's thoughts and feelings. Being genuine does not mean that the facilitator should necessarily say the first thing on her mind to the participant. The genuine facilitator can be said to be "authentic" when he is, in part, involved in the relationship and yet not attached to any relational outcomes. Genuineness requires self-awareness and self-acceptance and is best tempered with empathy and warmth.

Warmth is about intent. My friend Jim Magelby used to say that if you do not both love your client and *show* that you love your client, you cannot help her. Warmth is holding the intent of loving kindness and expressing that intentional quality through loving presence with the other.

Empathy can be described as "walking in the other's footwear." The word *compassion,* which is related to the concept of empathy, literally means to "suffer with." But empathy (literally "in-feeling") is not just about suffering with the other; it also is about rejoicing with the other, as the context changes. Empathy involves not just the intellectual understanding of the other's experience but also the actual feeling of the other's experience below the neck, in the rest of the body.

EXPERIENTIAL LEARNING 8.3

(1) Have you had the experience of someone else being deeply present with you in a helpful way? Describe the experience.

(2) What are the typical obstacles that keep you (or I) from being as present as we could be with each other? (Also see discussion in Chapter 4)

(3) What do you value most, genuineness, warmth, or empathy? Why?

One-Person Psychodrama Between Internal Voices ("Vertical")

The facilitator may ask a participant to carry on a conversation by speaking from different voices within herself. The facilitator may have the participant sit in different chairs, or stand in different positions, as she gives different "parts" of herself a voice. Voices often have different levels of power in the personality. Perls (1969) called the bully voices the "top dog" and the bullied voice the "bottom dog." The facilitator can encourage the bottom dog to stand up to the top dog in the dialogue.

For example, a participant (Mary) once shared that she was "bummed" that she had broken up with her boyfriend. I asked her to show us what her internal conversation was like. We put one chair in the middle of the circle. I asked Mary to stand in front of the chair and to yell at herself about how the breakup was all her fault. She pointed a finger at the chair and said, "You screwed it up again . . . you should have tried harder. He wasn't that bad, you may never find any better . . . what will people think?" Then I asked Mary to sit in the chair and choose someone in the group to play out the position (she asked Sally to play "the parent," which is a form of doubling described earlier in the chapter). She was also asked to choose another person to stand behind her as she sat, with their hands on her shoulders, who could support her seated "inner child" (she asked Jane). Then Sally pointed at Mary and said, "You screwed it up again . . . you should have tried harder. He wasn't that bad, you may never find any better . . . what will people think?" Mary, with the help of Jane, talked back to the parent, saying, "I don't care what you think. I am going to trust how I feel and move on."

Two-Person Psychodrama Between External Voices ("Horizontal")

In one dialogue on the religious divide, a young woman (JoDee) in the group became furious at an older man (Sam). Sam was a clergyman who had a daughter who, against her father's wishes and her father's religious beliefs, decided to come out as a lesbian woman. JoDee had recently come out as lesbian and experienced rejection from her own family.

I put two chairs in the middle of the circle and asked them to sit facing each other. I also asked the circle of participants to feel free to get up, come in the middle, and stand behind either JoDee or Sam, if they wanted to add something to their voices (another example of doubling). JoDee starts the conversation and says, "I would like your blessing." Sam replies, "I can't give you a blessing because I believe that homosexuality is a sin." Another woman jumps up and stands behind JoDee and says, "I don't care if you bless me or not then!" A man stands behind Sam and responds, "I am sorry, but you have to understand that I am acting on my principles." The facilitator can also join in such conversations, and I stand behind JoDee and ask, "I need to know who you value most, your daughter or your God." Sam replies, "I must put my God first." Instead of getting more angry, JoDee starts to cry and thanks Sam for his honesty.

Two-Person Psychodrama Involving Both Internal and External Voices ("Two-Dimensional")

The facilitator can help create a more complex psychodrama that gives participants an opportunity to simultaneously play out, in a safe community, both the internal and external conversation that exists in all human interactions. Such conversation requires some preparation time, so that participants understand the purpose of the exercise and the roles they are playing. In the following example, the students were able to do a complex role-play because they had practiced such role-plays before and had seen how such work could lead to transformation.

In a diversity dialogue, a Muslim man (Hakeem) told a story about an experience he had on campus, in which he had been stereotyped by other students who belong to the dominant culture and religion. One of the students (Robert) in the class said sarcastically, under his breath but loud enough to be heard, "I am sure it was another White man who messed things up again."

As the facilitator, I did not want to only "manage" the difficult conversation that was happening but instead try to help use the difficulty as an opportunity for transformation in the group. I asked Hakeem and Robert to come and sit in two chairs in the middle of the circle. Robert started to talk about how, as a White male, he was tired of being "blamed by everyone for all the troubles in the world." We agreed to try a two-dimensional dialogue, where both Hakeem and Robert would each ask other people in the group to help play the parts of their own "child" and "parent" ego states (see Chapter 5).

Hakeem asked Azad to play his inner parent and Martin to play his inner child. Robert asked Janet to play his inner parent and Frank to play his inner child. Azad and Martin were asked to stand behind Hakeem, while he sat in his chair. Janet and Frank stood behind Robert.

The conversation went on only for a few minutes, but we discovered many facets to Hakeem and Robert's experiences. For example:

Robert's inner child (Frank) said, "I feel sad that Hakeem was teased by other White men, and I am afraid he will think I am racist because I am a White man, too."

Robert's inner parent (Janet) said (to his own inner child), "Yes, and you should feel guilty about that."

Hakeem's inner parent (Azad) said, "I did not know Robert felt sad."

Hakeem's inner child (Martin) said, "I feel less angry now at Robert."

Whole-Group Psychodrama Involving Both Internal and External Voices ("Three-Dimensional")

In the last exercise, the dialogue focused on only two people, Robert and Hakeem, and each had two helpers who gave voice to the parent and child ego states. In the three-dimensional psychodrama, the dialogue involves more than two people and can even involve everyone in the group. Instead of asking other participants to play such parts as "inner child" and "inner parent," the speakers can represent their own parts by themselves. The best way to do this is to have each participant practice speaking from her or his observing/supervisory self (see Chapter 5).

In such a dialogue, a typical comment might be, "I am noticing that my inner parent is telling me to feel guilty and my inner child is feeling quite angry." Such communications can help people understand themselves and each other in a more intimate, deeper way.

Theatrical Psychodrama and Dialogue

Finally, dialogue can be used as a follow-up to theatrical psychodrama, which involves the group audience in a potentially powerful learning experience. One way to combine theater and dialogue is to have the dialogue group (or a smaller subgroup) put on a performance that dramatizes a difficult situation involving sociohistorical trauma. The drama is stopped at a particular scene and the audience (or larger dialogue group) is asked to join in the theater and "play out" alternative ways of dealing with the difficult situation.

For example, a campus group does a theatrical psychodrama on date rape. In the scene, a woman and man are on a date, and the man asks for sex. The woman says no, but the man persists. At this point, the psychodrama is stopped, and the audience (dialogue group) is asked to participate in the psychodrama. One man might say, "I think the guy should honor what the woman said!" The facilitator invites him to go up on the "stage" and play out that voice. Later, a woman says, "That woman should just leave!" She is also invited to play out that option and also reenter the psychodrama where it stopped.

In these theatrical psychodramas, the audience can be an outside group that the dialogue group decides to perform with, a larger dialogue group itself, or both.

EXPERIENTIAL LEARNING 8.4

(1) Have you ever participated in a psychodrama? What was it like? Consider the possibility that in a sense all human interactions are psychodramas.

(2) Which of the four kinds of psychodrama dialogue is most interesting to you? In what kind of dialogue would you use this technique?

REFERENCES

Armstrong, T. (2010). *The power of neurodiversity: Unleashing the advantages of your differently wired brain.* Cambridge, MA: DeCapro.

Bauman, S., & Kopp, T. G. (2006). Integrating a humanistic approach in outpatient sex offender groups. *Journal for Specialists in Group Work, 31*(3), 247–261.

Brizendine, L. (2006). *The female brain.* New York: Three Rivers Press.

Brizendine, L. (2010). *The male brain.* New York: Three Rivers Press.

Community Education Team. (1999). Fostering relationality when implementing and evaluating a collective-drama approach to preventing violence against women. *Psychology of Women Quarterly, 23*(1), 95–109.

Dayton, T. (2005). The use of psychodrama in dealing with grief and addiction-related loss and trauma. *Journal of Group Psychotherapy, Psychodrama, and Sociometry, 58*(1), 15–34.

Diener, E., & Tov, W. (2007). Subjective well-being and peace. *Journal of Social Issues, 63*(2), 421–440.

Horvath, A., & Symonds, B. D. (1991). Relation between working alliance and outcome in psychotherapy: A meta-analysis. *Journal of Counseling Psychology, 38*(2), 139–149.

Howard, L. A. (2004). Speaking theatre/doing pedagogy: Re-visiting theatre of the oppressed. *Communication Education, 53*(3), 217–233.

Itin, C. M. (1999). Reasserting the philosophy of experiential education as a vehicle for change in the 21st century. *Journal of Experiential Education, 22*(2), 91–98.

Johnson, R. A. (1993). *Owning your own shadow: Understanding the dark side of the psyche.* San Francisco: Harper San Francisco.

Kafewo, S. A. (2008). Using drama for school-based adolescent sexuality education in Zaria, Nigeria. *Reproductive Health Matters, 16*(31), 202–210.

Kipper, D. A. (1998). Psychodrama and trauma: Implications for future interventions of psychodramatic role-playing modalities. *International Journal of Action Methods, 51*(3), 113–121.

Kipper, D. A., & Ritchie, T. D. (2003). The effectiveness of psychodramatic techniques: A meta-analysis. *Group Dynamics: Theory, Research, and Practice, 7*(1), 13–25.

Koehn, C. V. (2007). Experiential work in group treatment for alcohol and other drug problems: The relationship sculpture. *Alcoholism Treatment Quarterly, 25*(3), 99–111.

Lazarus, R. S. (1982). Thoughts on the relations between emotions and cognition. *American Physiologist, 37*(10), 1019–1024.

LeDoux, J. (2002). *Synaptic self: How our brains become who we are.* New York: Penguin.

Lewis, M., Haviland-Jones, J. M., & Barrett, L. F. (2008). *Handbook of emotion* (3rd ed.). New York: Guilford.

Martin, D. J., Garske, J. P., & Davis, M. K. (2000). Relation of the therapeutic alliance with outcome and other variables: A meta-analytic review. *Journal of Counseling and Clinical Psychology, 68*(3), 438–450.

Mikulincer, M., & Shaver, P. R. (2005). Attachment security, compassion, and altruism. *Current Directions in Psychological Science, 14*(1), 34–38.

Moreno, J. L. (1985). *The autobiography of J. L. Moreno, M.D.* (Abridged). Boston: Moreno Archives, Harvard University.

Page, R. C., Weiss, J. F., & Lietaer, G. (2002). Humanistic group therapy. In D. J. Cain & J. Seeman (Eds.), *Humanistic psychotherapies: Handbook of research and practice* (pp. 339–368). Washington, DC: American Psychological Association.

Patterson, C. H. (2000). *Understanding psychotherapy: Fifty years of client-centered theory and practice.* Herefordshire, UK: PCCS Books.

Perls, F. (1969). *Gestalt therapy verbatim.* Moab, UT: Real People Press.

Pettinelli, M. (2011). *The psychology of emotions, feelings and thoughts.* http://cnx.org/content/m14358/latest/

Polster, E., & Polster, M. (1973). *Gestalt therapy integrated: Contours of theory and practice.* New York: Brunner-Mazel.

Ponzetti, J. J., Selman, J., Munro, B., Esmail, S., & Adams, G. (2009). The effectiveness of participatory theatre with early adolescents in school-based sexuality education. *Sex Education, 9*(1), 93–103.

Rogers, C. (1951). *Client-centered therapy: Its current practice, implications and theory.* London: Constable.

Schechtman, Z., & Pastor, R. (2005). Cognitive-behavioral and humanistic group treatment for children with learning disabilities: A comparison of outcomes and process. *Journal of Counseling Psychology, 52*(3), 322–336.

Schneider, K. J., Bugental, J. F. T., & Pierson, J. F. (2001). *The handbook of humanistic psychology.* Thousand Oaks, CA: Sage.

Shor, R., & Sykes, I. J. (2002). Introducing structured dialogue with people with mental illness into the training of social work students. *Psychiatric Rehabilitation Journal, 26*(1), 63–69.

Smokowski, P. R., & Bacallao, M. (2009). Comparing psychodramatic and support group delivery formats. *Small Group Research, 40*(1), 3–27.

Stanovich, K. (2009). *What intelligence tests miss: The psychology of rational thought.* New Haven, CT: Yale University Press.

Tauvon, L. (2002). Psychodrama: Active group therapy, using the body as an intersubjective context. *Body, Movement, and Dance in Psychotherapy, 5*(3), 257–267.

Yalom, I. D. (2010). *The gift of therapy.* New York: Perennial.

Zaratas, Z., & Gokcakan, Z. (2010). A comparative investigation of the effects of cognitive-behavioral group practices and psychodrama on adolescent aggression. *Educational Sciences: Theory & Practice, 9*(3), 1441–1452.

Transpersonal Dialogue

Talking From Spirit

In this chapter, transpersonal exercises for dialogue are presented, along with a background on transpersonalist theory and methods.

TRANSPERSONAL DIALOGUE

Like emotions and cognitions, spirituality can also be thought of as a dimension of human development that we all share. Transpersonal dialogue opens the door to adding spirituality to conversations. Although spirituality is difficult to define or describe, most people relate to such spiritual concepts as life purpose, desire for connectedness, inner peace, sacred experience, sense of oneness, and beyond the ego.

Although most people have spiritual experiences, we often are reluctant to talk about them. Perhaps spirituality is one of the most private of all human experiences. When we get together in our work locations, extended families, and even in our religious communities, we may keep at least some of our spiritual experiences to ourselves. This silence may be in part caused by the lack of safety we feel to be honest in front of others about our own unique spiritual experiences, especially those that may seem to be different from the norm.

In transpersonal dialogue, participants have the opportunity to explore and share what may matter most in their lives. The facilitator creates a space where participants can do such exploring and sharing without having to be afraid that they will be judged or excluded from the group.

SPIRITUALITY AND RELIGIOSITY

All healing was originally spiritually oriented. Most of our ancestors, all over the Earth, consulted shamanic healers for their illnesses. These shamans would journey into ecstatic states of consciousness to assist their clients, often using visualization, drumming, and sometimes sacred medicines to assist in their healing rituals (Harner, 1990).

Early Western psychologists recognized the spiritual dimension of human thought and behavior. In fact the word *psychology,* invented in the 16th century, has the root *psyche,* which means "soul" in Greek. However, the spiritual dimension became less fashionable in the 20th century as many social workers and psychologists yielded to pressures to appear more scientific and professional and less spiritual (Derezotes, 2011).

Since the 1980s, there has been a global religious resurgence. Over two thirds of the human world now self-identifies as religious, more than ever before in history. The United States is now one of the most religious nations in this pious world (Armstrong, 2006). A parallel spiritual resurgence also has developed in the United States over the past decades. Maslow (1973) anticipated this resurgence of interest in spirituality and called it the psychology of transcendence or the fourth force of psychology.

This fourth force of psychology, now called transpersonalism, reintroduces the concept of spirituality into professional helping and adds spirituality to the list of such psychological concepts as insight, cognition, social behavior, and emotion. The word *transpersonal* literally means to "go beyond the mask" of the personality. From this perspective, every human has a personality that he wears, like a mask. As a person "disidentifies" from her roles, possessions, beliefs, and other personality traits, she finds that she still has a "soul" or "center" or "spirit" left inside.

A number of transpersonal authors have informed social work and psychology. Perhaps most important is Wilber (1977, 1986a, 1986b, 1987, 2006), who introduced a theory of lifelong consciousness development called the spectrum model, which in part describes the process of personality formation and disidentification. Washburn's (1988) transpersonal theory of human development, Assagioli's (1965) psychosynthesis, and Hillman's (1975, 1991) Jungian approaches helped introduce transpersonalism into mainstream psychology.

WHAT ARE THE DIFFERENCES AND RELATIONSHIPS BETWEEN RELIGION AND SPIRITUALITY?

Religion can be thought of as a social function in which people come together to share rituals, beliefs, and doctrines. Religion may help or interfere with the spiritual development of an individual (or do both, to different extents). In contrast, spirituality can be thought of as an individual dimension of human development. Every person has a spiritual component, with a different set of spiritual experiences and interests. Spirituality can be seen as the search for reverent connectedness with the inner world (e.g., the physical, emotional, cognitive) and outer world (e.g., the other person, other living thing, ecosystems). Spirituality can also be associated with the need of the individual to make meaning of her life experience and find a life purpose (Derezotes, 2005). Not all religious people see themselves as spiritual, and not all spiritual people identify themselves as religious. Figure 9.1 illustrates how people can be divided into four groupings based on their relative identification with spirituality and religiosity.

Figure 9.1 Grouping Based on Spirituality and Religiosity

Very spiritual Not so religious	Very spiritual Very religious
Not so spiritual Not so religious	Not so spiritual Very religious

EXPERIENTIAL LEARNING 9.1

(1) Do you see yourself as a spiritual person? As a religious person? Explain.

(2) If you have been involved in a religion at some time in your life, did your religion either support or hinder your spiritual growth?

(3) In the past year, in what situation (if any) did you feel the most spiritual? Explain.

(4) Do you have any relationships or communities where you feel safe to talk about your spirituality? If so, can you explain what makes you feel safe?

EVIDENCE FOR THE TRANSPERSONALIST APPROACH

Spiritual issues have been found to be factors in the etiology of most biopsychosocial problems, and spiritually oriented interventions can help foster positive outcomes (Ano & Vasconcelles, 2005; Pargament, 2007). In most studies, people with high scores in spirituality and religiosity also tend to have higher scores on such indicators of wellbeing as happiness, life satisfaction, life purpose, self-esteem, and optimism. In addition, high scores in spirituality and religiosity are also correlated with low scores on such indicators as anxiety, depression, substance abuse, criminal activity, loneliness, and marital dissatisfaction (Koenig, McCullough, & Larsen, 2001).

Spiritual and religious coping skills and values are associated with positive psychological adjustment in over 50 studies (Ano & Vasconcelles, 2005). For example, mindfulness has been shown to improve psychological functioning and to reduce mental health symptoms (Lazar, 2005). The use of yoga and breath work has even been shown to be effective in work with such challenging populations as adolescent sex offenders (Derezotes, 2000). Meditation can help people reduce the effects of trauma (Hanh, 2011).

Some researchers think they have located a module in the human brain that evolved as our biological spiritual or religious center (Alper, 2001; Hamer, 2004). Other researchers remain skeptical that spirituality or religiosity will be explained by the function of any isolated part of the human brain (Beauregard & O'Leary, 2007).

SPIRITUALITY IN SOCIAL WORK

Like psychology, social work had early roots in spirituality that were later abandoned. The first social workers were mostly women who were volunteers for religious organizations. In the early 20th century, calls for professionalism in social work and a focus on science seemed to make many social workers reluctant to talk about or study spirituality.

Spirituality reappeared in the literature in the 1980s and 1990s. For example, Joseph (1988) introduced concepts for social work practice and religion, and Cowley's seminal article on transpersonal casework appeared in 1993. Implications of spirituality and religion for social work education were also developed (e.g., Canda, 1988; Cowley & Derezotes, 1994). Surveys of practitioners in the mid-1990s showed that social workers value spirituality and desire more training (e.g., Derezotes & Evans, 1995; Sheridan, Bullis, Adcock, Berlin, & Miller, 1992). Practice principles for spirituality in social work were developed (e.g., Bullis, 1984; Derezotes, 1995; Loewenberg, 1988) and tested (Derezotes, 2000). A text on religious traditions in social work practice was also produced (Van Hook, Hugen, & Aguilar, 2003).

SPIRITUAL INTERVENTIONS FROM THE WORLD'S WISDOM TRADITIONS

The spiritually oriented practitioner does not need to be perfect to be of help to others. The effective practitioner is aware and accepting of her own imperfections, as well of her strengths. She is able to be transparent with the client about these strengths and limitations, when such transparency supports the client's progress. The practitioner may have her own spiritual practice(s) that she engages in. The practitioner respects the diversity of client religiosity and spirituality and is aware of her own spiritual and religious countertransference reactions (see Chapter 3 and Derezotes, 2011).

All of our world's major religious traditions share an ethics of reciprocity that in the Christian tradition is called the Golden Rule (Religioustolerance.org, 2011). Buddhists, for example, are encouraged by some teachers to offer *metta* (loving kindness and compassion) to people who have attacked them and to refuse the gift of aggression when it is offered to them in a group (Grady, 2011). Similarly, in the Sermon on the Mount in the Gospel of Matthew, Jesus tells his disciples to turn the other cheek when someone is violent, rather than to insist on an eye for an eye, a tooth for a tooth. Martin Luther King Jr. echoed the words of Jesus when he said that darkness cannot drive out darkness; only light can do that. Hate cannot drive out hate; only love can do that.

A person living in the United States in the early 21st century has access to a diversity of spiritual traditions and teachers. For example, the Dalai Lama teaches students to distinguish between the conventional self and the "nonexistent" self. He teaches that the nonexistent self believes that I am separate from the Other and that this is an illusion that leads to unnecessary suffering. The student works to raise his consciousness that only the conventional self is real. Thich Nhat Hanh (2011) counsels trauma victims to use mindfulness techniques to stay in the present moment. In such a state, he says, we can recognize the ghosts of the past for what they are and know that we are now safe. Instead of repressing memories, some people thus may benefit from bringing the things they fear the most closer to themselves.

Peter Kuhn (2011) writes about his meditations at Auschwitz II (also called Birkenau), which is the site of a World War II German concentration camp. He was able to imagine being both a prisoner and a Nazi camp guard, and he was able to have compassion for both positions. He states that such meditation, which he calls seeing the tyrant or seeds of war within myself, helped in his own healing process. Such visualization might have implications in dialogue work.

Other writers emphasize the use of imagination and intent to revision the way we see ourselves and our relationships with other people. Matt Fox (2000), for example, writes about an Original Blessing from God, which refers in part to the idea that human beings are born basically whole, and loving and kind toward each other. Similarly, Mipham (2012) suggests that humans share a basic (fundamental) communal goodness. She states that most people think that humans are basically bad and that this belief inhibits us from forming true communities.

EXPERIENTIAL LEARNING 9.2

(1) If you went to see a counselor, how would you feel talking about your spirituality with her? Explain why.

(2) How would you feel about seeing a counselor who seemed perfect? How would you feel seeing a counselor who was aware of her imperfections? Can you explain why?

(3) When someone has hurt you (when you are a victim of sociohistorical trauma), have you tried experimenting with using forgiveness or loving kindness as a response? If so, how did this response work for you?

MINDFULNESS

Mindfulness is a method used in many spiritual traditions, and now in transpersonal work as well, to help foster the development of consciousness, or the reverent awareness of self and the world. As we saw in Chapter 7, mindfulness is now being incorporated into some cognitive-behavioral therapy (CBT) techniques as well. There are currently many different approaches to mindfulness in use (Begley, 2007). Most approaches teach that mindfulness is essentially just paying full attention to everything inside and outside of myself without judgment or criticism (Boyce, 2011).

Mindfulness was traditionally taught in some major wisdom traditions as a form of meditation. According to many sources, there are basically two kinds of meditation. The first involves training and focusing the mind, and the other is mindfulness meditation, which involves being a witness to everything, including my own mind. Some authors liken the first form to a laser beam, and the second form (mindfulness) is more a like a search-light, that is, open to seeing whatever comes into view (internal and external) from the widest possible illumination of awareness.

Mindfulness approaches may use such techniques as sitting in an erect posture, body scanning, focusing on breath, and focusing on sensations, emotions, and thoughts. Sometimes, participants also work on letting go of resistance (ego fears), tuning in to cre-ative consciousness, opening the mind, and moving forward with a practical plan for trans-formation (Alexander, 2008). People can practice being mindful during their entire day, as they work and play. Like any technique, mindfulness does not address every life issue, so teachers may warn students to avoid spiritual bypassing, which may involve the use of mindfulness to avoid feelings, psychological issues, and life development tasks and feelings (Welwood, 2011).

There is increasing evidence that mindfulness brings benefits to people who are suffer-ing. Many of these benefits have particular relevance to dialogue. For example, mindfulness practice has been found to help people have less reactivity to others and become more open, accepting, and curious in relationships (Boyce, 2011). Mindfulness techniques have been used successfully in dealing with stress and with physical pain and illness (Kabat-Zinn, 1991).

Mindfulness also stimulates neurogenesis, which is the growth of neurons. Studies of people who use mindfulness show that their hippocampus grows an average of 15%, which may indicate improvements in processing novel experiences and memory. There are also recorded changes in electrical activity (shown in the electroencephalogram or EEG) and blood flow (shown by functional magnetic resonance imaging or fMRI). Monks who regularly practice mindfulness have high levels of gamma waves and other significant brain changes. Mindfulness can result in less reaction when startled, as well as overall more positive emotions. Three months of meditation training was shown to produce more activ-ity in the left prefrontal cortex (associated with activity, joy, altruism, interest, enthusiasm) and 20% improved immune response.

Mindfulness has even been linked to reduced symptoms associated with such disor-ders as obsessive-compulsive disorder, borderline disorder, and drug addiction. With ongoing practice, these changes can become long lasting (Ricard, 2011; Siege1, 2011). Ultimately, mindfulness may help foster personal and collective transformations. Through mindful self-reflection, I can study my reactions to others and their reactions to me.

Some researchers think that mindfulness techniques may help us use relationships as mirrors that can teach us who we really are (Ponlop, 2011). By being more mindful of real-ity, I ultimately can also learn to love myself and the world more deeply. Thus, as the Dalai Lama (2011) has said, mindfulness can help us each take more responsibility for the world's well-being.

EXPERIENTIAL LEARNING 9.3

(1) What benefit, if any, do you see in having reverent and nonjudgmental awareness of self and the world?

(2) Have you ever tried mindfulness techniques? If so, what was your experience like?

TRANSPERSONAL EXERCISES FOR DIALOGUE

Sharing Intentions

Many spiritual exercises begin with an intention. An intention is the purpose, aim, or desired outcome of the exercise, which may be held individually by one person or collectively by a group of people. The facilitator can ask group members to talk about their intentions before a dialogue begins. For example, the facilitator might begin a dialogue on the religious divide by asking for people to take turns going around the room and offer, if they like, an intention for the meeting. One person might begin by saying, "I hope that we are all honest and respectful." Another might say, "I wish that I learn more about all of you, and that you learn more about me." A third might add, "My intent is that we all love each other more, regardless of our beliefs."

The facilitator does not necessarily need to help the group agree on one intention but can make space for the many intentions that usually emerge. Often, however, the group gradually discovers some commonalities as they go around the circle sharing. In another dialogue with American Indians and White people, for example, one of the Indian leaders brought a talking stick, which she passed around the room. She asked us to take turns declaring our intentions for the meeting as we each in turn held the stick.

Sharing Imagination

In spiritual work, imagination is often used to foster development. Imagination can be thought of as intentional creativity, which can be either left wild and open or focused on a desired outcome or goal. For example, in one dialogue, the facilitator played a tape of drumming that the group listened to for 20 minutes, with the intent to simply be open to notice what came up for them in their bodies, hearts, and minds. Then participants were given an opportunity to talk about what they experienced as they listened to the tape. Comments were varied, and participants commented later that they felt closer with each other after sharing what came up in their imagination. In a more focused exercise, participants in a community dialogue were asked to focus upon imagining the perfect community. We learned that people had many different ideas, but we also identified some common elements such as public safety, economic stability, and equal opportunities for everyone.

Another form of imagination is guided imagery. Guided imagery can be used in dialogue to foster conversations about particular topics. For example, in one dialogue on spiritual diversity, I asked participants, with their permission, to prepare for a guided imagery. I showed them the disidentification drawing, illustrated in Figure 9.2, and explained what disidentification is. Then I asked them to close their eyes in a comfortable position. Some lay on their backs on the carpet while others stayed in their chairs. Then I asked them to imagine that they were making a journey toward their centers or souls. The first direction was, "Imagine first all the possessions that are important to you in your life . . . now imagine that you no longer have them and ask yourself, what is left of me now?" I repeated this direction for each of the "layers" as they headed inward. When they reached the center, I asked them to notice what it was like to have "let go as best you could today" of what you identify with. Then we reclaimed each layer back as we headed out again from the center. Afterward, I asked participants to open their eyes and dialogue about what "parts" of their personalities they had the hardest time letting go of, and why.

Figure 9.2   Disidentification Drawing

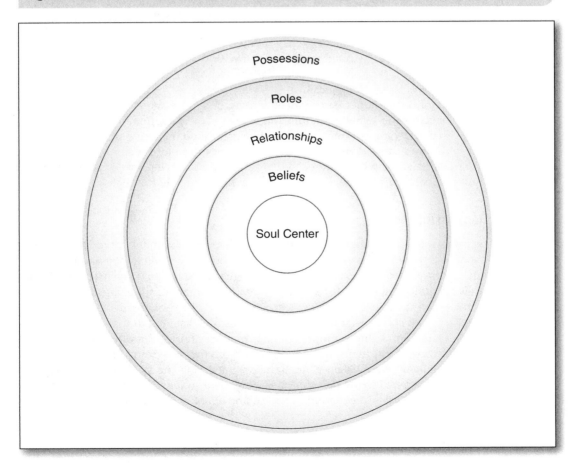

Mindfulness

Mindfulness techniques enhance dialogue. Before the dialogue begins, the facilitator can ask participants to sit quietly and practice nonjudgmental awareness of their own inner worlds. Then the mindfulness can be expanded to include nonjudgmental awareness of the other people in the circle, and then gradually the local community, local ecosystem, and even the world. Finally, the facilitator asks participants to practice mindfulness at the same time that they are engaged in actual dialogue interactions. As participants learn to stay in their nonjudgmental or witness ego state during the dialogue, they are able to be more respectful listeners for each other.

What Do You Know to Be True?

In this exercise, the facilitator asks participants to go around the circle and share one thing that they know to be true. The facilitator does not comment on the responses, but just listens, and asks the group members to do the same thing. In one dialogue, on the religious divide, I asked participants to respond to this question. There was a wide range of answers, both within the group of people who identified as religious and within the group of people who identified as not religious. Religious people, for example, had responses including "That Jesus is my Lord and Savior," "That I am on this Earth to love and serve others," and "That I am constantly growing." This kind of exercise can help participants start to develop more trust and safety in the group. For some people, this is the first time that they have ever felt safe saying what they really believe, in a true community of spiritual diversity.

Living Funeral

In this exercise, the group agrees to focus on one person at a time. Participants are asked to share what they would have said about the person if they were attending their funeral. Statements can be positive or negative, but all must be truthful and said with care for the recipient. The person who agrees to have her funeral also has a chance to talk about what unfinished business she might have in her life, including unfinished business with group members. I have done this exercise with a dialogue group that had met for an extended time. The exercise helped participants find deeper connections and meanings in their relationships with each other that were surprising, despite the fact that they had known each other for months or even years.

Giving Blessings

A blessing is a wish of the highest good for the Other. Blessings can be specific, such as a wish that the Other find a meaningful job or a loving partner. A participant does not necessarily have to have a particular religious belief or position to give or receive a blessing. The facilitator can invite blessings in a dialogue. Such exercises can be very emotionally moving and can help foster deeper relationship and community.

REFERENCES

Alexander, R. A. (2008). *Wise mind: Open mind: Finding purpose & meaning in times of crises, loss, and change.* Oakland, CA: New Harbinger.

Alper, M. (2001). *The God part of the brain: A scientific interpretation of human spirituality and God.* New York: Rogue.

Ano, G. A., & Vasconcelles, E. B. (2005). Religious coping and psychological adjustment to stress: A meta-analysis. *Journal of Clinical Psychology, 61,* 461–480.

Armstrong, K. (2006). *The great transformation: The beginning of our religious traditions.* New York: Knopf.

Assagioli, R. (1965). *Psychosynthesis: A collection of basic writings.* New York: Penguin.

Beauregard, M., & O'Leary, D. (2007). *The spiritual brain: A neuroscientist's case for the existence of the soul.* New York: HarperCollins.

Begley, S. (2007). *Train your mind, change your brain.* New York: Ballantine.

Boyce, B. (2011). Introduction: Anybody can do it and it changes everything. In B. Boyce (Ed.), *Mindfulness revolution: Leading psychologists, scientists, artists, and meditation teachers on the power of mindfulness in daily life* (pp. xi–xviii). Boston: Shambhala.

Bullis, R. K. (1984). *Spirituality in social work practice.* Washington, DC: Taylor & Francis.

Canda, E. R. (1988). Spirituality, religious diversity, and social work practice. *Social Casework, 69*(4), 238–247.

Cowley, A. S. (1993). Transpersonal social work: A theory for the 1990s. *Social Work, 38*(5), 527–534.

Cowley, A. S., & Derezotes, D. S. (1994). Transpersonal psychology and social work education. *Journal of Social Work Education, 30*(1), 32–41.

Dalai Lama. (2011, Winter). Seeing ourselves clearly. *Buddhadharma,* pp. 34–39.

Derezotes, D. S. (1995). Spiritual and religious factors in practice: Empirically based recommendations for social work education. *Arete, 20*(1), 1–15.

Derezotes, D. S. (2000). Evaluation of yoga and meditation trainings with adolescent sex offenders. *Child and Adolescent Social Work Journal, 17*(2), 97–113.

Derezotes, D. S. (2005). *Spiritually oriented social work practice.* Boston: Pearson/Allyn & Bacon.

Derezotes, D. S. (2011). Spirituality and mental health. In V. Vandiver (Ed.), *Best practices in mental health: A pocket guide.* New York: Lyceum Books.

Derezotes, D. S., & Evans, K. E. (1995). Spirituality and religiosity in practice: In depth interviews of social work practitioners. *Social Thought: Journal of Religion in the Social Services, 18*(1), 39–56.

Fox, M. (2000). *Original blessing: A primer in creation spirituality presented in four paths, twenty-six themes, and two questions.* New York: Tarcher.

Grady, N. L. (2011, Winter). Ask the teachers. *Buddhadharma,* pp. 21–22.

Hamer, D. (2004). *The God gene: How faith is hardwired into our genes.* New York: Doubleday.

Hanh, T. N. (2011). *Peace is every breath: A practice for our busy lives.* New York: HarperOne.

Harner, M. (1990). *The way of the shaman.* New York: HarperOne.

Hillman, J. (1975). *Revisioning psychology.* New York: Harper Colophon Books.

Hillman, J. (1991). The cure of the shadow. In C. Zweig & J. Abrams (Eds.), *Meeting the shadow: The hidden power of the dark side of human nature* (pp. 239–240). Los Angeles: Jeremy P. Tarcher.

Joseph, M. V. (1988). Religion and social work practice. *Social Casework, 60*(7), 443–452.

Kabat-Zinn, J. (1991). *Full catastrophe living: Using the wisdom of your body and mind to face stress, pain, and illness.* New York: Delta Trade Paperbacks.

Koenig, H. G., McCullough, M. E., & Larsen, D. B. (2001). *Handbook of religion and health.* Oxford, UK: Oxford University Press.

Kuhn, P. (2011, Winter). The tyrant within. *Buddhadharma,* pp. 17–18.

Lazar, S. W. (2005). Mindfulness research. In C. K. Gerner, R. D. Giegel, & P. R. Fulton (Eds.), *Mindfulness and psychotherapy* (pp. 220–238). New York: Guilford.

Loewenberg, F. M. (1988). *Religion and social work practice in contemporary American society.* New York: Columbia University Press.

Maslow, A. (1973). *The farther reaches of human nature.* New York: Viking.

Mipham, S. (2012, January). Joined at the heart. *Shambhala Sun,* pp. 17–19.

Pargament, K. I. (2007). *Spiritually integrated psychotherapy: Understanding and addressing the sacred.* New York: Guilford.

Ponlop, D. (2011). The great mirror of relationship. In B. Boyce (Ed.), *Mindfulness revolution: Leading psychologists, scientists, artists, and meditation teachers on the power of mindfulness in daily life* (pp. 193–195). Boston: Shambhala.

Religioustolerance.org. (2011). The "golden rule" (a.k.a. ethics of reciprocity): Passages from various religious texts. http://www.religioustolerance.org/reciproc2.htm

Ricard, M. (2011). This is your brain on mindfulness. In B. Boyce (Ed.), *Mindfulness revolution: Leading psychologists, scientists, artists, and meditation teachers on the power of mindfulness in daily life* (pp. 126–135). Boston: Shambhala.

Sheridan, M. J., Bullis, R. K., Adcock, C. R., Berlin, S. D., & Miller, P. C. (1992). Practitioners' personal and professional attitudes and behaviors toward religion and spirituality: Issues for education and practice. *Journal of Social Work Education, 28*(2), 190–203.

Siegal, D. J. (2011). *The whole-brain child: 12 revolutionary strategies to nurture your child's developing mind.* New York: Random House.

Van Hook, M., Hugen, B., & Aguilar, M. (Eds.). (2003). *Spirituality within religious traditions in social work practice.* Pacific Grove, CA: Wadsworth.

Washburn, M. (1988). *The ego & the dynamic ground: A transpersonal theory of human development.* Albany: State University of New York Press.

Welwood, J. (2011, Spring). Human nature, Buddha nature. *Tricycle,* p. 437.

Wilber, K. (1977). *The spectrum of consciousness.* Wheaton, IL: Theosophical Publishing House.

Wilber, K. (1986a). The spectrum of development, the spectrum of psychopathology, and treatment modalities. In K. Wilber, J. Engler, & D. Brown, (Eds.), *Transformations of consciousness: Conventional and contemplative perspectives on development* (pp. 651–659). Boston: New Science Library.

Wilber, K. (1986b). Treatment modalities. In K. Wilber, J. Engler, & D. P. Brown (Eds.), *Transformations of consciousness* (pp. 127–160). Boston: New Science Library/Shambhala.

Wilber, K. (1987). The spectrum model. In D. Anthony, B. Ecker, & K. Wilber (Eds.), *Spiritual choices: The problem of recognizing authentic paths to inner transformation* (pp. 237–265). New York: Paragon House.

Wilber, K. (2006). *Integral spirituality: A startling new role for religion in the modern and postmodern world.* Boston: Shambhala.

CHAPTER 10

Biological and Environmental Dialogue

Communicating With Our Bodies and Nature

Throughout the text, I have suggested that there is an ecobiopsychosocialspiritual or body-mind-spirit-environment connection in everyday human life. Biological and environmental dialogue can both (1) help foster connections between people and (2) help foster connections between people and other animals or ecosystems. Often work in one of these areas may also foster the work in the other.

Dialogue involves both spoken language and nonverbal expressions, and both forms are offered in this chapter. The first half of the chapter includes the use of such body techniques as movement, dance, music, and art in dialogue. The second half provides approaches to environmental dialogue with nonhuman animals, nonliving things, and the rest of the cosmos.

WHOLE-BODY DIALOGUE

We humans are in conversation with the body all the time, both with our own bodies and with the bodies of other people. Our own bodies can tell us nonverbally, if we listen, when we need to sleep, eat, exercise, and relax. Other people's bodies nonverbally communicate information to us, about their health, their emotions, their attitudes, and so on. Most of us have had the experience of feeling a reaction in our own body to another person, which might involve (for example) fear, sexuality, love, or even disgust. In everyday interactions, we may ignore or completely deny these communications. The purpose of whole-body dialogue is to make these communications more conscious and translate them into verbal communications that help us further develop our relationships and communities.

Body-Mind Connection

A wealth of research demonstrates the connection between the body and the mind. We know that the mind can influence body functions and that body functions influence the mind (Murphy, 1993). The body also communicates through natural movements that others can read.

Research supports this idea that we can communicate and even help heal by using the body-mind connection. Studies show, for example, that people can interpret the emotions of others through nonverbal physical movements (Clarke, Bradshaw, Field, Hampson, & Rose, 2005). The medical profession has found that healers and patients make more effective treatment teams when they can dialogue about disease and well-being. Effective body work by complementary and alternative medicine (CAM) practitioners includes listening to "body-talk" and "body stories," where their patients have the opportunity to talk about their illnesses and other body experiences (Gale, 2011).

Psychotherapists often pay attention to the language of their clients' bodies. For example, built upon the pioneering work of Reich (1945), bioenergetics is a model of psychology that uses physical techniques to work with body tensions to foster psychological healing (Lowen, 2005). There are also now many studies that show that people can evoke a "relaxation response" in the body by using simple mind focusing techniques (Benson, 2012).

EXPERIENTIAL LEARNING 10.1

(1) Have you ever experienced a body-mind-spirit-environment connection? Explain.

(2) What has your body told you about yourself today? Did you listen?

(3) Do you ever "people watch" when you are in a public space? What kind of things do you notice? Do you ever check out these body intuitions to see if they are accurate?

Dance and Movement

Dance and movement are relationship-building activities that can help bring people into community. Dance and movement have been used throughout history and prehistory. Our ancestors often used dance to tell stories and included sacred dances in their rituals (Oesterley, 2002). Today, we still see examples of sacred dance in such traditions as American Indian dance, the Whirling Dervishes from Sufi ceremony, and Christian liturgical dance. Women in many cultures have used scared dance to develop their own spirituality, and these rituals are now becoming more popularized again in the West (Stewart, 2000). Dance still may carry very different meanings in different cultures and traditions. One of my African students told me, for example, that in his country, dance is part of a sacred ceremony and that people never use dance as "a way to show off for dating like people do in the United States."

Christian theologian Matt Fox (1990, 1991) uses circle dances in his workshops and presentations. He has participants hold hands in a big circle and move around the meeting room, creating an almost "instant community" as people interact. The popular Dances of Universal Peace (2011) also uses dance from many world traditions to help people connect in new communities.

Dance and movement therapy (DMT) has been used to promote well-being for decades. Marian Chace introduced DMT to the USA in the 1940s, and by the 1970s, increasing numbers of American therapists used DMT in their practices (Chace, Sandel, Shaiklin, & Lohn, 1993). DMT assumes that there is a body-mind connection and that the person can express her psychological history through movement (Payne, 1992). The therapist may first help the client relax and warm up, and then she can create a safe space for spontaneous expression, perhaps mirror the client's movements, and later help the client make meaning out of the experience (Behar-Horenstein & Ganet-Sigel, 1999).

Dance scholars have found many relationships between dialogue and dance. Dance research has been characterized as a dialogue that includes library activities, focus group interaction, and writing activities (Dils & Crosby, 2001). Effective dance education has also been viewed as a dialogue, in which the teacher interacts with students and community to design, implement, and evaluate innovative programs (Anttila, 2007).

EXPERIENTIAL LEARNING 10.2

(1) Do you believe that you can tell things about people by how they move their bodies as they walk by? Explain.

(2) What did you think about the idea of a circle dance? Have you ever had the experience of feeling quickly "in community" when involved in some kind of group dance or movement?

(3) How do you feel about doing movements in front of other people? Explain.

WHOLE-BODY EXERCISES FOR DIALOGUE

Movement Between Whole Group and Small Group

The facilitator frequently shapes and shifts the physical structure of the dialogue circle. If the group size is between 8 and maybe 28 people, people may be seated in a large circle. The advantage of a large circle is that everyone can participate in the conversation, and the disadvantages are that a larger group reduces the length of time each person will have to speak and may also reduce the sense of safety for some participants. The facilitator can experiment by shifting the format from one large circle to multiple smaller circles and back to one circle.

Figure 10.1 illustrates three kinds of circle arrangements that can be used. In case A, everyone is arranged in one circle. In B, one subgroup is seated inside the larger circle, and people in the outside circle listen silently to the dialogue in the smaller circle (usually called a "fishbowl"). In C, the group is divided into multiple smaller circles, each with a separate conversation. In cases B and C, the size of the smaller circles may vary (this can be called the "circle of circles").

Figure 10.1 Large Group—Small Group

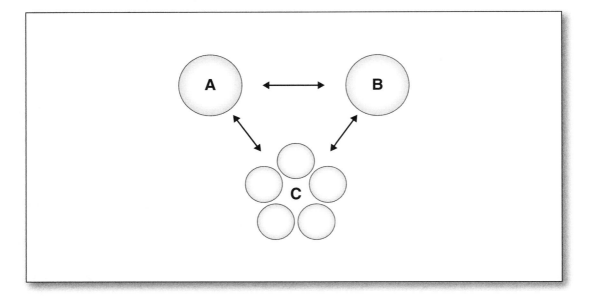

Expressing With the Whole Body

The facilitator can use body movement at any time in the dialogue process. The basic technique is to ask participants to show how they are feeling or thinking through a body movement. For example, in a warm-up exercise, I sometimes ask participants to take turns showing us through a body movement how each is feeling coming into the session. One person might stand up and then twirl around joyfully. Another might collapse onto the floor. A third might hold her head and bend over.

After a difficult session, the facilitator could also ask the participants to do a brief "checkout" through a similar movement. After the movements, people might be given additional time to ask questions or explain what their movements meant to them. As with any other exercise described in the text, participants always have the right to pass on their turn.

I have found these movements to often help uncover and release feelings and thoughts that were "deeper" than the conscious mind of people. Participants often say that they did not even know what they were feeling until their bodies moved.

Listening With the Whole Body

Sometimes I have asked people to stop the verbal conversation in the room and to pay attention to what they are feeling in their bodies. Often, some people in the room will say that they feel tension, and if I ask them, they might say that the tension is in their neck or back. Others might say that they have an upset stomach or a headache. Then, now that the group is perhaps more aware, we might to start to talk more deeply about how we are feeling and thinking about the conversation. When people realize that their bodies are constantly "talking" with each other, they often feel more connected with each other.

Body Image Dialogue

We know that poor body image is common in the United States (Gimlin, 2002). Although (or perhaps partly because) we spend a good deal of our wealth and time in dieting, grooming, and beautifying our bodies, many people struggle to accept their bodies. Dialogue can focus on our relationship with our own bodies and related issues of self-care.

For example, I have invited people to go around the circle and speak if they wish about their own relationships with their body. One way to foster this conversation is to lay out on a table a number of art cards, which could be either purchased at a bookstore or made out of pictures cut out of magazines. People could be asked to select a card that draws them, or the direction could be to pick out a card that reminds them of themselves. Then they can use the picture to talk about their relationship with their own body and own body self-care. As typical, people should be allowed to share without being judged or analyzed, and a general open dialogue can follow the structured sharing.

Sexuality as Dialogue

Most human beings experience sexual feelings toward and from other people. Like other intense feelings (such as anger or fear), we do not necessarily express them in a direct and assertive manner, especially without expectations or judgments. Our cultures often have taboos against such open expressions. People also may feel extremely vulnerable in a conversation about sexuality, perhaps in part because these feelings have rarely if ever been discussed in a safe environment. There may be dialogue situations where sexual feelings could be safely owned, for the purpose of deepening mutual understanding and relationship. The facilitator can create exercises that are relatively safe, where there is no judgment or pressure to respond to comments.

For example, in dialogues on sexual diversity, I have asked people to write down on a sheet of paper a socially inappropriate sexual fantasy that they have. Then people fold the sheets of paper and I collect and redistribute them. Then we take turns reading them out loud. I ask participants to respond to two questions: (a) If I had this fantasy, what would I be afraid people would think or do, and (b) if I had this fantasy, would I try to hide it from others or would I feel comfortable sharing it? One participant read his anonymous sheet of paper, which said, "I would have sex with someone of the same gender as I." The participant then said, "If I had this fantasy, I guess I would be scared that my family would be angry with me and say I am a sinner, or worse . . . and yes, I would for sure hide it from others. I wouldn't want to lose my job or family."

Another, more direct exercise that a group might try is to give participants an opportunity to volunteer to hear from other people in the group about their own sexual energy. The opportunity to volunteer protects everyone, because no one is forced to either receive or give feedback about sexuality. For example, if Bob raises his hand and volunteers, then other people, if they wish, can talk honestly with Bob about what sexual feelings they may have about him or how they respond to his sexual energy. They can also ask him questions about how he feels toward them. After Bob volunteered, Marcia said, "Bob, I feel like I have to put up a protective shield around me when you are in the same room with me, because sometimes I sense that you view me only or at least primarily as a sexual object . . . is that true?" If Bob wants to respond to that statement, the facilitator might have to help him notice and own any defensiveness or anger that comes up for him. Bob might be able to say, for example, "I appreciate that feedback, and you are not imagining things because I do find you attractive. Although I also really like you as a person, both things are true at the same time. But I have tried to hide my sexual feelings toward you and it sounds like I did not do a very good job of hiding that."

In the example above, Bill might also want to speak with Bob. Bill might say, "Bob, I imagine that you are very threatened by and judgmental of my sexuality, since I came out to the group that I am gay. Can you speak to that?" Bob is able to respond, "Thanks for bringing that up. You are right, I am uncomfortable around you, probably mostly because I am afraid that you will make a pass at me, and I do not know how to respond." These kinds of communications can stimulate further dialogue with other participants, and the facilitator can provide a space for such a follow-up conversation with the whole group.

EXPERIENTIAL LEARNING 10.3

(1) Do you feel more comfortable doing a dialogue with one other person or with a group? Why do you think?

(2) Do you think a dialogue on body image could help some people deal with their own lack of acceptance about their bodies?

(3) Why are people often so private in talking about their sexuality? Can you think of a circumstance where you might want to have such a dialogue? How would you facilitate it?

DEEP ECOLOGY DIALOGUE

We humans are in constant nonverbal interaction with other living things and with the ecosystems that support all life. Most of us have favorite flowers, animals, landscapes, and ecosystems, for example. Many of us also sense that other animals have feelings, and we will often talk to animals and imagine that they may be responding back to our words. We might say, "What's wrong?" to a pet dog, for example, or "Hi, little guy" to a dragonfly that lands on a walking stick. We also seem to respond to plants, the seasons, weather, the sun, the local landscapes, or the night sky as we daily interact with such natural "Others" and systems.

The purpose of deep ecology dialogue is to make these communications more conscious and translate them into verbal communications that help us further develop our relationships, communities, and connections with our world.

DEEP ECOLOGY

Deep ecology philosophy values all living beings equally and emphasizes the interconnectedness of all living things with the ecosystems that support life (Tobias, 1988). There is growing scientific evidence that the physical and psychological well-being of human beings is interconnected with the well-being of other living things and ecosystems (e.g., de Steiguer, 2006). The ways we think and communicate as humans may in fact be intimately connected with the evolution of natural ecosystems (Abram, 1996). Ecofeminists have added androcentrist theory to deep ecology and suggest that our overemphasis of the masculine perspective in our worldview has helped create our disconnection with and destruction of the environment (Nelson, 2006). Ultimately, deep ecologists recognize that humans need to recognize our interdependence with nature before we cause irreversible damage to the ecosystems that support our existence (Bender, 2003).

Our ancestors called to sacred plants, animals, and landscapes in their healing ceremonies (Roszak, 1992) and were also able to intuitively sense their medicinal and nutritional qualities (Clinebell, 1996). Similar experiences are reported by many indigenous peoples today, who often say they listen to nature with their hearts. As modern humans have increasingly lost this connection with other living things and ecosystems, we may also have lost our connection with our own bodies, sensuality, and language (Abram, 1996).

Some scientists today believe that the heart itself may actually be able to listen. The electromagnetic field of the heart has been found to be 5,000 times stronger than that of the brain and is measurable up to 10 feet from the body. Such fields may be able to "dialogue" in "heart entrainment" with the fields of other organisms. In addition, 60% of heart cells are neural cells, with all the ganglia, axons, and dendrites that brain cells have. These heart neural cells are hardwired into the brain's amygdala, thalamus, hippocampus, and cortex, which suggests that the heart may interact with such brain functions as meaning making, problem solving, reasoning, learning, emotional memories, and sensory experience (Buhner, 2012).

Masanobu Fukuoka (1978), the celebrated farmer and philosopher from Shikoku, Japan, has written and spoken about how farmers can intuitively sense the qualities of their crops and natural environment. Biologists have found that our own bodies have in fact evolved in intimate concert with other animals and plants. "Our bodies and lives only make sense in the context of other species. Only by looking at other lives do we really understand our own" (Dunn, 2011, p. 258). Even eating is a dialogue. For example, at least 50 different kinds of plant microRNA have been found in human blood samples by scientists at Nanjinj University in China. Some of these microRNA strands are helpful (e.g., by killing the flu virus); others may be harmful.

Conversations Between Local Wildlife, Ecosystems, and Humans

Many people want to feel reconnected to nature and feel better when they experience such connection. The dialogue facilitator can set up psychodramas that give other living things and ecosystems a "voice" that we humans can listen to.

One way to do this is to divide the dialogue group up into roles. In one dialogue, half of the group can pick specific local plants (forest, wild flowers), animals (birds, fish, bears), or land forms (rivers, hills) to role-play. The other half can take on roles of environmentalists, politicians, ranchers, Big Oil company executives, and so on. Then everyone can dialogue from the position they took on.

The dialogue in this example might become complex, loud, and emotional, and it might go like this. Marcus, who is a forest, says, "I am tired of being cut down more and more. I give you oxygen, nutrients in the soil, and beauty, but all you do is cut me down for more houses and roads." Then Debra, who is a developer, says, "Look, we cannot afford in this economic downturn to not keep building and expanding our economy." At the end of this exercise, the group can process the experience together.

Dialogue With Pictures of Living Things

Another method of fostering a dialogue of deep ecology is to use drawings or photos of living things and landscapes. These can be arranged on a table, and participants can be asked to choose a card or picture that they are especially drawn to. After people have returned to their seats, the facilitator can ask them to take turns explaining why they identify with the animal they have chosen. Kathy might say, "I chose the seahorse because I love the way they are so gentle and calm, which is the way I am when I am at my best." Then Ben says, "I chose the coyote because he is kind of a trickster like me."

Dialogue of Sacred Landscapes

For many people, elements of the natural world have a spiritual or sacred quality to them. In this exercise, the facilitator asks participants to close their eyes for a minute and reflect on their favorite landscape, which some might even call "sacred." Then the group is asked to share what their landscapes are and explain why. Susan says that she has a beach she visits in Central California, which is sacred to her. "The water is turquoise, and the beach and cliffs behind are often golden. I feel everything is alive, and I feel most alive when I am there." Doug says, "My sacred landscape is up in the Wasatch Mountains when I am skiing. I love the crispness of the air and the stillness of the mountains. I feel calm."

Sensing the Seasons

The facilitator can ask participants to share what they feel and think about the season they are currently in. One day, in a group I was facilitating, we had reached the shortest day of the year, the winter solstice. I asked participants how the season affected their bodies, minds, and spirits. Some people said they loved the cold weather and the snow. Others said they were always sad and more socially withdrawn this time of year.

EXPERIENTIAL LEARNING 10.4

(1) Have you ever felt like you could communicate with another living thing that was not human? Do you believe that other living things have feelings? Explain.

(2) Do you have a special connection with a particular landscape (location that you have been to)? What kind of "dialogue," if any, have you had with this landscape?

REFERENCES

Abram, D. (1996). The spell of the sensuous: Perception and language in a more-than-human world. New York: Pantheon.

Anttila, E. (2007). Searching for dialogue in dance education: A teacher's story. *Dance Research Journal, 39*(2), 43–57.

Behar-Horenstein, L. S., & Ganet-Sigel, J. (1999). *The art and practice of dance/movement therapy.* New York: Pearson.

Bender, F. L. (2003). *The culture of extinction: Toward a philosophy of deep ecology.* Amherst, NY: Humanity Books.

Benson, H. (2012). Tracking the mind body connection. *Brain World, 2*(3), 40–43.

Buhner, S. H. (2012, January). How you really can listen with your heart. *Spirituality and Health: The Soul/Body Connection,* pp. 79–83.

Chace, M., Sandel, S. L., Shaiklin, S., & Lohn, A. (1993). *Foundations of dance/movement therapy: The life and work of Marian Chace.* Columbia, MD: American Dance Therapy Association.

Clarke, T. J., Bradshaw, M. F., Field, D. T., Hampson, S. E., & Rose, D. (2005). The perception of emotion from body movement in point-light displays of interpersonal dialogue. *Perception, 34,* 1171–1180.

Clinebell, H. (1996). *Ecotherapy: Healing ourselves, healing the planet.* New York: Haworth.

Dances of Universal Peace. (2011). http://www.dancesofuniversalpeace.org/home.shtm

de Steiguer, J. E. (2006). *The origins of modern environmental thought.* Tucson: University of Arizona Press.

Dils, A., & Crosby, J. F. (2001). Dialogue in dance studies research. *Dance Research Journal, 33*(1), 62–72.

Dunn, R. (2011). *The wild life of our bodies: Predators, parasites, and partners that shape who we are today.* New York: HarperCollins.

Fox, M. A. (1990). *Spirituality named compassion and the healing of the global village, Humpty Dumpty and us.* Minneapolis, MN: Winston Press.

Fox, M. (1991). *Creation spirituality: Liberating gifts for the peoples of the Earth.* San Francisco: Harper San Francisco.

Fukuoka, M. (1978). *The one-straw revolution.* Emmaus, PA: Rodale Press.

Gale, N. K. (2011). From body-talk to body-stories: Body work in complementary and alternative medicine. *Sociology of Health and Illness, 33*(2), 237–251.

Gimlin, D. L. (2002). *Body work: Beauty and self image in American culture.* Berkeley: University of California Press.

Lowen, A. (2005). *The voice of the body.* Alachua, FL: Bioenergetics Press.

Murphy, M. (1993). *The future of the body: Explorations into the further evolution of human nature.* Los Angeles: Tarcher.

Nelson, C. (2006). *Ecofeminism vs. deep ecology, dialogue.* San Antonio, TX: Saint Mary's University Dept. of Philosophy.

Oesterley, W. O. E. (2002). *Sacred dance in the ancient world.* Chelmsford, MA: Courier Dover.

Payne, H. (1992). *Dance movement therapy: Theory and practice.* New York: Routledge.

Reich, W. (1945). *Character analysis* (T. P. Wolfe, Trans.). New York: Orgone Institute Press.

Roszak, T. (1992). *The voice of the earth: An exploration of ecopsychology.* New York: Touchstone.

Stewart, I. L. (2000). *Sacred woman, sacred dance: Awakening spirituality through movement and ritual.* Rochester, VT: Inner Traditions.

Tobias, M. (Ed.). (1988). *Deep ecology.* San Marcos, CA: Avant Books.

Dialogue Applications

INTRODUCTION TO SECTION III

In Section III, an inclusive approach to dialogue practice is applied to five dialogue practice areas. In each chapter, a different community challenge is addressed through dialogue methods. The area of healing divides is discussed in Chapter 11. Chapter 12 is about diversity and social justice work. Peace, reconciliation, and conflict resolution are covered in Chapter 13; Chapter 14 looks at family and community building across the life-span; and community therapy is explored in Chapter 15.

WHAT IS THE INCLUSIVE APPROACH?

The inclusive approach to dialogue uses interventions drawn from any and all of the dialogue models, as the changing dialogue situation may require. As described in Chapter 5, an inclusive or integrated approach does seem to be effective in helping people. The inclusively oriented facilitator does not have to draw from *every* model, however. Few of us believe equally in every model or feel equally comfortable with them all. We do know that when a professional helper believes in his method and can convince the client that the method works, then the method is more likely to work.

Each method does give us a different approach to dialogue and therefore may prove useful in certain situations. The following figure resummarizes the basic differences between the models, as described in Section II.

Dialogue model	Dialogic situations where interventions drawn from each model might be useful
Psychodynamic Chapter 6	When stories about past sociohistorical trauma still need to be processed
Cognitive-behavioral Chapter 7	When healthier beliefs and behaviors are required

(Continued)

(Continued)

Experiential-humanistic Chapter 8	When greater awareness and expression of emotions is required
Transpersonal Chapter 9	When further spiritual development is required
Biological and ecological Chapter 10	When the body-mind-environment connection needs to be fostered

Often interventions drawn from most or all of the models can be used in the same dialogue session. For example, in a dialogue on the religious divide, the conversation intensifies when Jenay says to William, "It really bugs me that you think your religion is the only true religion."

The facilitator might then start with a psychodynamic (Chapter 6) exercise: "What if we go around the room and every person who wants to can share a brief story about what (and how) you were taught to believe about religion from your family and culture." After a process discussion in which the psychodynamic experience is discussed, the facilitator could follow up with a cognitive-behavioral therapy (Chapter 7) exercise. She asks participants who identify as religious to notice what beliefs they have about nonreligious people and for the other participants to notice the beliefs they have about religious people. Later, the facilitator asks Jenay and William to sit in chairs in the center of the circle and process their child, observing self, and parent ego states in an experiential-humanistic psychodrama (see Chapter 8). A later transpersonal (Chapter 9) exercise might ask participants to take turns sharing "one thing that each of you know for sure." Finally, the facilitator might initiate a body-mind exercise (Chapter 10) and have them take turns drawing a crayon picture that shows what the relationship between their religiosity and spirituality looks like.

CHAPTER 11

Bridging Divides Through Dialogue

Transforming Our Spaces of Misunderstanding

What is a divide? There are always going to be differences between individuals and between groups, such as age, gender, religion, and sexual orientation. Such differences can enrich our lives. However, just like the North American Great Basin is slowly widening and spreading California further and further apart from the Wasatch Front of Utah, any difference between people can become wider, and this widening space can be filled with misunderstanding, stereotyping, oppression, and even overt violence.

Often, sociohistorical trauma helps widen differences into divides. When people are mistreated because of their age, gender, religion, sexual orientation, or any other difference, then greater spaces of misunderstanding tend to form. These spaces may be filled with stereotypes, mistrust, hostility, and sometimes even violence.

Dialogue can help bridge these spaces of misunderstanding, or divides. Bridges are relational connections made across differences. Bridges do not erase the differences they cross, but they make it possible for people to form relationships across differences, which may be some of the richest relationships they ever form. In this chapter, dialogues that help bridge divides are described. These dialogues can help fill the spaces of misunderstanding with mutual understanding and even friendship.

Why would people in a community or family want to bridge the differences that divide them? The people I know who are most committed to this work tell me that they are responding to the pain they feel from the disconnection. In other words, whether most of us are aware of it or not, probably everyone in a community suffers when there is a significant divide. They also often say that establishing relationships with people who are different from them truly enriches their lives.

The basic approach to bridging a divide is to create a space where people can safely and gradually get to know each other in increasingly authentic ways. The intimacy that can develop in dialogue tends to reduce the misunderstandings, stereotypes, fears, and aggression that often separate people. Years ago, I helped evaluate a gang diversion program that used midnight basketball games to reduce intergang violence. One of the young men told us, "It is harder to shoot someone after you play ball with him." In a way, this young man summarized what happens in dialogue; as people "play" together, whether through sports or dialogue, we tend to establish bridging relationships.

A growing body of research supports the efficacy of dialogue as a method in bridging divides. Student interactions with diverse peers, for example, result in positive social, cognitive, and democratic shifts by the sophomore year of college (Hurtado, 2005). Intergroup learning across diverse student groups helps reduce prejudice and promotes acceptance of diversity (Nagda, Kim, & Truelove, 2004). Efforts to bridge divides through intergroup dialogues (see Chapter 3) have been found to result in positive changes in student beliefs, attitudes, and behaviors (Alimo, Kelly, & Clark, 2002; Gurin & Nagda, 2006).

What happens with dialogue participants that promotes such change? Researchers are beginning to understand what this change process entails. Factors that seem to predict such positive changes across human divides include the (1) engagement of self in conversation, (2) critical self-reflection, (3) appreciation of diversity, and (4) alliance building (Nagda, 2006).

Dialogues that address divides will use the basic phases of dialogue described in Chapter 5. Issues specific to dialogues that address divides are summarized in Table 11.1, broken down by each dialogue model. The right-hand side has five lists of issues that can be addressed, drawn from the five dialogue models. In each row, at least one question addresses the negative impact of the divide, and one question addresses a way to move forward.

Table 11.1   Work Tasks and Issues in Dialogues That Address Divides

Models (see Section II)	Issues to Address (Drawn From Each Model)
Psychodynamic	What is the shared history of the divide in our community? What are our individual stories about the divide? What sociohistorical trauma exists in these histories and stories? How have these trauma stories caused us unnecessary suffering?
Cognitive-behavioral	How do people behave toward the other side of the divide? What stereotypes do we carry about the other side of the divide?
Experiential-humanistic	What emotions do we carry about each other? How have these emotions also harmed me emotionally? How do we want to feel toward ourselves and each other?
Transpersonal	How has the divide affected our spirituality? How does the divide challenge each of us to grow spiritually?
Body-mind-environment	How has the divide affected our bodies? How has the divide affected our living environment? What physical or environmental activities help bridge the divide?

In the rest of the chapter, descriptions of dialogue work with specific examples of various kinds of divides are described.

(1) What divides exist in your community, family, work, or school setting? What sociohistorical trauma is at the root of these divides?

(2) How do these divides affect you and others? Explain.

(3) How could they be transformed? What would change if they were transformed?

GENDER DIVIDES

With a new dialogue class, one of my favorite approaches to begin with is the gender divide dialogue. I usually ask either the women or men to volunteer to fill maybe six empty chairs arranged in the center of the room. If I do not get enough volunteers, I might designate some "volun-tolds." Once this "fishbowl" is filled, I set some rules for the exercise. People in the center circle may talk but have the right to pass on questions or issues. People in the outside circle are not allowed to speak but can listen deeply and respectfully. At the end of the fishbowl, the whole class will be allowed to join in the dialogue.

I then sit in the middle circle with the participants and ask a question, to provide structure to help participants to start speaking. If the men are in the circle first, I might ask, "What is the hardest thing about being a man?" Usually someone is willing to start. The kinds of things men often bring up include a pressure to be financially successful, a pressure to act "manly," bullying by other men, and competition in the workplace. When the men are finished, the women often want to respond with many questions and comments. The whole group processes the experience. Often, the women will say that they were impressed with and moved by the openness of the men.

Then I would ask for six women to sit in the inner fishbowl circle. The same rules apply. The women often bring up such comments as pressure to look beautiful, pressure to be successful at both work and home, low wages, sexism, expectations to do all the housework, and expectations to be the primary caretaker of the children and any aging parents. The whole group processes again. Usually the class indicates that they liked this exercise, learned more about the opposite sex, and thought a lot about what was said after class.

RELIGIOUS DIVIDES

There is probably at least some tension between religions in most diverse communities today, and there are usually at least some people who want to help bridge religious divides.

My community is not an exception. As in any other dialogue technique, the facilitator has to find a balance between encouraging safety and risk taking, and it is always a challenge to find the right timing and approach to encourage authentic sharing and deeper respectful listening across religious divides.

I use structure to create safety. Sometimes I ask the religious minority in the room to speak first (there is usually one majority and at least one minority group). Often people will naturally sit next to their friends when they enter the dialogue space. Instead of automatically moving people or using a fishbowl (which might make them feel even more surrounded and oppressed), I might ask them to stay in their chairs and speak to the question, "What is it like being a member of the XYZ Church?" I will ask the other group to remain silent and listen until the group has finished. Then, the whole group can process the exercise. As usual, I will then reverse the dialogue and ask the majority religion members to answer the same question, and then have another group dialogue.

Some comments that people who identify as belonging to the "minoritized" group might make include, "I feel alone when the majority religion has their community events" or "I feel the most angry when my children are ostracized." Comments that people identifying in the majority group might make include, "Others seem to think we are all bigots and rigid in our beliefs" and "It seems to be OK in this community to say nasty things about our religion."

After this round, we might move to more difficult conversations, perhaps in future dialogue sessions. I might ask each group to address the following question at the next meeting: "What are some painful stories you might tell about being a member of your church in this community?" Another question that can be helpful is, "What things have each of us thought, said, or done that might have caused suffering for members of other religions?" As people start to see that the other group has also suffered and that they have contributed to that suffering, new openings for connection may occur. A typical comment might be, "I often remain silent when people put down folks from the other church. I will not do that anymore because I realize now that my silence is giving them permission to make those stereotypes."

I have also led dialogues on religion at my university, which is located in a region that has a strong religious majority (let's say the "XYZ Church"). However, members of the XYZ Church are also actually in the minority in some departments on campus. In one dialogue, situated in such a department, I asked for volunteers who were members of the XYZ Church to gather in a fishbowl and talk about what it was like for them to teach in our college. As usual, the rule was that people in the outside circle had to listen quietly. After they finished, we moved to a fishbowl with a group of participants who were not members. In both fishbowls, I sat with the people in the inner circle and helped start the conversation. For the last 45 minutes or so, we had a large group discussion (which was mostly an intellectual or cognitive interaction), during which practically everyone spoke about the divide that had opened up in the department over the years. We realized that we all have the experience of being the minority group in some of our life settings.

POLITICAL DIVIDES

One week, I invited representatives of one very conservative political organization to come on campus and visit my dialogue models class. Our guests seemed very tense, and the students also seemed unusually uncomfortable as we participated in the check-in exercise (which was, "What did you have for breakfast this morning, and what would you have liked to have had instead?"). I thought we should pay attention to the tension somehow, and I asked our guests to follow up on the check-in by commenting on "What is it like to be here today in our classroom for this dialogue?"

One of the visitors talked about how he felt like he was entering "enemy territory" when he came on campus, and another visitor said that she had heard that all the faculty on campus hated people in her political organization. Later on, another visitor talked about how the university was sometimes described as the "bowel of the devil" in their organization's meetings. These kinds of comments helped my students realize how vulnerable our guests were feeling. They did a good job of listening, and some responded when the visitors were finished by being very supportive and understanding. I was proud of them that they did not act defensive or angry (although they might have had those feelings inside, of course). My students' behavior also seemed to help our visitors participate more openly. Their feedback at the end of the dialogue was that the classroom experience was the most friendly environment they had ever visited on campus.

After the visitors had talked about their feelings and fears, and we had finished processing as a large group, I asked the students to also go around and talk about how they had been feeling when they first walked in. Interestingly, most of the students said that, although they were initially nervous, they now felt better.

One point of this story is that our culture can be very divided by political ideology, and perhaps because of our own intense emotions, we may forget how frightened the Other is of us. I have learned to not be surprised to hear that other people may see me very differently than I see myself. I cannot assume that others will see my good intentions, and I must be patient with their initial fears, if I hope to eventually make a relational connection with them.

Another point is that people can usually pick up on the nervousness (or other feelings) of others in the room. Usually people will feel sensations in their own bodies when others are, for example, fearful or angry. If the facilitator can help just one person start talking about what she feels in her body, then others will be more likely to do the same. When people become more aware of their body sensations, then they can start to deal with the emotions they are having and begin to relate with each other.

DIVIDES ABOUT SEXUAL ORIENTATION

Few issues seem to divide populations like sexual orientation. In my community, many people feel fiercely about the subject, and even families can develop long-lasting, even seemingly permanent divides about sexual behaviors. In our monthly religious divide dialogues, which are open to the public, the subject comes up almost every meeting.

In one dialogue, a participant was talking about his experience of coming out as a gay man to his parents. We decided to co-create a psychodrama about his experience. One person (Jill) volunteered to play the teen child, a young woman. An older man (Stan) volunteered to play the father, who also happened to be a member of the clergy of a local church. They sat in chairs facing each other, inside the circle. The woman tells her father that she is in love with another woman and asks for his blessings. The man says he cannot give her a blessing, because his God says that she is committing a sin.

Many people in the group wanted to participate (see psychodrama in Chapter 8). One woman jumped up and stood behind Jill and said angrily to Stan, "You are such a bigot! Jesus would not have acted this way!" A man stood up and walked behind Stan, put his hand on Stan's shoulder, and said quietly, "I love you, but I cannot bless your behavior. I must stay true to my own beliefs." Another man stood behind Jill, saying, "Then I bless myself!"

Later, the group came back together into one circle. More than one person had tears in their eyes. We talked about how most of us could relate to the psychodrama, although the parent-child conflicts we have experienced were not all about conflicts in sexuality. The feeling of universality about parent-child conflict seemed to bring us all closer together, and a number of participants said that they thought it was possible for children and parents to stay in relationship with each other, even when there are significant ideological differences.

DIVIDES ABOUT JOB RANKINGS

Most of us who work in a university setting know how job rank can divide tenure track faculty from non–tenure track faculty, staff from faculty, and administrators from faculty. Job ranking can be divides in many work locations, of course.

Dialogues can help people bridge these divides, especially when there is support from campus leadership for this kind of work. If the facilitator can get a "buy in" from the most powerful people on campus, then there is a possibility that enough safety can be established for the less powerful to talk with authenticity about their experiences. Without such safety, transforming dialogue may not happen, because many people are naturally fearful for their job security and thus do not want to talk about what they really feel and think at work.

A relatively safe way to begin such a dialogue is to start by meeting separately with different groups. The facilitator can first meet, for example, with non–tenure track faculty and ask them to discuss among themselves what it is like to have the lowest status faculty positions in the college. Then a separate dialogue can be held with tenure track faculty, to discuss their experiences. Eventually, if there is a mutual commitment to work toward transforming the divide, both groups can be brought together. As in most dialogue processes, the groups will probably need to meet multiple times so that trust and honesty can be built.

EXPERIENTIAL LEARNING 11.2

(1) Which of the divide dialogues you read about above appealed to you the most? Why?

(2) Do you have any friends who belong to the other side of any of the divides in your community? What do you especially value about that kind of a friendship?

FOLLOWING UP DIALOGUE WITH ACTION FOR SOCIAL CHANGE

Often participants in my groups have wanted to follow up their dialogues by engaging in some kind of social change activity. These activities may be collective or individual.

Some participants in religious divide dialogues have become more actively engaged in their own churches. One participant I know also happened to be a leader in his church, where he has become increasingly active in promoting greater understanding of and compassion for nonmembers. Since he is well respected in his church, he has influenced many of his co-members.

Often, social workers, psychologists, and other psychotherapists have told me that the way they practice has been changed because of their participation in dialogue work. They report that they are more sensitive to issues of diversity when they assess their clients and that they use dialogue techniques when they work with individuals, couples, families, and groups. They also report becoming more committed to engaging their clients in conversations about oppression, privilege, and social justice.

REFERENCES

Alimo, C., Kelly, R., & Clark, C. (2002, Fall). Diversity issues in higher education: Intergroup dialogue program student outcomes and implications for campus radical climate: A case study. *Higher Education,* pp. 49–53.

Gurin, P., & Nagda, B. A. (2006). Getting to the what, how, and why of diversity on campus. *Educational Researcher, 35*(1), 20–24.

Hurtado, S. (2005). The next generation of diversity and intergroup relations research. *Journal of Social Issues, 61*(3), 595–610.

Nagda, B. A. (2006). Breaking barriers, crossing borders, building bridges: Communication processes in intergroup dialogues. *Journal of Social Issues, 62*(3), 553–576.

Nagda, B. A., Kim, C., & Truelove, Y. (2004). Learning about difference, learning with others, learning to transgress. *Journal of Social Issues, 60*(1), 195–214.

Dialogue In Social Justice Work

In this chapter, dialogues are described that may foster the relationships necessary for social justice work.

WHAT IS SOCIAL JUSTICE WORK?

Social justice work is about co-creating more fairness in community. Our word *justice* has Old French and Latin roots that referred to "equity" and "righteousness." Social justice work is based on many of the same values that guide dialogue work; both see the worth of every person and respect the diversity of perspectives and characteristics. According to the National Association of Social Workers (2012), "Social justice is the view that everyone deserves equal economic, political, and social rights and opportunities." A just society is a sustained and fair system of human cooperation (Rawls, 1993).

There are at least three forms of social justice. The first, legal justice, is about what I, as an individual, owe society. The second, communicative justice, is about what people owe each other. The third form, distributive justice, is about what society owes its members and is the form most affiliated with social justice in social work (Van Soest, 1995). Social justice also arguably includes economic justice, which provides values for guiding economic institutions (e.g., National Center for Law and Economic Justice, 2012).

Although the United States has made progress in dealing with social justice issues, more progress is still required. Significant disparities still exist between racial cultural linguistic groups in such categories as school achievement, poverty, and opportunity (Cochran-Smith, 2004). Recent research ranks the United States 27th out of 31 member nations in the Organisation for Economic Co-operation and Development (OECD, 2012), higher than only four other nations: Turkey (31st), Mexico (30th), Chile (29th), and Greece (28th). The inequality of economic wealth and income in the United States was a large contributor to this poor ranking.

SOCIAL JUSTICE WORK AND SOCIOHISTORICAL TRAUMA

Sociohistorical trauma tends to create social injustice in our communities and institutions. When there are divides of misunderstanding between peoples, people are more likely to fear and devalue those on the other side of the divide and treat them (or allow them to be treated) unjustly. Those who happen to be in power may be more likely to abuse their power, if they believe that they have been victimized by, or fear, other groups with less power.

Research in Social Justice Work

There is increasing evidence to support the contact hypothesis, which suggests that intergroup contact, including intergroup dialogue, can reduce prejudice (Dovidio, Gaertner, & Kawakami, 2003; Gurin, Nagda, & Sorenson, 2011). Intergroup dialogue has been successfully used to promote social justice work (Dessel, Rogge, & Garlington, 2006; Nagda & Zuniga, 2003). "Sexual orientation dialogues" remain uncommon but show promise in helping to reduce misunderstanding between sexual minorities and sexual majority populations (Dessel, Woodford, & Warren, 2011).

Why Do Social Justice Work?

Social justice work is often challenging work. Those who are privileged may not be ready to feel the pain of carrying privilege, and those who remain oppressed may not be ready to feel the pain of being oppressed. I have often heard, for example, people of color talk about the fatigue they feel from having to constantly educate White people. I have also often seen White people react with guilt, defensiveness, or anger when they hear stories of oppression.

Social justice work is often painful work, but I believe that we suffer even more from living in an unjust world. Even those of us who are the most privileged suffer from injustice, because we tend to live with a sense of separateness from and fear of the Other, a guilt and shame about the unfairness of what we have, and an often all-consuming need to protect what we think is ours. The purpose of social justice work is not to make the privileged feel worse but to help them feel the world that already *is*. As a White man, the more I am aware of injustice, the more I am freed from any attachment I still have to holding on to my privileges.

I have often heard participants in social justice work talk about the benefits they have received from doing the work (see also Chapters 2 and 3). Many talk about the friendships that they developed with people different from them. Others talked about the satisfaction and empowerment they experienced in doing something about social injustice in their world.

EXPERIENTIAL LEARNING 12.1

(1) What social injustices exist in your community, family, work, or school setting? What sociohistorical trauma is at the root of these injustices?

(2) How do these issues directly affect you? Explain.

(3) How might they be transformed? What would change if they were transformed?

Table 12.1 Dialogue Work in Social Justice

Focus Area	Dialogue Topics
Beginnings	Warm-ups Finding commonalities and reasons for commitment Practice dialogues Dealing with challenging reactions
Dialogues of privilege	What is privilege? Intergroup dialogue Intragroup dialogue
Dialogues of oppression	Sharing stories of sociohistorical trauma Transforming challenging reactions
Developing multicultural competence	What is multicultural competence? Understanding motivations Understanding obstacles
Becoming allies	Understanding what an ally is and is not Allies in social justice dialogue
Cooperative social action	Planning cooperative actions Dialogue actions Debriefing

Table 12.1 summarizes the six areas of social justice work that are discussed in the next sections of this chapter. In each section, some background and practical dialogue exercises are offered.

BEGINNINGS

Warm-ups

Before any dialogue begins, introductions can help people start to relate to each other, across the differences that divide us, and are best done with relatively nonthreatening sharing (see Chapter 4). For example, participants may share about their favorite food or music, which are common interests most people can relate to.

Finding Commonalities and Reasons for Commitment

I like to establish some simple commonalities in the first meeting. In addition to the initial warm-up exercises described above, participants can be asked to respond to different kinds of questions that are still relatively nonthreatening. Examples of these might include the following:

1. For a group of on-campus participants, please describe your favorite class that you ever had and why you liked it.

2. What landscape do you most relate to in the world? This "sacred landscape" might be, for example, a river location, a beach, a field, or a mountaintop.

3. If you had to listen to only one album of music for a month, what would it be?

The group also often benefits from some kind of introductory remarks by a leader or leaders. When I make such remarks, I try to keep them as brief as possible, and then ask others to add what they would like to the conversation. These remarks should help explain the purpose and history of the group.

At some point in the first meeting(s), the reasons for commitment to the dialogue can be discussed. The facilitator can talk about how important commitment is in any relationship, essentially because it creates a safer environment for sharing. One of my favorite ways to foster motivation and commitment for social justice work is to show inspirational films. One of my favorite films is *Two Rivers: A Native American Reconciliation* (Mitchell, 2007). This film offers reasons for privileged groups to do social justice work, demonstrates the importance of listening and speaking from the heart, and gives a vivid example of a reconciliation process that included dialogue as a key component.

Practice Dialogues

Practice dialogues are "real" dialogues, but they usually occur *within* a homogeneous group (intragroup dialogue), before the facilitator brings that group together with a different group for a heterogeneous dialogue *between* those groups (intergroup dialogue). The purpose of practice dialogues is to help participants learn values, skills, and knowledge necessary for them to be successful in the difficult dialogues they are planning to participate in. Some of these are described below.

The *values* of justice work dialogue are the values of dialogue described throughout this text. Every participant is valued. Human diversity is always respected, including differences of opinion and ideology. Listening to understand is the most important activity in dialogue, and when we speak, we speak to share our own (or "little t") truths, rather than to presume to teach others any universal (or "capital T") truths. Ultimately, dialogue process supports each participant's self-awareness, self-acceptance, and responsibility for both his own behavior and the well-being of the larger community.

The *skills* of social justice dialogue include many of the same dialogue skills offered throughout this text. The facilitator models self-awareness, self-acceptance, self-disclosure, genuineness, and empathy. The facilitator offers a combination of psychodynamic, cognitive-behavioral therapy, experiential-humanistic, transpersonal, or ecobiological techniques to help participants interact.

The most important *knowledge* necessary for social justice work is self-knowledge. When participants know and accept themselves, they are more able to create relationships with each other. Knowledge about others is also important, and each participant will be open to learning from others to the extent that he is also open to learning about himself.

In practice dialogues, participants practice listening to both the inner dialogue (self-knowledge) and the outer dialogue (knowledge of the Other). These dialogues begin with a conversation about relatively safer issues. We might have the oldest class members talk about what it is like to be older, for example, while the younger half listens. Even in such "practice dialogues," participants' inner dialogue might include intense feelings of guilt or anger. They learn in class how to slow down their reactions to others by observing their own feelings and striving to understand them, rather than just acting them out with defensive or aggressive behaviors. They start to appreciate in class how they can listen to each other and at the same time listen to their inner reactions, without judgment.

When new outside groups are invited to the dialogue class or group, they may also need some practice dialogues. The facilitator might begin by asking them to talk about the purpose of the dialogue and how they feel and think about participating. Concerns can be raised and addressed. The new participant group also gets a chance to see how I operate and can start to build trust in my values, intentions, and skills.

Anticipating Challenging Reactions

In practice dialogues, as in all the dialogues described in this chapter, challenging emotions and related behaviors will almost certainly arise from time to time. When these emotions and behaviors appear, the dialogue facilitator uses them as opportunities for further dialogue, growth, and social justice work. The facilitator wants to help privileged groups work through their difficult reactions and also keep a focus on the suffering of oppressed groups. This balance may also be challenging to achieve, because both groups want attention for their pain.

Some of the most common challenges are dealt with below.

In earlier chapters, I wrote about how the work of a relationship, or the work of intimacy, can be thought of as the process of co-discovering where you end and I begin. When there is an angry or defensive reaction, for example, the participant who is upset has the responsibility to look at how much of his emotion is about himself (his own sociohistorical trauma) and how much is about the Other (what the other person said or did in the dialogue). The facilitator's role is in part to help the angry person process his reactions in front of the group and then to return the group to the voices of other people in the group who may have triggered him. The facilitator wants to help the angry person process his emotions, but does not want to reward the anger or defensiveness by focusing too long on his reactions to others in the group.

Expressions of anger and defensiveness usually go together. Any intense emotion like anger can be thought of as a river with two major tributaries, which are the past and the present. During a dialogue, anger or defensiveness can be triggered for many different reasons, but the intensity of anger may often have more to do with past sociohistorical trauma than the current trigger. I have found that participants usually express anger or defensiveness when they feel attacked or threatened by events in the dialogue. In practice dialogues, participants can practice locating what feelings may lie "underneath" their anger or defensiveness.

Guilt and shame are other challenging reactions that tend to go together. Participants who belong to privileged groups often experience guilt and shame when they hear stories of oppression from more disadvantaged groups. When they experience guilt and shame, they often talk about their pain and may share tears. Again, the role of the facilitator is to help the participant to deal with his reactions without necessarily moving the focus of the group away from the stories of oppression that triggered the reactions.

Participants are often not aware that their guilt and shame are more about themselves than about the other person. Guilt, as discussed in previous chapters, can be thought of as a "pseudo-feeling" that I experience in my head, instead of the "real" feelings that are located more below my neck. In other words, guilt is the refusal to experience the world the way it really is. I have found that my guilt seems to shift when I reflect on my feelings, so when I facilitate, I ask participants to reflect on whether they might feel sad, mad, glad, scared, or excited. Often people discover they have many of these feelings, in reaction to the stories they have heard. I want them to see that they do not have to feel guilt to listen to others for understanding, and that guilt often shifts the focus away from my listening for understanding to my demand to be understood.

Another way to help participants with guilt is to ask the group to consider what they experience when a person reacts to *them* with guilt. Most people say that they feel annoyed or even angry when people react to them with guilt. They say that it is hard to trust their guilt, because it seems to be based more on fear than on genuine empathy for the other.

Participants also can become submerged in shame during a dialogue, and in fact, shame may be one of the greatest obstacles to dialogue during difficult conversations. Shame (or "toxic shame") can be thought of as my belief in my own inferiority. I have always liked Bradshaw's (2005) idea that "toxic" shame is transformed into "healthy" shame when I start to understand and accept my own limitations. I have found that people usually are embarrassed about feeling embarrassed. When I own my shame in front of others, I am no longer as afraid of it, and that shame seems to diminish.

DIALOGUES OF PRIVILEGE

What Is Privilege?

I especially like Paula Rothenberg's (2012) definition: "White Privilege is the other side of racism. Unless we name it, we are in danger of wallowing in guilt or moral outrage with no idea of how to move beyond them. It is often easier to deplore racism and its effects than to take responsibility for the privileges . . . once we understand how white privilege operates, we can begin addressing it on an individual and institutional basis." A significant part of social justice work is owning privilege, which is looking at the benefits that tend to arise because of such characteristics as male, White, class, and heterosexual (Anderson, 2011).

Privilege can be thought of as status given to a group of people by the larger culture that affords them special advantages over others. Privileges might include advantages in receiving respect, status, power, wealth, and safety. If there is a disadvantaged group, then there must be a relatively privileged or advantaged group. To illustrate this concept to the dialogue group, ask them to imagine the two columns of Figure 12.1 to be two sides of a coin.

Figure 12.1   Privilege and Disadvantage: Two Sides of the Same Coin

"Back"	"Front"
Group A	Group B
Privileged group	Disadvantaged group
Gets more than Group B	Gets less than Group A

Intergroup Dialogue

Dialogue techniques can be used to help people with privilege become more aware of their status and advantages, so that we can then use our privilege to help co-create more social justice. I have found that participants can come to recognize their privilege in many ways. One of the most powerful techniques is intergroup dialogue, between groups with different levels of privilege.

Such groups are best led, I believe, by co-facilitators who approximate the different diversities of the larger group. In our dialogue training group (DTG), my co-facilitator and I have co-facilitated a year-long series of meetings with a group consisting of about half people of color and half White people. Participants have told us that they appreciate the fact that she is a woman of color and I am a White man. Our participants have also told us that they like how we have modeled dialogue in front of them, and that our co-facilitation has helped them develop trust of people different from them.

As a facilitator, I can help participants do social justice work by modeling the work myself and by being transparent about my own internal process. In our DTG, for example,

I have often shared with the group information about my own racist thoughts and feelings, and owned the privileges that I enjoy. Often, other participants start to share their thoughts and feelings, after I have done a little of this kind of public sharing. As I will argue in the last chapter of the book, effective facilitation may be thought of as simply public learning (or learning in public), during which I share my own process in ways that support the growth of others.

Intragroup Dialogue

As an older White male, I may also be especially positioned to model privilege work with younger White males. In my White Male Privilege Group (WMPG), I have enjoyed co-creating a space in which younger White men can feel safe to explore their own privileges with me. Again, I often offer self-disclosures and modeling in this group. The participants have told me that such behaviors are especially helpful to them, encouraging them to also work on noticing their own privileges.

Another dialogue technique that has furthered the process in the WMPG is the acknowledgment of our behaviors, both those that have served to promote social justice and those that have directly or indirectly contributed to further injustice. The group members take turns sharing these stories. For example, one man told us about how he had not said anything when people were putting down a particular religious group in his presence. Another talked about how he had stood up for a friend of color who had suffered a micro-aggression in a restaurant, when she was the only one in the party who was asked for her identification. We usually discover that most of us have been heroic in some situations and cautious in other situations.

Sometimes facilitators are asked to provide diversity trainings for groups who are not necessarily motivated yet to look at their privilege. For example, some members of my DTG were invited to provide a training for a classroom of White men. They were all required to take the training, and few of them were enthusiastic. Usually, when confronted with a group of "nonvoluntary" participants, I begin a dialogue with a conversation about how they got into the class and how they think and feel about their nonvoluntary status. When their resentment about being forced to take a diversity class is acknowledged, most participants are better able to focus on the dialogue itself. We then asked the participants to dialogue about the benefits and costs of their race and gender. Luckily, a few participants took the lead in responding to these questions. We supported them, and I also modeled my own self-reflections on these questions. One man said that he was aware that he was automatically respected as a White male in some communities in the state. His comment helped others feel more comfortable sharing more openly.

DIALOGUES OF OPPRESSION

Sharing Stories of Sociohistorical Trauma

Oppression can be thought of as a pattern of unjust use of authority or power. If I experience such sociohistorical trauma long enough, I can start to internalize the oppression and begin to believe that I deserve to be oppressed.

What are stories of oppression? In these exercises, participants share personal experiences that exist within a larger context of ongoing unjust treatment or control. For example, I might tell a story I heard from my father about when he was discriminated against years ago, or I might tell a story about a micro-aggression that just happened to me in the grocery store last night.

Dialogues of oppression are often difficult, both for the people sharing stories and for the people hearing the stories. I have experimented with many different forms of dialogue that offer different mixtures of safety and risk taking for participants.

Overall, perhaps one of the best ways to structure these dialogues is to provide an opportunity for the stories of oppression to be told by one group, while the other group is instructed to listen for understanding, without responding verbally. After everyone in the first group has had a chance to speak, then the listening group is given an opportunity to respond. The two groups can be arranged in many different configurations. Sometimes I have created a large circle, and people sit wherever they wish; sometimes we have separated the group into two half-circles; and sometimes the first speakers are in the middle, in the smaller "fishbowl" circle.

When the listening group starts to respond, I often have to help them deal with their difficult emotions. Some participants may feel guilty, others perhaps angry. Everyone expresses these emotions differently, sometimes through withdrawal, others through tears or words. As further described in the following section, I usually try to help participants "slow down" their initial reactions so that they better understand themselves and learn new ways of thinking, feeling, and acting.

The facilitator strives to keep a balance between doing dialogue activities and processing those activities. He also wants to balance the focus between internal and external dialogue. These two sets of dialogue processes, when put together, create four possible combinations of work. These cells are not mutually exclusive (for example, the facilitator could do an activity with both internal and external dialogue). Hopefully, a balanced dialogue will contain at least some content in each of the four cells, illustrated in Figure 12.2.

Figure 12.2 Four Modes of Dialogue Work

Doing activity with internal dialogue	Doing activity with external dialogue
Processing activity with internal dialogue	Processing activity with external dialogue

Figure 12.3   Moving Back and Forth Between Groups: Four More Modes

Disadvantaged group speaks	Privileged group responds
Disadvantaged group processes their challenging reactions	Privileged group processes their challenging reactions

Group attention also needs to be balanced and fair. The facilitator wants to try to balance the four modes, presented in Figure 12.3. These modes represent four different ways that the facilitator can focus the dialogue. I try to give each mode about the same amount of focus, so that each group and individual feel that dialogue time is fairly distributed. If one group receives more time, I usually make sure that it is the disadvantaged group.

Transforming Challenging Reactions

Inevitably, members of privileged groups will have reactions to hearing stories of oppression, even when they have participated in practice dialogues and privileged group dialogues. No matter how "evolved" an individual is, he is still going to have challenging responses to others from time to time. When this happens, it is an opportunity for the participant to put into action the skills he learned in earlier dialogues. I have learned that the very most difficult conversations often lead to the most rewarding outcomes for participants.

In working with these reactions, to be as fair as possible to individual learning styles and group identities, I try to move back and forth between activity and process, between internal and external, and between advantaged and disadvantaged, as discussed above.

When people have difficult reactions, I try to first notice them in front of the group, in a mindful way (aware but not judgmental, as described in Chapter 8). I try to avoid interpretations or suggestions. I might, for example, say, "Jamie, what is happening for you right now?" when I see him rolling his eyes, rather than, "Jamie, are you angry right now?"

Then, if I think he can do the work of internal and external dialogue, I might ask the participant to use assertive language to describe his thoughts, feelings, and emotions. Jamie might say, "I think I am getting a little angry, but am not sure why." I might then ask, "Would it be OK if we explored this further to try to find out?"

If I do not think that the participant is ready to do the work, I might ask if he would like some help, either from me or from others in the group. Sometimes participants are just not ready to explore their internal reactions and do the work of relationship building (discovering where you end and I begin). Maybe the dialogue is bringing up past trauma in a way that feels too overwhelming or vulnerable. If the participant can acknowledge his difficulty, I always appreciate that and maybe add, "Thanks for saying that are not ready *yet*. Maybe we can get into this later at some point if you want to." My addition of the word *yet* may provide some hope and encouragement.

As discussed in Chapter 4, the dialogue facilitator strives to be aware of his own reactions so that he does not project them onto others, or otherwise confuse them with the reactions of others. So when there is conflict, the facilitator recognizes and accepts his own initial reactions but still strives to find ways to help participants get *their* needs met.

Often, facilitators want to make peace in the group before the conflict can really emerge and be dealt with. This may be because the facilitator is uncomfortable himself. For example, when Candace is talking about the oppression of women by men, Desmond gets angry and says, "Maybe it is time to get over it!" The group gets quiet; no one has yet shown anger this directly. The facilitator does not try to "make peace" by silencing Desmond but instead responds by saying, "Desmond, can you talk with Candace about what you were feeling and thinking?" Desmond responds, "I was angry because she goes on and on about how women are oppressed, and she does not realize that men have it hard too. I am kind to women, but I seldom get any recognition for it!" The facilitator asks, "How have you had it hard as a man, Desmond?" The facilitator lets Desmond talk for a while about his painful experiences of what he calls "reverse discrimination" in applying for a job, and helps him explore why he felt defensive, but eventually steers the conversation back to Candace again, so that Desmond does not take all the attention away from Candace's voice.

Eventually, Desmond may be able to see that he is defensive and angry because he feels attacked by the women in the group. Desmond may also realize that he does in fact want to have a relationship with the women that he can feel good about, and that this will take some ongoing and often hard work. The group can help him find new ways to handle his feelings that do not silence others but rather open up possibilities for more satisfying relationships with women.

DEVELOPING MULTICULTURAL COMPETENCE

What Is Multicultural Competence?

Multicultural competence can be thought of as the ability to communicate and work with others, especially with those who are different from me. I think that the mark of an educated person today should be that he can develop relationships with people different from himself. The way I like to introduce these topics to a class or group is to pose them as questions and see if the group can co-discover these definitions themselves. The word *educate* means to "draw out" in Latin, and I think the dialogue facilitator is in this sense a true educator, drawing out meanings from participants whenever possible. Many theorists believe that multicultural competence should be grounded in social justice work, which may include such activities as advocacy, outreach, and prevention (Vera & Speight, 2012).

Understanding Motivations

Why would someone want to develop multicultural competence? Again, I would pose this question to the group and let a cognitive dialogue develop among participants. I have found that most people are naturally curious about other cultures and communities.

Understanding Obstacles

When I ask my participants and students about the obstacles that make multicultural competence more difficult, they usually talk about their fears. I remember President Clinton talking about how most of us have a natural fear of people who are different and that perhaps this is a trait that evolved in our early ancestry. He was optimistic that we could work on changing this attribute.

EXPERIENTIAL LEARNING 12.2

(1) What are your reactions to reading about work in privilege and oppression? Are you interested in doing more of this work? What are your fears? Your hopes?

(2) What do you think about the idea that the mark of an educated person today should be that he can develop relationships with people different from himself? Has this set of skills and values been taught in your educational experiences? Explain.

BECOMING ALLIES

Understanding What an Ally Is and Is Not

When approaching the topic of allies, I like to start by asking participants to dialogue about the following questions:

1. What is an ally to you?

2. When you have been in a tough time in your life, how have people been good allies for you?

3. How have people not been good allies?

4. Who do you consider yourself to be an ally for today?

Allies in Social Justice Dialogue

Kivel (2002) has provided a useful list of what disadvantaged people often say they look for in an ally. These include, respect, listening, sharing of power, taking risks, honesty, admitting errors, speaking up, and commitment. In social justice dialogue, I like to ask participants to dialogue with each other about what they want and expect in an ally.

COOPERATIVE SOCIAL ACTION

Planning Cooperative Actions

Not every dialogue will result in social action, but some do. Some dialogues begin with a shared commitment that the conversations will lead to additional social action. In other dialogues, social action may evolve spontaneously from the conversations and relationships that develop.

Social actions are social justice activities that challenge inequality and oppression and support fairness and equality. Social justice dialogue can be considered a social action, but social actions can also take place outside the group meeting and in the larger community. Examples of social actions in the larger community include lobbying, public demonstrations, educational workshops, and media events.

If some participants in a dialogue are interested in moving toward a social action orientation outside of the group, the facilitator can help the group talk about this idea and come to some kind of resolution. Sometimes only some participants will move toward community-level actions, and sometimes the entire group will participate.

In both my dialogue training group and my White Male Privilege Group, the intention from the beginning was that members could volunteer to participate in outside social action activities. These activities have involved mostly educational workshops.

Dialogue During Events

One effective way of conducting social action is to bring the dialogue group to a larger audience, in a fishbowl kind of format. In other words, instead of offering a didactic panel, the participants will sit in a circle in front of the larger audience and talk among themselves as if they were back in their dialogue circle.

For example, I brought my DTG to a large social work class. There were about 11 participants at the meeting and about 60 students in the class. I arranged the chairs in one large half-circle (for students) and one small circle (for participants). Then, I asked the dialogue group to talk about what their experience had been while participating in the DTG social justice dialogues for 1 year. Just like in a fishbowl activity, the class watched without speaking, in this case for about 40 minutes. Then I set out extra chairs in the dialogue circle, and students could come and sit in the circle and participate in the dialogue themselves. Later, in the evaluation, students told me that this had been the single most meaningful class they attended that semester.

Debriefing

The dialogue group will usually benefit from an opportunity to talk about their outside social action experiences. Participants can compare experiences and give each other feedback and support regarding the experience.

EXPERIENTIAL LEARNING 12.3

(1) Respond to the questions about allies in the text:

a. What is an ally to you?

b. When you have been in a tough time in your life, how have people been good allies for you?

c. How have people not been good allies?

d. Who do you consider yourself to be an ally for today?

(2) Are you interested in participating in social justice action? Explain.

REFERENCES

Anderson, S. H. (2011). *Explorations in diversity: Examining privilege and oppression in a multicultural society.* Belmont, CA: Cengage Learning.

Bradshaw, J. (2005). *Healing the shame that binds you.* Deerfield Beach, FL: Health Communications, Inc.

Cochran-Smith, M. (2004). *Walking the road: Race, diversity, and social justice in teacher education.* New York: Teachers College Press.

Dessel, A., Rogge, M. E., & Garlington, S. B. (2006). Using intergroup dialogue to promote social justice and change. *Social Work, 51*(4), 303–309.

Dessel, A. B., Woodford, M. R., & Warren, N. (2011). Intergroup dialogue courses on sexual orientation: Lesbian, gay, and bisexual student experiences and outcomes. *Journal of Homosexuality, 58,* 1132–1150.

Dovidio, J. F., Gaertner, S. L., & Kawakami, K. (2003). Intergroup contact: The past, present, and the future. *Group Processes and Intergroup Relations, 6*(1), 5–21.

Gurin, P., Nagda, B. A., & Sorenson, N. (2011, Spring). Intergroup dialogue: Education for a broad conception of civic engagement. *Liberal Education,* pp. 46–51.

Kivel, P. (2002). *Uprooting racism: How White people can work for racial justice.* Gabriola Island, Canada: New Society Publishers.

Mitchell, R. (Director). (2007). *Two rivers: A Native American reconciliation* [Motion picture]. United States: Greenleaf Street Productions.

Nagda, B. A., & Zuniga, X. (2003). Fostering meaningful racial engagement through intergroup dialogues. *Group Processes and Intergroup Relations, 6*(1), 111–128.

National Association of Social Workers (2012). Social justice. http://www.naswdc.org/pressroom/features/issue/peace.asp

National Center for Law and Economic Justice. (2012). *Fighting for fairness for people in need.* http://www.nclej.org/

Organisation for Economic Co-operation and Development (OECD). (2012). Social justice in the OECD. http://www.sgi-network.org/pdf/SGI11_Social_Justice_OECD.pdf

Rawls, J. (1993). *Political liberalism.* New York: Columbia University Press.

Rothenberg, P. (2012). The White Privilege Conference, University of Colorado at Colorado Springs. http://www.whiteprivilegeconference.com/white_privilege.html

Van Soest, D. (1995). Peace and social justice. In R. Edwards (Ed.), *Encyclopedia of social work* (19th ed., pp. 1810–1817). Washington, DC: NASW Press.

Vera, E. M., & Speight, S. L. (2012). Multicultural competence: Social justice and counseling psychology: Expanding our roles. *The Counseling Psychologist, 31*(3), 253–259.

Dialogue in Peace and Conflict Work

Dialogue does not create peace or resolve conflict; people do that. However, dialogue can help participants develop the kinds of relationships that facilitate peacemaking and conflict resolution. This chapter offers such dialogues for peace and conflict work.

WHAT IS PEACE?

Peace is not the absence of conflict but is an ongoing nonviolent, relationship-oriented approach to conflict.

Conflict is unavoidable; there is always conflict between people, even between those who love and like each other. There is also always conflict between a human being and other living things and between a human being and her environment. Living things are linked together in complex ecosystems, but we also can compete for resources, status, and mates. Our natural environment nurtures our lives but also can threaten our well-being through extreme weather and geologic events.

Violence, however, is avoidable; people are able to learn new ways of resolving conflict that are not destructive to themselves or others. Peace between myself and the Other requires mutual understanding and acceptance, even love.

Peacemaking fosters inner peacemaking. As I strive to foster peace between and within others, I tend to also foster the qualities of inner peace inside myself. Inner peace is associated with the cultivation of such qualities as self-awareness, self-acceptance, self-forgiveness, equanimity, and joy (see Chapter 9 for descriptions of these qualities).

Dialogue Is Peace Practice

Dialogue is a peacemaking practice. In dialogue, people relate in a two-way conversation with each other. In contrast, violence is a one-way conversation, or monologue, that silences the Other.

Dialogue is both an internal and external practice. Dialogue involves interpersonal work that can promote mutual understanding and acceptance between people, as well as intrapersonal work that can foster self-understanding and self-acceptance.

Peace and Sociohistorical Trauma

Sociohistorical trauma can ultimately lead to either violence or dialogue. Violence is a poor weapon of revenge that is meant for the perpetrator but ultimately harms me the most. In contrast, peacemaking practice is arguably the best "revenge," because I find the greatest joy when I offer joy to others.

Peace and Conflict Studies

Peace and conflict studies (PCS) look at how individuals and communities become more violent or more peaceful (Dugan, 1989). PCS, which are related to diversity and social justice work, help students deal effectively with threats to peace, justice, and human dignity. In the first decades of PCS, programs emphasized conflict resolution approaches, cross-cultural issues in conflict, alternative security approaches, and issues of violence within and between states (Lopez, 1985). Although university-based PCS programs are still being introduced to new campus locations, the idea of peace is not new. All the world's major religious traditions have supported peace and peacemaking for millenniums (Gordon & Grob, 1988).

Just like dialogue can offer diversity students tools for the application of theory, a dialogue class is the laboratory class for PCS. Most peace education is "head first" rather than "feet first" and aims especially at changing the minds of participants. There is less emphasis directed toward changing behaviors (Firer, 2002) as well as hearts. Dialogue offers powerful opportunities for experiential learning in the prevention and management of violence, which is integral to PCS (Galtung & Jacobsen, 2000).

Dialogue work is increasingly included in PCS programs. Dialogue can help promote relationships, civic participation, and ultimately social change (Dessel & Rogge, 2008). Dialogue may have special relevance in PCS today, in a world where people struggle with issues of intergroup relations, increasing diversity, and social problems that are too complex for any one person to resolve (Schoem & Hurtado, 2001).

In the rest of this chapter, five interrelated dialogue approaches to peace and conflict work are forwarded, as summarized in Table 13.1.

Table 13.1   Dialogue Approaches in Peace and Conflict Work

Peace and Conflict Area	Brief Description of Dialogue Work
Approaches to peaceful conflict resolution	Resolving conflicts effectively
Mediation and reconciliation	Resolving disputes between two or more parties
Reconciliation	Reestablishing peaceful relations between former enemies
Major peace and conflict studies (PCS) curriculum areas	Creating opportunities for dialogue across differences that divide people
Dialogue models class for PCS program	Providing dialogue lab for students

APPROACHES TO PEACEFUL CONFLICT RESOLUTION

Psychodynamic Dialogue Approaches

Psychodynamic dialogue may help people work together to resolve conflict peacefully. Participants can be asked to tell stories of past experiences that were painful, while others are asked to listen without commenting. I have used this technique to start difficult dialogues between groups in conflict. For example, in working with a congregation that had experienced ongoing conflicts, we asked participants to each share a story about a difficult experience they had in their church. Often people have seldom if ever had the opportunity to talk about such issues while others just listen to understand. This conversation brought up some laughs and tears that seemed to help the group pull together again.

Participants also may find it useful to explore their own inner dynamics, identifying the voices of their child, parent, and observing self ego states in the larger conflict. For example, in a dialogue between proponents and opponents of legislation that would ban same-sex marriage, there were two people who really "got into it." Malcomb was a proponent of the legislation and represented himself as straight and as a member of the "ABC" Church. Toni was an opponent of the legislation and represented herself as a lesbian and an atheist. They began to attack each other in front of the group, so I had to intervene.

Both Tonie and Malcomb had learned in an earlier dialogue how to do transactional analysis work (see Chapter 6). I asked them to sit facing each other in the middle of the circle and speak to each other from each of the three voices. They did a wonderful job, and their responses are described in Table 13.2.

After the group listened silently to this fishbowl exercise with Malcomb and Toni, there was a follow-up conversation. Most people said that they could relate to the voices that Malcomb and Toni shared. Some began to share these personal voices.

Cognitive-Behavioral Dialogue Approaches

The facilitator can ask participants to share beliefs that they have held about the conflict and about their opponents, while others listen. For example, in one dialogue with members and nonmembers of a particular dominant culture, participants shared the stereotypes that they held about each other's groups. Some people in the minority culture group owned that they stereotyped the other group as being power-hungry, rigid, and unable to think for themselves. Some majority group members stereotyped the minority group as adolescent,

Table 13.2   Ego State Dynamics in a Conflict About Legislation That Bans Same-Sex Marriage

	"Malcomb" (proponent of legislation and identifies as straight and as a member of the "ABC" Church)	**"Toni" (opponent of legislation and identifies as a lesbian and as an atheist)**
Child	"Toni, I am scared and angry that you want to take away my religious freedom!"	"Malcomb, I am scared and angry that you want to limit my freedom to marry who I want!"
Parent	"Toni, you are misguided and a sinner and should get help to change your homosexuality."	"Malcomb, you are a bigot and homophobic and should realize your actions are not Christian."
Observing self	"Toni, I notice that I am scared that I will lose my freedoms and also have judgments about your sexuality."	"Malcomb, I notice that I am scared that you will take away my freedoms and I also have judgments about your values."

angry, and rebellious. Many of the members were aware of these stereotypes but had never heard them expressed in such a straightforward but also caring way. The group seemed to shift; it was as if the shared awareness and acceptance of these stereotypes made them less powerful.

PCS students can identify old behaviors that were not so helpful and new behaviors that are more effective in promoting peaceful conflict resolution. In the first 30 minutes of my dialogue models class, I often ask students to bring up situations in their own lives that we can talk about. Often these involve conflicts with their roommates, lovers, parents, or supervisors.

We discuss how anger and defensiveness often are not helpful responses to conflict and how patience and listening may help develop relationships across divides.

Experiential-Humanistic Dialogue Approaches

The facilitator can ask participants to talk about their feelings about the people involved in the conflict. In the dialogue on the antimarriage legislation mentioned above, I also asked people to use feeling words to describe their experiences at the beginning and ending of the meeting. At the beginning of the meeting, for example, people were asked how they felt going into the dialogue. Many said "nervous" or "scared." They were given a chance to explain briefly why they felt the way they do. Some people started their sentence with "I feel . . . " but then finished their sentence with a you-message. When one person said, "I feel that a lot of the people here are really messed up," I asked her to try to use a word like *sad, mad, glad, scared, nervous,* or *disgusted* instead.

At the end of this dialogue, people were asked to check out by using another feeling word to describe their current state or experience. The responses varied but included words such as *hopeful, still nervous, gratitude, confused,* and *angry.* With the time remaining, some people explained why they had the feelings they reported. These experiential exercises often help people reach inside and become more aware of their own internal process, as well as the internal process of others.

Often in dialogue, one of the hardest things for people to do is to look at the Other directly in his eyes and say exactly how they feel about him, with the intent to communicate rather than to harm. Almost as difficult is to be the Other and simply listen to such a direct expression of emotion, with the intent to understand rather than to develop an immediate response. Such exchanges of emotional honesty seem to often help people make leaps toward greater intimacy.

Transpersonal Dialogue Approaches

Participants can share how they each view the conflict from their own spiritual lenses.

Spiritual lenses are often helpful because they offer the greatest perspectives of all. When I look at any conflict from a spiritual perspective, I think about conflict from the context of infinite time and space, which usually makes conflicts seem less daunting and more manageable. I may also try to see things with a more tempered ego, which enables me to not take the conflict so personally. These are the kinds of perspectives I hope to draw out from people when I invite a transpersonal approach to dialogue. Instead of lecturing or sermonizing to people about religion or spirituality (my own "Big T" truths), I find it works best in a dialogue to invite people to rediscover their own spiritual wisdom ("little t" truths).

Bioecological Dialogue Approaches

When possible, it is often useful to use what James Hillman called the "greatest healer" to help people make positive movement in difficult dialogues. The great healer, when all other healers fail, is nature. Since it is usually not convenient to take the dialogue group on a hike in a national park, the facilitator can find other ways to work with animals, plants, and landscapes indoors.

I like to bring in cards that have drawings or photos of animals, plants, and landscapes. I often will lay them face up on a table in the center of the room and have people pick up one (or more if there is time) that they are drawn to today. Then we go around the circle and people can talk about why they think they were drawn to the card(s) they selected. I have found that almost always people love this kind of exercise, and group cohesion and relationship are usually fostered.

EXPERIENTIAL LEARNING 13.2

(1) Try one of each of the five approaches described above.

(2) Which was the most helpful to you? Why?

MEDIATION

Mediation is an approach to alternative dispute resolution (ADR), a nonviolent way of resolving disputes between two or more parties. *Conciliation* refers to all mediation and dispute resolution processes. The mediator seeks agreement but is not so concerned with the exploration of feelings and past trauma. The mediator seeks to be neutral, considers all views, facilitates communications, models respect, and allows people a chance to explain their story. Ultimately, the goal is to identify participant issues and interests, evaluate options, and agree on the best solutions. Sometimes mediation can be used with arbitration, during which the mediator may pass on decisions about the best outcomes (Boulle, 2005; Cremin, 2007; Sourdin, 2002).

Can dialogue help facilitate mediation? Although dialogue facilitation and mediation have some different goals and methods (as highlighted above), the dialogue facilitator can contribute to the ultimate success of mediation. Mediation works best when people are willing to stay in relationship, which means in part that you and I seek to understand each other and respect our differences. I am more willing to compromise with you when I feel in relationship with you.

I like to use many of the standard dialogue models in mediation work. If the parties both know each other, introductions may not be necessary. With limited time, I may ask the participants to begin by explaining the *context* of their position in the dispute. I have always liked the idea that people do the best they can, in the context as they understand it. In other words, the way I perceive the history, the possible consequences, and the current circumstances of the dispute will tend to influence how I feel, think, and act.

For example, in one dispute between two partners, I asked Julio to talk first about his own perceptions of the context of his marriage and impending divorce. Then Richard had an opportunity to talk about his perceptions. It turned out that Julio felt abandoned by Richard and Richard felt abandoned by Julio. After listening to both of them speak to the trauma they both experienced in the relationship over the past years, I also asked them to speak to the love that had initially brought them together and distinguished love (a choice) from like (which is not a matter of choice). They were able to acknowledge to each other that they did once both love and like each other and that perhaps there was still love (in the sense that they wished each other well).

This process of beginning with words about pain, followed by words of love, seemed to help Richard and Julio move back toward relationship, so that they could begin to negotiate a "good divorce."

Some colleagues of mine participated in a series of mediation events that were offered to both sides of a major water dispute. There were not only strong feelings in the room during these events but also a sense that big money and future lifestyles were at stake. The facilitator at such events cannot, of course, force people to become friends or even to be civil with each other. One approach I used at a similar event was to ask participants to each tell a story about water from their own personal past. People really "got into it" and shared all kinds of narratives. One woman talked about playing in the waves at the ocean when she was a child, for example. Another talked about a downpour that broke a long drought on her parents' ranch. One man asked if he could be allowed to tell two stories, because he could not decide which was more dear to him. This conversation did not change the power dynamics of political positions in the room, but many people reported that the water stories dialogue was the favorite part of their participation in the mediation work.

RECONCILIATION

Reconciliation aims to create conditions for a lasting end to conflict. Through reconciliation (or restorative justice work), people can deal together with their past suffering and build relationships based on trust and cooperation (see Hauss, 2003). Perhaps one of the best-known reconciliation efforts occurred when the South African Truth and Reconciliation Commission (TRC) was created by the Government of National Unity to help the country work through the sociohistorical trauma of apartheid and to move toward lasting friendship and peace between the races and cultures (see Truth and Reconciliation Commission, 2012).

Some of the reconciliation work I have done was in my own community, between people of different faiths. Although there has not been the extent of violence between groups that has been seen in other parts of the world, my local community does have a history of significant tension. When I work with groups of people who want to find ways to get along, I like to ask them for examples of what inspired their desire for the work. For example, I think of the lyrics of a song written by Jimmy Hendrix entitled "We Gotta Live Together" that I used to listen to. I also think of a young man, who happened to be in a gang, who said "it is harder to shoot someone after you play ball [basketball] with them." It has been my experience that when people interact and get to know each other through positive interactions, foundations for lasting peace become more possible. Such stories and inspirations often reveal common values and can help groups work through difficult conversations.

Reconciliation work requires ongoing dialogue. If the conflicts took decades or centuries to develop, they are unlikely to go away in a few days. Sociohistorical trauma can be transformed, but it usually takes commitment and work to develop healthier relationships. People who stay committed seem to often be motivated by the dialogue experiences, in which they have a safe space to speak frankly, feel understood, and often develop rich relationships with people very different from them. I have often heard participants and students comment on how much they value these kinds of relationships, which go across the contexts of sociohistorical trauma that have divided our families, communities, and nations.

Large group dialogue may be required in reconciliation work. I have found that it is possible to do effective dialogues with one or two hundred people, using small group techniques discussed in the text. One technique I like to use when the group is over 100 people is to create a "tag team" circle in the middle or front of the room. Participants can talk only if they go into the circle and take a seat in the tag team circle (which has about 8–12 chairs). The facilitator can set rules for participation; for example, people can stay in the circle only for 5 minutes at a time, or you are allowed to tag someone to take that person's chair if he or she has already spoken at least once. At the end of the dialogue, the facilitator can open up the entire room for a whole-group discussion. A checkout exercise might be to ask everyone to pick a partner and talk about where they are at for 5 minutes in groups of two (or "two-dads").

Reconciliation dialogue can also be focused on a particular topic for each session. Such a focus can help people start talking about difficult issues. For example, in a conversation about a war that occurred, we asked participants to talk about the spiritual aspects of the war experience. We asked two participants to begin by talking about Tick's (2005) view that when war is waged for power or domination, instead of for the protection of home and loved ones, warriors suffer spiritual wounds and loss of identity. People were able to get into a cognitive dialogue about this interesting idea.

EXPERIENTIAL LEARNING 13.3

(1) Have you ever participated in mediation? If so, did it help? If not, do you think dialogue could help such a process move in a positive direction? Explain.

(2) What kind of reconciliation does your family, community, or region especially need?

(3) How would you design a dialogue to help foster such a process?

MAJOR PCS CURRICULUM AREAS

Dialogue can be used to foster relationship building in any of the PCS curriculum areas listed in Table 13.3. I have included further descriptions of some of these areas in this section.

Table 13.3 Selected PCS Curriculum Areas

Curriculum Area	Dialogue Examples
Daily interactions	Dialogue about family, work, and community conflicts
Social activism	Dialogue between local groups and across local divides
Globalization and global justice	Dialogue between members of different global entities, including wealthy, emerging, and poor nations
Diversity and social justice	Dialogue between people of different cultures, different socioeconomic status, or races
Nationalism	Dialogues across members of different nations or between people with different views of nationalism
Religion	Dialogues across religious divides
Politics	Dialogues across political divides
Environmentalism	Dialogues between environmental divides

People have conflicts in everyday situations. My PCS students understandably relate especially well to conversations about daily interactions. Dialogues for work with couples, families, and groups are discussed further in Chapters 14 and 15. Topics such as social activism, social justice, and diversity are related to those discussed in Chapter 12.

I also like to offer opportunities for students to practice conversations that have local, national, *and* global dimensions, such as religion, politics, nationalism, and environmentalism. One way to structure such a dialogue is to have the group count off by twos and then have the 1s go on one side of the room and everyone else on the other side. Each side is asked to take on the voice of one side of the issue to be discussed. After maybe 45 minutes, the facilitator can ask people to switch sides, so everyone has a chance to speak from both sides of the issue. At the end of the second dialogue, the facilitator can ask the participants to come back together and process the experience in small and then large group formats.

A DIALOGUE MODELS CLASS IN SUPPORT OF PCS OR DIVERSITY CURRICULUM

Purpose and Context

The dialogue models class can support the curriculum of a number of programs, including peace and conflict studies, diversity, and social work. Students learn the knowledge, values, and particularly the skills involved in the *practice* of dialogue. Dialogue is presented as a relationship-building communication strategy that can be used in many areas of professional helping, including community work, conflict resolution, psychotherapy, and peacemaking. Students have reported that a dialogue models class provides them with practical tools for work and life. Table 13.4 illustrates the major components of such a class.

Table 13.4 Dialogue Models Class

Weeks	Topics	Class Activities
Class 1	Introduction	Students meet each other in safe activities
Classes 2–3	Trainings in values, skills, knowledge	Students trained in dialogue values, skills, knowledge Students practice dialogue in role-plays and "real plays"
Classes 4–5	In-class dialogues	Students identify divides in class Students dialogue across divides
Classes 6–14	Visitor dialogues	Students dialogue with visiting group Students and visitors debrief dialogue
Class 15	Processing and termination	Students process the semester Students identify strengths and limitations in dialogue

Class 1 is structured to be a safe introduction to the course; students engage in warm-up activities. In the next two classes, students receive instruction from the facilitator on basic values, skills, and knowledge, and then they practice the skills in role-plays involving real situations from their own relationships and families. For example, if a student wants to do a dialogue on her family, I have her pick the students in the class who can best play her mother, father, and siblings. When there is an opportunity to do a dialogue between group members, we do a "real play" where people interact genuinely with each other. In Classes 4 and 5, the class identifies divides that exist in their own group. These may include divides of age, faith, gender, politics, or race. Then we practice dialogues across these divides, applying the skills we are learning.

This practice-oriented class involves students in the process of learning crucial intellectual, emotional, and social frameworks and strategies that are required of participants and facilitators of dialogue (and I believe also as human beings). Students are encouraged to assess and develop their own cognitive understanding, social maturity, and emotional sensitivity. Because dialogue is a set of processes that can be practiced at the dyadic, family, group, institutional, and global levels, students are also asked to participate in experiential learning exercises on all those levels, both in class and in community, that will enable them to communicate effectively in situations of value and other forms of diversity.

In Classes 6 through 14, we do dialogue with groups that we invite into the classroom. I try to invite a variety of groups that have characteristics different from most members of the class. I usually first spend time with the guests, to explain to them what we want to do. We almost always ask the guests to start. I will ask them a question and then give them each at least one chance to speak, before the students are allowed to interact with questions or comments. For example, we invited a group from the campus student Muslim Association. They sat together on one side of the circle, and I asked them to take turns responding to the question, "What is it like being a Muslim student on this campus and in this community?" When the dialogue is done, I give the class a break and meet with the visitors, to give them an opportunity to debrief and to follow up if any of them need some assistance or support. After the break, I debrief with the class. In the last class (Class 15), we debrief as a class about the entire semester. I also gave students a chance to give feedback about the strengths they have seen in each other.

Dialogue models is taught from a multidisciplinary perspective, using the lenses offered by such disciplines as social work, psychology, education, communication, political science, philosophy, and sociology. Commonalities and differences between various models of dialogue will be explored. Students study the five dialogue models described in this text and practice methods drawn from those models, including such key elements as

1. mutual understanding, respect, confirmation;

2. fluid and creative movement between small and large group interaction;

3. emphasis on process;

4. deep listening; and

5. sharing personal experiences and stories.

EXPERIENTIAL LEARNING 13.4

(1) If the class you are currently taking is a dialogue class, what kinds of benefits are you experiencing from it?

(2) Can you think of any reasons why all students should be required to take a dialogue class? Explain.

REFERENCES

Boulle, L. (2005). *Mediation: Principles, processes, practice.* Chatswood, Australia: LexisNexis Butterworths.

Cremin, H. (2007). *Peer mediation: Citizenship and social inclusion in action.* Maidenhead, UK: Open University Press.

Dessel, A., & Rogge, M. E. (2008). Evaluation of intergroup dialogue: A review of the empirical literature. *Conflict Resolution Quarterly, 26*(2), 199–205.

Dugan, M. (1989). Peace studies at the graduate level. *Annals of the American Academy of Political Science: Peace Studies: Past and Future, 504,* 72–79.

Firer, R. (2002). The Gordian knot between peace education and war education. In G. Salomon & B. Nevo (Eds.), *Peace education: The concept, principles, and practices around the world* (pp. 55–61). Mahwah, NJ: Lawrence Erlbaum.

Galtung, J., & Jacobsen, C. G. (2000). *Searching for peace: The road to TRANSCEND.* London: Pluto Press.

Gordon, H., & Grob, L. (1988). *Education for peace: Testimonies from world religions.* Maryknoll, NY: Orbis.

Hauss, C. (2003). *"Reconciliation": Beyond Intractability.* Conflict Research Consortium, University of Colorado, Boulder. http://www.beyondintractability.org/bi-essay/reconciliation/

Lopez, G. A. (1985). A university peace studies curriculum for the 1990s. *Journal of Peace Research, 22*(2), 117–128.

Schoem, D., & Hurtado, S. (Eds.). (2001). *Intergroup dialogue: Deliberative democracy in school, college, and workplace.* Ann Arbor: University of Michigan Press.

Sourdin, T. (2002). *Alternative dispute resolution.* Pyrmont, NSW, Australia: Lawbook Co.

Tick, E. (2005). *War and the soul: Healing our nation's veterans from post-traumatic stress disorder.* Wheaton, IL: Quest.

Truth and Reconciliation Commission. (2012). http://www.justice.gov.za/trc/

CHAPTER 14

Dialogue Across the Life Span

This chapter offers dialogue applications across the life span. Dialogue approaches with children, adolescents, adults, and the aging are described.

CHILDREN

Basics

Many children are capable of engaging in age-appropriate dialogue during their later grade school years (Grades 4–6), although they may have such limitations as less-developed attention span, self-awareness, emotional control, capacity for empathy, language skills, and social skills.

What does the facilitator especially want to pay attention to with people this age? First, dialogue should be focused on age-appropriate topics. What kinds of dialogue might be age appropriate for children between 8 and 13 years? The best answer is probably another question: What are these children usually most interested in? The wise facilitator asks each group of children about their own unique interests. At 10 years old, for example, I might want to talk about such things as vocational dreams, bullies, playground behavior, friends, video games, television programs, and food. Sometimes children will also identify much more sophisticated topics for dialogue.

Second, the facilitator wants to focus on helping the young people in the group start to develop age-appropriate and basic dialogue values, skills, and knowledge that these children can master. Basic dialogue values include the importance of our interconnectedness with our communities, the response-ability we all have for the well-being of our communities, the importance of listening, and the responsibility we all have to speak and act with integrity. Basic skills include the ability to identify and assertively express my thoughts and feelings, the ability to listen to others for understanding, the ability to be mindful (awareness without judgment), and the ability to listen to and accept my self. Basic knowledge includes the purpose of dialogue, the meaning of relationship, respect, community, and responsibility. These areas are summarized in language that may be understandable to most upper grade school-aged children in Table 14.1.

Table 14.1 Dialogue Values, Skills, and Knowledge for Upper Grade School-Aged Children

Values	1. We all are connected to each other in a community. 2. Each of us has something to offer to help our community. 3. It is more important to understand someone than to be understood. 4. I want to speak and act in ways that make me feel better about myself.
Skills	1. I can know what I am feeling and thinking and put it into words. 2. I can listen to someone else and understand what he or she is feeling and thinking. 3. I can watch myself and others and not make anyone wrong.
Knowledge	1. Dialogue is for making relationships and communities. 2. Relationships are when we can talk and listen and care about each other. 3. Respect is when I treat you like I want you to treat me. 4. Community is made of people in respectful relationships. 5. Responsibility is doing what I am able to do to help others and community.

I have found that this content is best taught in an experiential manner. I first ask the children to sit in a circle, ideally in a small group of maybe 8 to 20. I might ask for a story about something that happened to one of the children in the past week. Perhaps Cecelia says that her whole family has been sick with the flu. Then I might ask how Cecelia's family affects everyone else in the room (Value 1 from Table 14.1). When Billy says, "We could all get the flu?" I might ask him what he thinks and feels about that (Skill 2). He says that he feels a little scared. When I ask the group what they think Cecelia might be feeling, Fred says that maybe she is feeling sad (Skill 2). Then I ask, what could any of us do to help Cecelia's family (Knowledge 5)? Kenny says that maybe we could bring them some soup. This kind of conversation can help children learn experientially.

Third, children generally need significant structure in their dialogues. Structure usually helps children feel safe enough to work together in a group. Structure may include clear ground rules, supervision of turn taking, and frequent verbal reinforcement of positive behavior. *Ground rules* for children this age are described in Table 14.2.

Table 14.2 Ground Rules for Children

Do	**Do Not**
(1) Take turns speaking (2) Listen to other people when they talk (3) Be respectful when you speak	(4) Interrupt others (5) Speak longer than one minute at a time (6) Act like a bully (7) Talk about what happened outside group (may be exceptions to this)

Supervision of turn taking helps participants learn how to share the attention of the group. I sometimes use a talking stick with children in dialogue. Each child gets to take a turn as the stick is passed around the circle. A child who does not want to speak can pass the stick to the next person. Another way to supervise turn taking is to simply have participants go around the circle, one by one, and speak or pass.

Reinforcement of positive behavior is the most efficient way of leading children toward learning dialogue values, skills, and knowledge. This means that the facilitator generally pays more attention to children who are participating in an appropriate manner and less attention to children who are not. If the inappropriate behavior is abusive or threatening, then the facilitator has no choice but to directly stop and perhaps also redirect the behavior.

Examples of Dialogue With Children

One dialogue I like to do with grade school-age children is to have them talk about bullying. We know that participation of students in public schools in dialogue can result in positive shifts in attitudes, feelings, and behaviors (Dessel, 2010). Since bullying is not only common but can lead to all kinds of avoidable suffering for children, I like to deal with the subject through dialogue.

I might, for example, have the children first do a simple warm-up. Perhaps they share their names and what they had for breakfast (perhaps followed by what they wish they had for breakfast). I might ask for a volunteer to explain what bullying is. Then I give him the talking stick and ask him to tell a story about either experiencing or watching a bullying situation, while avoiding telling the names of any of the participants. After each child tells his story, I ask if anyone wants to make a comment or ask a question. Then I might ask all the children to take turns with the talking stick, making comments about how they feel and what they think about bullying.

Another dialogue that seems to often work well is the "emotion dialogue." We first write down the basic emotions onto a white board (sad, mad, sad, scared, excited, disgusted) and together define them briefly. Then we go around the room and ask each child to talk about the strongest emotion he felt this week. Robby, for example, might say that he was very sad when his pet fish died last weekend. This dialogue gives children practice in identifying, accepting, and assertively expressing emotions.

Another version of the emotion dialogue focuses more on listening to others than on listening to the self. The children take turns sharing a story about something that happened to them this week. Then the other children take turns guessing what emotions the story-teller might have felt during the situation. The storyteller gets to respond to these guesses.

I also like to ask children to talk about their Big Dreams, which are their long-term fantasies about love (relationships, family, community) and work (vocation). In this "Big Dream" dialogue, I might ask each participant to take a single sheet of paper and a handful of crayons. Then I ask them to draw a picture of their Big Dream of work on one side of the paper and their Big Dream of love on the other side. Then I have them break into groups of two (dyads) and take turns first guessing what their partner's drawings are about. After each person guesses, the person who drew the pictures gets to explain what they mean to the partner. After this dyad exercise, we come back to the large group and go around the circle, asking children to make comments about how they feel and think about the exercise they just did.

EXPERIENTIAL LEARNING 14.1

(1) What dialogues for children would have been most useful to you as a child? Why?

(2) What dialogues for children would make most sense to implement in your community? Explain.

ADOLESCENTS

Basics

I have discovered that adolescents generally seem to like dialogue. They still may need more structure than adults but usually not as much as grade school-aged children. The facilitator may need to group teens together who have similar maturity levels, since they often seem to feel safer around others with matching developmental characteristics. Although there are always individual differences, age is one predictor of maturity; many younger adolescents (13–15½ years) are far less emotionally, socially, and cognitively developed than most older adolescents (15½–19 years).

Usually adolescent groups work best when there are at least a few members who are committed to the process and follow the ground rules. The dialogue struggles when the informal group leaders are not as committed to the process and rules. The wise facilitator tries to build on the strengths of the committed core group, when it exists. When no such group exists, I try to build a group "from the ground up" by noticing the potential for such positive leadership in new members and supporting positive behaviors that emerge from them.

Dialogue is difficult enough for voluntary participants, but when involuntary participants meet in a group, they often feel especially unsafe and unprepared to engage in listening and self-reflection. Generally, the facilitator should try to help members find motivation for the dialogue at the beginning of the process. However, if the core leaders act in inappropriate or even antisocial ways, I try to refer back to the ground rules and reach for any motivation the participants may have for attending the group.

For example, as a social worker, I once facilitated a group of teen girls and boys who were assigned to the group by the school vice principal because they had all been involved in aggressive behavior. The agreement was that they had to attend five meetings to get back into school. A few of the most verbal participants quickly started to take over the group with comments like, "This is stupid" and "Can we go now?" I realized after a few minutes of unsuccessful facilitation that I could not get the group to engage in dialogue by simply ignoring or redirecting behaviors. So I told them that if they wanted to be in the group, I expected them to follow a set of ground rules and proceeded to offer them the kinds of rules outlined in Table 14.2. I was surprised that all of them became more cooperative when I reminded them that they had a choice. The alternative (expulsion from school) was apparently worse than five group sessions.

When one member acts out "inappropriately" during a dialogue, I usually try a four-part series of interventions. First, I try to *ignore* the youth who is acting out and give my attention to the participants who are engaged appropriately. Second, if ignoring does not work,

I try to *distract* the acting-out teen to more appropriate activity. Third, I might try to *call attention* to the behavior (in a respectful way) and ask the group to talk about what it is like for them to experience the acting-out behavior. Finally, I might have to *set a limit* on the behavior and then *follow through* on a consequence if the limit is not respected.

Examples of Adolescent Dialogue

Adolescents are usually able to do and enjoy more complex dialogues than younger children. This ability and interest allow the facilitator to experiment with a wide range of topics.

I like to start new groups out with dialogues across the gender divide, between boys and girls. I usually have one group start in the middle of the group in a fishbowl. For example, I might have some or all of the boys (perhaps six to eight teens) go in the middle circle first with me. I then might ask the boys to take turns responding to the question, "What is difficult about being a boy?" Another question might be, "What do girls not seem to understand about boys?" After about 15 to 20 minutes, I will have the boys return to the large circle and have six to eight girls sit with me in the small circle. They then respond to the questions, "What is difficult about being a girl?" and "What do boys not seem to understand about girls?" After another 15 to 20 minutes, the girls return to their seats and the entire group can process the conversation. Usually, there is much interest, laughter, and conversation generated by the fishbowl activities. When invited into a new classroom, this activity is a great introduction to dialogue for the teens.

Another dialogue that adolescents often enjoy is about the teen-adult divide. I might ask the group to talk about what they feel and think about the adults in their lives. Most adolescents have many things to say about this topic. We might go around the room with the talking stick. Then I might have half of the teens pretend to be adults and ask them to respond the way their parents or teachers might respond to what was said. The other half of the room "pretend to be themselves" and respond to the adults. This kind of dialogue, which becomes a kind of theater, gives the teens an opportunity to practice speaking and listening and imagining the other.

Many teens and other younger people are deeply concerned about environmental well-being. They have more years ahead of them than do adults and understandably want to be able to breathe clean air and drink clean water. I like to invite them to talk about their thoughts and emotions about their own local ecosystems. One way to get at this subject is to ask participants to respond to the questions listed in Table 14.3.

Table 14.3   Questions for Dialogue on the Environment

(1) Can you tell a story about a time in your life when being out in nature was especially fun, healing, or helpful to you? (This could be when you were sad and took a walk out in the sun.)

(2) What natural landscape is your most sacred? (This could be a mountain you visited, a beach you swam at, a forest you walked in.)

(3) What kind of environmental problem bothers you the most? (This could be pollution in a river, smog in the air, or a forest that has been cut down.)

EXPERIENTIAL LEARNING 14.2

(1) What dialogues for teens would have been most useful to you when you were a teen? Why?

(2) What dialogues for teens would make most sense to implement in your community? Explain.

YOUNG ADULTS

Basics

The majority of the students who take my peace and conflict studies dialogue class are in their 20s. They tend to be enthusiastic about entering into dialogue but are also often unfamiliar with what dialogue really is. Dialogue can help young adults to learn how to deal with common life challenges in effective ways (McCoy & Scully, 2002).

In the dialogue models class, we spend a considerable amount of time practicing both interpsychic and intrapsychic dialogue, as well as understanding how they are interrelated and complementary. Table 14.4 illustrates some examples of how what people say in the interpsychic dialogue (column 1) actually may reflect an intrapsychic dialogue (column 2) that is more complex or even different in content. Young adults are often open and mature enough to start to look at the differences and relationships between our actions and internal experiences. The facilitator can engage students in practice dialogues in which the dialogue is frequently "slowed down" so that the intrapsychic dialogues can be examined. Thus, when a participant makes a comment, the facilitator might sometimes ask the participant to try to share his intrapsychic dialogue with the group. Such sharing can enrich the conversation and deepen the relationships in the group.

Table 14.4 Relationship Between Interpsychic and Intrapsychic Dialogue

Interpsychic Dialogue	Intrapsychic Dialogue
I'm mad at you. . . .	I feel a complex mixture of emotions inside of me, including hurt, fear, and anger.
I want to be friends with you. . . .	Although I do want to get closer to you, I am ambivalent about you. I am not sure I trust that you like me, and you frighten me a little.
I could not disagree with you more.	I feel threatened by your certainty about your position and worry that maybe you are right.
What you said is very interesting. . . .	I am having all kinds of judgments about you that I am uncomfortable having and do not want to admit to.
This reminds me of a quote from Gandhi. . . .	I am feeling overwhelmed by this conversation and do not know why, and I'd feel much safer if I went up into my head.

Dating Issues

Most participants in their 20s are interested in dating and welcome conversations about their relationships with their lovers. The facilitator should make sure these conversations include relationships that reflect both GLBTQ (gay, lesbian, bisexual, transgender, and questioning) and "straight" interests. The facilitator can ask for a volunteer to first discuss an issue he is facing in a relationship. Then the group can psychodrama the relationship and follow up with a processing discussion.

For example, one of my students (Amanda) was talking about her experience of having her new lover (Jenay) tell her that she loved her. Amanda told us that her interpsychic response was "I love you too" but that her intrapsychic conversation was more ambivalent and complex. I asked Amanda to pick someone in the circle who could play Jenay, and she picked Samuel. We put two empty chairs in the middle of the group and played out the scene again. Then Amanda picked out three people to play out the child, parent, and observing self ego states (Chapter 6) in both Jenay and Amanda's intrapsychic dialogues. They stood behind either Amanda or Samuel and offered voices to add to the dialogue. The conversation that followed included the dialogue voices in Table 14.5. The interpsychic voices (in the second column) were what was actually said in the initial conversation. The inner child, inner parent, and observing self (columns 3, 4, and 5) were intrapsychic voices that the six student helpers offered.

Table 14.5 Voices in Dating Dialogue

Person	Interpsychic	Intrapsychic: Inner Child	Intrapsychic: Inner Parent	Intrapsychic: Observing Self
Jenay (played by Samuel)	I love you	I like you so much that I am afraid that I will lose you	I should tell you that I love you	I like you a lot, and this makes me scared and excited
Amanda (played by herself)	I love you too	I do like you but am not sure I love you yet, yet fear you will leave me if I don't say that I love you	I should tell you back that I love you	I like you too, thanks for telling me this; I am scared and excited too

After the psychodrama was done, I asked Amanda to talk about her process. She felt that the dialogue had helped her become more aware of what she was feeling and thinking, and she thanked the class. Then I opened the dialogue up to the six helpers and asked them if they wanted to add anything. Several of them felt that the dialogue was easy to relate to and that they had had similar experiences. I liked how the "straight" people in the group were able to relate as well as the people who identified as GLBTQ.

MIDDLE AGE

Basics

Most adults between ages 35 and 65 have the capacity to engage in dialogue. By middle age, many adults have also become more aware of the existence and impact of any socio-historical trauma in their past. In addition, middle-aged adults often have significant responsibility to children, parents, partners, work settings, and larger communities, and such response-abilities may be on their minds and in their hearts.

With the developmental maturity that tends to arrive by middle age, this population often includes leaders who can have a significant impact on the people they serve and care for. In working with this age group, therefore, the facilitator can challenge dialogue participants to take active leadership roles in modeling dialogue in their families, work settings, and communities.

Bridging Transgenerational Divides

Since so much of conflict in midlife is with people who are much younger or older, I like to focus on transgenerational divides with this age group. Two forms of intergenerational dialogue are midlife parent–younger child dialogue and midlife child–aging parent dialogue. Some approaches are described below for the first meetings of these dialogues. As these groups meet over time, they tend to become more self-directing, and the facilitator's role gradually changes from setting group structure to facilitating difficult conversational moments. Ongoing dialogue groups such as these can help people learn to resolve conflicts using democratic and nonviolent approaches (Carcasson, 2010).

Midlife Parent–Younger Child Dialogue

This kind of dialogue gives participants an opportunity to interact with many other parents and children who are also experiencing a transgenerational divide. Sometimes it is easier to listen or speak to someone else's child or parent than to one's own family members.

As is usually true, the setup of this group will affect the results. When planning this group, I try to get an equal number of midlife parents and their children to commit to attend, so that the conversations are balanced. Many of the participants might bring their own biological parent or child with them, but that is not required. I also might set an age range for the children, for example, perhaps only latency children, or teens, or children in their early 20s can attend.

When the group meets, I might first have the group go around the circle and do a simple introduction and warm-up exercise. Then I will have them go around again and take turns identifying the issues that seem to most divide the children and the parents.

The children might be invited to go into a central fishbowl circle first. As usual in the fishbowl, only those in the inner circle (children) can speak, while the outer circle (parents) needs to just listen quietly. I will sit with them and will start with the question, "What are the things about your lives that are most difficult for your parents to understand?" A good follow-up question might be, "What are the most annoying things about your parents?" After the children respond to these questions, we might return to the big circle and dialogue as a large group. Then it is the parents' turn to enter the fishbowl. I might ask them to respond to the same two questions, "What are the things about your lives that are most difficult for your children to understand?" and "What are the most annoying things about your children?"

Midlife Child–Aging Parent Dialogue

There are many ways to do these dialogues. One way to facilitate the midlife child–aging parent dialogue is to begin by assigning each midlife child to sit with one aging parent. Biologically related children and parents are asked to not sit together. By arranging for people to sit with someone only *similar* to their biological relative, we create a dynamic that may allow for greater intimacy and deeper dialogue. Then I ask each parent-child dyad to respond to the following directions:

(1) Each aging parent can begin by telling a story about when he was misunderstood or mistreated by his midlife child.

(2) Each midlife child can then tell a story about when she was misunderstood or mistreated by her aging parent.

(3) Then the two people can dialogue about these two stories, considering how all the players might have felt in the stories and how each might have handled the situation differently.

Then I ask participants to process this dyad exercise as a whole group again.

Partners Dialogue

As discussed above, life partnerships are very important to many people in midlife, and midlifers often have conflicts with their lovers or life partners. Many people have sociohistorical trauma associated with intimate relationships that can be addressed in dialogue. A dialogue group can be set up to facilitate conversations about typical conflicts within partner relationships. Groups can include all heterosexual partners, all GLBTQ partners, or mixed groups. The same techniques used in the transgenerational dialogues described above can also be used in these partner dialogues.

For example, people can be assigned to dyads with another person with whom they do not have a relationship. Then these dyads can be given conversational assignments that stimulate dialogue, such as to discuss what they like and do not like about their partners.

Or, fishbowl exercises can be designed. In a mixed group of participants, couples can be asked to split up, so that one person sits on Side A of the circle and the other on Side B. Then Side A can do a fishbowl exercise, in which each person has the opportunity to tell a story about a conflict or issue in his or her relationship. In an all-heterosexual group, males and females can take turns in the fishbowl.

(1) Choose a dialogue for adults from the above sections and implement it in your own class or group.

(2) What was your experience of doing this dialogue?

AGING

Basics

Aging people can be the elders of our families and communities who offer love and wisdom to younger people. Unfortunately, in the current culture in the United States, the aging population is often isolated from other populations, which limits the possibilities of their sage-ing (Schachter-Shalomi, 1997). Dialogue can give aging people an opportunity to be of assistance to other people.

I have found that many people who are at first reluctant to sit down with the elderly ultimately find that their lives are enriched by building relationships with them. The first professional social work position I had was as an Adult Protective Services worker. I would make weekly visits to aging people who mostly lived in cheap apartments downtown. One of my discoveries in doing that work was that I got more out of my relationships with those clients than they did.

Aging people can also be isolated from each other. Dialogue can give them opportunities to share common experiences and offer mutual understanding and support. When I was a young social worker, for example, I served as a grief counselor for a hospice organization. In the first grief group that I ran, I asked the participants, who were all older than 60 years, to share stories about their experience of the loss of their spouses. I still remember an older man talking about how he felt the presence of his deceased wife in his house from time to time. Although I had heard that people sometimes have these kinds of experiences, I was surprised to actually hear such a story in a grief group. While I sat, not knowing what to say, another participant said, "Well I have had that happen to me, too." In fact, in that group, all of the participants eventually told a story of how they had at least once felt the presence of their deceased spouse. I had learned that group members will usually try to take care of each other and that usually one person's experience is shared by others.

Transgenerational Dialogue

One way to begin a transgenerational dialogue is to simply invite aging people to a location that would be relatively comfortable and even already familiar to the aging participants. I especially want to protect the aging people and focus on building a sense of safety for them, since many of them are traumatized by the aging experience itself and by the ageism they have experienced in this society that still worships youth. The aging participants can meet separately for several times until they begin to co-create a common purpose. Then other groups of younger members can be invited to join the aging group for dialogues.

Dialogue Training Groups

Elder dialogues can be designed to provide opportunities for relationship building and teaching between elders and other community members. My favorite example of such dialogue is the work of the International Council of Thirteen Indigenous Grandmothers (2010), a group of elderly women who travel around the world offering wisdom and inspiration about such topics as deep ecology and peacemaking. There is no reason why local communities can not also co-create grandmother and grandfather councils who go visit local schools, churches, and businesses to hold dialogues on important local topics. The facilitator can help co-create and manage these dialogues.

I helped co-create a similar dialogue training group of refugees, many of whom were elders, in my local community. The refugee people were from a number of different countries. A process involving dialogue on the past, present, and future led to a service mission for the group. They first wanted to share stories about sociohistorical trauma in their *past,* stories of war trauma and stories of refugee camps. Then the dialogue moved to conversation about their *present* life in the United States and the economic and social difficulties they encountered. Finally, they shared about their hopes and fears about their *future.* After these conversations, the group realized that they wanted to be of *service* to other refugees. They began a service component, where as a group, they traveled to schools and campuses to speak about the refugee experience.

Dialogues of Life and Death

Many aging people may become more aware of their own death and desire to have a better relationship with their death. Rather than being a "downer" for people, dialogues about life and death seem more often to be a freeing and uplifting experience for participants. I have tried a number of exercises with aging populations that have had such positive outcomes:

(1) Participants each share an important experience they had regarding death in their own life.

(2) Participants share what they believe the purpose of their own life is.

(3) Participants share what they think happens after death.

(4) Participants share what the biggest surprise about life has been.

(5) Participants share what their biggest fears about life and death are.

(6) Participants share what their biggest hopes and dreams about life and death are.

(7) Participants participate in a mock funeral (see Chapter 9).

EXPERIENTIAL LEARNING 14.4

(1) What dialogues for aging people would be most useful for the aging people in your own family or community? Why?

(2) What are your thoughts and feelings about doing a mock funeral?

REFERENCES

Carcasson, M. (2010). Facilitating democracy: Centers and institutes of public deliberation and collaborative problem solving. *New Directions for Higher Education, 152,* 51–57.

Dessel, A. B. (2010). Effects of intergroup dialogue: Public school teachers and sexual orientation prejudice. *Small Group Research, 41*(5), 556–592.

International Council of Thirteen Indigenous Grandmothers. (2010). http://www.grandmotherscouncil.org/

McCoy, M. L., & Scully, P. L. (2002). Deliberative dialogue to expand civic engagement: What kind of talk does democracy need? *National Civic Review, 91*(2), 117.

Schachter-Shalomi, Z. (1997). *From age-ing to sage-ing: A profound new vision of growing older.* New York: Grand Central Publishing.

CHAPTER 15

Community Therapy

Transforming Mental Health Challenges Through Dialogue

I have often thought when I have sat with clients in the role of a psychotherapist that, if I could only give them one thing, I would give each of them a *community*. Most of the people I know are more alone than they want to be. Most of us live in community poverty.

In this final chapter, the concept of community therapy is introduced, which is an approach that uses dialogue to prevent and respond to mental health issues in the family, local community, ecosystem, and global community. As shown in Chapter 1, although the etiology of what we today call mental illness is complex, we do know that trauma can be associated with symptoms of many "disorders." Through the use of dialogue models, community therapy provides both a prevention approach and a response to our mental health challenges.

Why include a chapter on mental health in a book on trauma and dialogue? First, I believe that dialogue can help bridge the current divide that exists between what is called direct (or micro/mezzo) practice and indirect (or macro) practice. In social work education, for example, most practice classes focus on one or the other form; few integrate all the levels of practice in meaningful and effective ways. Dialogue, as we have seen, can incorporate the individual, group, and community levels in the same meeting, at the same time. Such inclusion makes sense, since most mental health challenges involve individual, group, and community factors. For example, the etiology of depression observed in an individual may include such factors as her own childhood trauma, the limitations of her parents, and cultural factors in her community. The best response to such complex etiology is an equally inclusive program that addresses individual, group, and community factors.

Second, as discussed throughout this text, the symptoms of what we now call mental illness are often linked to traumatic events, and transformation involves in part the fostering of individual mental health. Third, mental health and mental illness are concepts that can deeply divide families and communities. When we have negative experiences or beliefs about the Other, we often say that a person or a group of people are "crazy." Many of us fear "the mentally ill," and we may well believe that they are far more dangerous than they actually are. Fourth, it is my hope that schools and colleges will eventually include dialogue as a legitimate approach to treating people who are suffering mental illness symptoms, as a result of their sociohistorical trauma.

WHAT IS MENTAL HEALTH AND ILLNESS?

This question, "What is mental health?" is one that would could fill a multiple-book-length exploration, but some principles can be summarized in this brief introduction. Essentially, a relatively broad and inclusive view of mental health is forwarded below.

1. Mental health and illness are *socially constructed* concepts and thus vary across such *contexts* as culture and time. Our definitions, symptoms, and medicines for life's challenges reflect the small part of the world we currently live in. Currently, our understanding of mental disorders represents the consensus of a select group of professionals.

2. Mental health and illness must always be seen *in context,* including the historical context and the body, family, institution, community, and ecosystem contexts that the individual currently interacts with. To the extent that certain characteristics are inherited, these traits may have evolved to serve some function in the distant past. To the extent that certain characteristics are learned, the individual may be reacting to his interactions with other people, including sociohistorical trauma. Mental illness characteristics may be tolerated or even highly valued in some families or cultures and devalued in others.

3. One important context, addressed by community therapy, is the extent to which the attitudes and behaviors of the community that the person lives in affect our view of whether she is mentally healthy or mentally ill. In other words, the community context is an important factor in how we view mental health.

4. The word *health* originally referred to the concept of *wholeness*. Although the term *mental* reveals our current emphasis on mental functioning, mental health involves much more than just the mind. As ecobiopsychosocialspiritual beings, our individual well-being is always interconnected with the body, spirit, and environment. Healthy people are thus more whole or more connected with their body-mind-spirit-environment.

5. Mental health and illness involve much more than symptoms. Today, mental health professionals are taught to choose a disorder for a client that most closely matches the client's symptoms. However, just like a runny nose could have many different root "causes" (such as a bacterial infection, an allergy, or the flu), in the same way anhedonia (the inability to experience pleasure) could have many possible root causes as well. A person is viewed as being "more than his symptoms." Thus, in mental health practice, the professional assesses and builds upon the person's strengths, as much as she works with the person's symptoms.

6. Thus, instead of being a "shrink" who reduces people to symptoms that reflect mental disorders, the community therapist might be an "expand" who sees people as whole humans first, with strengths and limitations, and connections with their internal and external contexts.

7. Since the number of disorders as well as the number of people with disorders has rapidly increased in the past decades, some have argued that the line between distress and disorder has become increasingly vague. For example, in a society where now up to 90% of the adult population has posttraumatic stress disorder (PTSD) symptoms, have we lost a sense of where common distress ends and "disorder" begins? (McNally, 2011). Thus, in mental health practice, the professional strives to normalize symptoms when appropriate and sees most disorders as continuums (locating many points between moderate distress through stronger challenge) rather than as categories (you either have the disorder or you do not).

8. Trauma can often be linked to what we call mental illness. People with childhood trauma, for example, seem to be more likely to develop the symptoms of mental illness that professionals currently treat (Everett & Gallop, 2000). We now know that PTSD can be associated with many kinds of traumatic events (Herbert, 2012), especially when a combination of genetic predisposition and environmental factors makes the person more vulnerable. Many trauma events have been linked to psychosocial difficulties that people have (Bussey & Wise, 2007), and such sociohistorical trauma may eventually be shown to be associated with many of the biggest mental health challenges.

9. Mental health challenges are always community health problems, and community health problems are always mental health problems. For example, widespread domestic violence occurs most in a culture that allows such behavior (Violence Prevention Initiative, 2006).

10. Mental health challenges are also always individual challenges. Views of past sociohistorical trauma as well as beliefs about the future can both change (Herbert, 2012).

In this chapter, when I use the phrase *mental health,* I am thus referring to "body-mind-spirit-environment health," and when I use the term *mental illness* I am referring to "body-mind-spirit-environment illness."

COMMUNITY THERAPY IS A TRANSFORMATIVE RESPONSE TO SOCIOHISTORICAL TRAUMA

As we have seen in the text, just about all of us have at least some kind of sociohistorical trauma from our past. The symptoms associated with these traumas are as diverse as the people who have them. These traumas can lead to endless cycles of retribution and revenge, which now threaten the well-being and very existence of an increasingly crowded and technologically sophisticated global society. Most sociohistorical trauma can be transformed, although not everyone is able and willing to transform their own trauma. Such posttraumatic growth can lead to improvements in individual and collective well-being.

Although there are many dialogue models, the common denominator of all the models is listening with self-awareness for understanding of the Other and speaking with authenticity and loving kindness. These skills and values can be learned by most people across most of the life span.

We have also seen how dialogue can be used in the helping professions, with individuals, families, and local and global communities. Dialogue can help build the relationships that are necessary for cooperative change. Ultimately, there is no divide that we cannot bridge through dialogue, although some divides are broader, and the necessary bridges may thus take more time to construct. All of these ideas form a foundation for the idea of community therapy.

What Is Community Therapy?

Community therapy uses dialogue to transform sociohistorical trauma toward increased individual and collective well-being. In addition to dialogue, community therapy draws upon other skills used by helping professionals to address the complex challenges that face our current local and global communities. Community therapy can help people learn about and respect all forms of human diversity and can help people promote social justice.

Since dialogue can be used with individuals, families, and small to very large groups, community therapy bridges the divide between micro- and mezzo-level practice (such as psychotherapy) and macro-level practice (such as community organization). Like dialogue, community therapy always has both an intrapsychic and interpsychic component, because participants are challenged to participate in both internal dialogue and dialogue with the other.

In this dialogue model, participants are seen as co-facilitators, co-teachers, co-learners, and co-evaluators. The community therapist learns to share power, status, knowledge, and skills. Community therapy does not take the place of other forms of care and self-care, such as psychotherapy, psychotropic medication, aerobic exercise, and nutrition. Rather, it *adds* an additional approach that integrates the micro, mezzo, and macro levels of care.

Community therapy could be seen to have five phases (see Table 15.1). In the *planning* phase, the facilitator/therapists and community planning group meet to dialogue about community needs. In my community, for example, the issue identified was the need to bridge the religious divide between members and nonmembers of the local dominant religion. The planning group also co-develops the goals, participants, and meeting locations and times. We found in our religious divide dialogues that it was helpful to have both sides of the divide equally represented. Our first meetings involved the planning of light dinners, since food often helps to bring people together. We eventually decided to meet for about 2 hours, once a month.

In the *introduction* phase, the community therapy participants meet for the first dialogues. The therapists help participants do initial introduction exercises. Participants also learn about the purpose, nature, and ground rules of dialogue.

Most of the work occurs in the *dialogue* phase. Participants start to have the kinds of difficult conversations often necessary for individual and community transformations. The therapists may be especially needed in these first dialogues, to help participants successfully engage in these deeper conversations. Although evaluations are conducted at the end of each dialogue, a final evaluation is also conducted after the last dialogue. In the *ending* phase, this evaluation is completed, and planning for follow-up activities is conducted.

In community therapy, participants are empowered to take leadership roles in transforming sociohistorical trauma in their communities. In the *follow-up* phase, some of the participants may want to become community therapists themselves, facilitating dialogues in their homes, institutions, and local communities. One of my doctoral students, for example, created a program designed to prevent campus date rape. Her work included psychodramas, and participants in these psychodramas planned to help facilitate future psychodrama activities themselves.

Table 15.1   Phases of Community Therapy

Stage	The Work
Planning	Co-identify need (what issues, populations, and challenges most need attention) Co-plan (identify participants, goals, and meeting space)
Introduction	Participants introduce themselves Participants learn elements of dialogue
Dialogue	Participants tell their stories Participants share their hopes and fears
Ending	Participants decide on follow-up goals Participants co-evaluate (evaluations done at the end of each meeting)
Follow-up	Participants become facilitators Participant-facilitators create new community therapy initiatives

The Community Therapist

The community therapist is a dialogue facilitator and a generalist who uses skills and theories drawn from many overlapping disciplines, including social work, psychotherapy, group facilitation, human diversity, community organization, conflict resolution, and international relations. Above all, the community therapist is willing and able to know himself. He cares about individual and collective well-being and about the future of all our descendants. He is especially skilled at the conscious use of self, which enables him to form helping relationships with other people. The community therapist is a dialogue facilitator who can work in many settings, with people from all walks of life.

COMMUNITY THERAPY APPLICATIONS

In the following chapter sections, examples of community therapy are forwarded that address symptoms found on individual, family, local community, institutional, ecosystem, and global community levels. The goal is not necessarily to reduce or eliminate symptoms, although such change may occur. The goal is, as in any dialogue, to build the kinds of relationships and communities that can support transformation of sociohistorical trauma.

The community therapist takes the suffering of people seriously but does not emphasize the elimination of all suffering, since much of the suffering that human beings have cannot be avoided. We all grow old, have illnesses and accidents, experience losses, and have to deal with constant change and uncertainty, for example. Community therapy is especially directed toward reducing avoidable suffering, such as patterns of isolation, competition, and retaliation.

In the following sections, applications for working with mental health issues at different levels are forwarded. These levels are listed in Table 15.2.

Table 15.2   Levels of Community Therapy

Individual applications
Family applications
Local community applications
Institutional applications
Ecosystem-level applications
Global-level applications

INDIVIDUAL APPLICATIONS

The following are examples of dialogues that can be done with people with symptoms of selected disorders. These community therapy applications are again not meant to necessarily take the place of other approaches but rather should be used in addition to existing approaches.

Depression

Depression is one of the most common complaints that people bring to therapists in the United States today, across the life span from childhood and adolescence (Kronenberger & Meyer, 2001) through old age (Sakauye, 2008). From a community perspective, depression can be viewed as a natural reaction to an unfriendly or traumatized social environment. The community therapist works on the collective issues that may be associated with what we call depression. For example, in my community and state, we have a rate of depression in women significantly higher than the national average. Instead of accepting the notion that there is something "wrong" with each individual woman, the community therapist asks the women in a dialogue to talk about the issues that are depressing to them.

In one such dialogue, I began by asking the women to define what depression is to them. We found that some themes were common (such as lack of energy, social withdrawal) and some not as common. I then asked the participants to dialogue about what "bums them out," and they talked about such issues as patriarchal attitudes of the men in their lives, lack of opportunity for leadership in their places of employment and churches, gender inequities in wealth and power, and other institutional biases against women. In such a dialogue, the emphasis is not on alleviating symptoms but is about mutual understanding, relationship building, and community.

Anxiety

We also know that complaints of anxiety are also very common in the United States (Herson, Turner, & Beidel, 2007). From a community perspective, anxiety could be seen as a natural reaction to unsafe and traumatic social environments. I have found that most people like to talk about their worries, if they have a safe place to have such conversations. As a community therapist, I like to bring a group of people together and ask them to dialogue about such questions as

1. What is anxiety?

2. How do you know you have it?

3. Why do you think it is so common today?

4. What are your current biggest worries?

5. What seems to trigger your anxiety the most?

6. What helps bring you peace of mind?

Personality Disorder: Borderline and Narcissistic

I have often heard people describe their ex-partners as being either borderline or narcissistic, which are today considered personality (or "Axis II") disorders. These "disorders" have become useful labels to use to make others wrong, because we associate the personality disorders with traits we view negatively, such as manipulation, a sense of specialness, and selfishness. From a community perspective, the traits we call borderline and narcissistic are actually natural reactions that are in most of us to a community in which people often feel manipulated, undervalued, and ignored. Most of us can also transform such traits into attitudes and behaviors of caring, altruism, and cooperation.

One dialogue technique I have used in communities is to ask each participant to "own my own personality disorder." Often we professional helpers are especially reluctant to avoid owning these kinds of traits, probably because we think that we should not have them. As people hear how most of us sometimes manipulate others, put ourselves first, and want to be special, we normalize our Axis II traits and take a step toward transforming them. The best way to keep myself stuck in having some trait seems to be to hate the trait and carry deep guilt and shame about the trait. Conversely, when I start to understand and accept the trait, I can begin to work on it and ultimately transform it.

Bipolar Disorder

There has also been an increase in diagnosis of what we now call bipolar disorder (Herson et al., 2007). As any diagnosis becomes more popular during a particular time period, it seems to become especially tempting for us professionals to label even more clients with that disorder. I have had quite a number of students and clients tell me in recent years that they were given a bipolar disorder diagnosis and also have frequently heard people label their ex-partner, business associate, or family member as "a bipolar."

Community therapy can help the many people who currently "own" a popular diagnosis experience many of the factors that Yalom (2005) has found to be therapeutic in group processes (see earlier chapters). These include hope, universality, interpersonal learning, and intrapersonal learning. The approach used with people owning bipolar symptoms can be used in work with other diagnoses.

For example, in a group for people who have been given bipolar diagnoses, I might ask them to start the dialogue by talking about their experience of how professionals, family, and friends treat them. Then we might talk about what each person's internal experience is like (including thoughts, feelings, internal conflicts, etc.). We might talk about the gifts and burdens associated with the symptoms they have in their lives and how their relationship with their symptoms may have changed over time. All these kinds of conversations can have the therapeutic group effects mentioned above.

Psychosis

Most of us would not want to be called "crazy," although perhaps most of us also worry that we are at times. Nonmedical, interpersonal approaches have been found to be helpful with people diagnosed as psychotic, in a variety of studies, in multiple cultures and countries (Calton, 2009). More than 100 different programs for people labeled with psychosis use at least some dialogue techniques. Programs with the best recovery rates include the Open Dialogue Treatment in Finland, the Soteria in Alaska, the Family Care Foundation in Sweden, and England's Hearing Voices Network (Mackler, 2012).

In one dialogue, a woman told the group that she was hearing voices during the session. When people told her that they did not know that she was "hallucinating," she replied that she spends a lot of energy hiding her symptoms. I asked her what her life would be like if she did not feel like she had to hide her symptoms, and she said, "*Much* easier!" It made me wonder what transformations we might see in our "chronically mentally ill" populations, if we were more accepting of them.

Community therapy could be focused on changing family and community attitudes as much as on working with the people who have the diagnoses. I wonder how well people with psychosis diagnoses might become if they lived in a more loving community that accepted their symptoms and gave them meaningful roles to perform in their work and love lives. The community therapist could create neighborhood dialogues during which people talked about these issues and got to know each other.

Pervasive Developmental Disorder

Life is hard enough for most of us who do not have significant disabilities. Children and adolescents who grow up with symptoms of pervasive developmental disorders often have to face many challenges that most of us never even think about. They may not have the same opportunities in work and love that most of us expect. Their families also may suffer as they strive to help as much as they can and also accept the suffering that they cannot alleviate.

I was involved in a series of dialogues that included young adults with diagnoses of pervasive developmental disorder (PDD) who had successfully navigated relationships and parents with children with PDD diagnoses. The young adults talked about their struggles, joys, and sorrows, and the parents listened and later asked questions. The parents reported that these dialogues were very useful in informing them about what to do and not do with their own children. The young adults reported that they felt empowered, after having an opportunity to be teachers for others.

FAMILY APPLICATIONS

Community therapy can be used with families to help foster individual and collective transformation of sociohistorical traumas.

Ideological Divides

Just like the larger communities they exist in, families are often divided by political, religious, cultural, and other ideologies. Perhaps especially in these times of radical change, family members may tend to strongly identify with ideologies that provide a sense of stability and safety. People who hold other ideologies may be viewed in a very negative way. The community therapist can offer opportunities for individuals and families to meet together and dialogue about their beliefs, so that they can stay in relationship despite their ideological divides.

One way to work with political divides is to meet with a single family and co-create a dialogue with them in which members take turns sharing their political views on various subjects. The therapist realizes that the family has probably *debated* politics before and that such conversations have probably only further widened the divides. The community therapist explains briefly to the family about how a dialogue is different from a debate in both process and outcome. Debate is about winning an argument, and the debater can use any communication strategy to win, including fighting with facts, emotions, or theories. In dialogue, people can also share facts, emotions, or theories, but the goal is, as Martin Buber said, the "confirmation of otherness," which is to seek to understand and respect each other (Friedman, 1983). When people come together with such intent, they can learn to be in relationship, despite their differences.

Then basic ground rules of dialogue are presented. After these preparations, the dialogue begins. The therapist asks family members to listen silently as participants each speak for 2 to 3 minutes. For example, in one blended family, the mother and father and their four adult children meet together to talk about the upcoming presidential election with the therapist. The first speaker is the oldest daughter, who also happens to be a dedicated Republican. She begins the dialogue by explaining why she is a Republican. Her brother, the next speaker in the circle, feels just as strongly that he is a Democrat. It turns out that the family has two Democrats, two Republicans, and two Independents. When the first round is completed, the therapist has the family do a second round, during which people are allowed to speak again for 2 to 3 minutes about the reactions they had to the first round. When the family finishes the second round, they evaluate the session with the therapist. The therapist learns that the family members now have hope because for the first time, they think they may have some skills to use to talk about difficult things.

Helping Families Deal With Sexual Minorities

In another family, there is a single mother who is worried that her only child, a 16-year-old son, is gay. The mother was taught in church that homosexuality is a sin, but her son has left their church. When the community therapist asks the mother and son whether they want to stay in relationship with each other, however, they both say yes. This commitment for relationship creates a foundation for the dialogues, because they both value relationship more than ideology. The therapist might have them begin practicing dialogue about their views on sexuality and religion. Again, the difference between debate and dialogue is described, and ground rules are offered. In one such conversation I was involved in, the parent and child were both able to listen to each other and then express their love for each other.

Sometimes some family members value ideology more than relationship. Dialogue can help clarify each person's hierarchy of values, so that members know where they stand with each other. I still remember vividly one dialogue in which a father told his daughter that he valued his relationship with his God more than he valued his relationship with her. Instead of being angry or hurt, she cried and thanked him. She explained that she had suspected the truth about her father's value hierarchy but that she appreciated his truthfulness and now felt more free to move on without his approval. Usually, honesty, delivered with love, seems to be the best therapy.

Multiple Family Dialogue

Family dialogues can also involve multiple families. I was asked, for example, by local refugee leaders to help their people deal more effectively with the parent-child conflicts that they encounter in the United States. Many of the children of first-generation refugees knew English and the culture better than their parents did, which often created power shifts in their families. We decided that a powerful way to help families deal with these shifts was to collect a group of parents and children together in the same dialogue circle. The support of the leaders was vital in bringing people to the early evening meetings. A light dinner helped make people more comfortable, each night before the dialogues began. In the dialogues, we asked the children to sit in the center in a fishbowl and talk about their lives while their parents listened. Later, the parents had an opportunity to talk in front of the children. Finally, the entire group engaged together in dialogue.

Child Custody Issues

In this era of litigation over child custody, community therapy can offer win-win alternatives to the often win-lose scenarios seen in the courtroom. Preceding the dialogue, as part of a conflict resolution process, I like to show people one of two films that dramatize this process, *I am Sam* (Nelson, 2001) and *Losing Isaiah* (Gyllenhaal, 1995). In both of these films, the people in conflict eventually learn that they can and must cooperate in raising the child they have been fighting about. The films are so well done and realistic that most people seem to relate to them. Such films can help give people hope that relationship is possible.

EXPERIENTIAL LEARNING 15.2

(1) Identify one of the mental disorders and have a dialogue regarding that diagnosis, as described above. See if you can create a safe space for people to talk about their depression or anxiety, for example. Describe your experience.

(2) If your family of origin could have been involved in a multiple family dialogue (with other families) when you were a child or adolescent, what kinds of topics and conversations would have helped you? Explain.

(3) What kind of family dialogues would you like to be involved in today? Why?

LOCAL COMMUNITY APPLICATIONS

Mental health is associated with the well-being of the local community. The following paragraphs provide brief examples of dialogues that can help transform community well-being.

Conflicts Between Pedestrians, Bicyclists, and Motorists

One of the most common complaints women have made about their husbands in my office is about their road rage. Why would this be such a common issue for so many men and women? I think that we may sometimes unconsciously transfer our anger about past socio-historical trauma upon strangers in other vehicles. Perhaps it is relatively safe or seems more acceptable to be angry at a stranger than at the people we are most angry at. One man told me once that he "hates bicyclists, since they all think they are better than everyone else." This man had a history of being made to feel inferior in his family and community of origin. I also wonder if our anger about the stresses and pressures of everyday life ends up intensifying driving on our roads, making "getting ahead" literally a life-or-death issue.

As town, suburbs, and cities create more routes for pedestrians and bicyclists, tensions and even dangerous incidents between some pedestrians, bicycles, and motorists may also increase. Community therapy may help reduce tension and increase understanding, cooperation, and safety. One way to do such a dialogue is to use psychodrama to stimulate the conversation.

The community therapist, for example, starts out by meeting with a group of interested bicyclists and motorists. The therapist asks both groups to describe common situations of tension and danger that occur on community roads. These are written on the board by a volunteer participant. Then the group reaches consensus on what incident to psychodrama. People volunteer to take on certain parts of the situation. A decision is made to do a situation where a bicyclist is riding down a busy street, blocking the lane for a motorist behind him. When the motorist finally is able to pass, he cuts off the bicyclist, narrowly missing him. The two people start to swear at and then threaten each other. The two actors play the scene out, and then dialogue group members are invited to join in the psychodrama and offer alternative ways that the two people could have played out the scene. Later, the entire group dialogues about the experience.

Dialogue as an Alternative to the Legal System

Local communities sometimes seek alternative treatments for people who have committed such crimes as child abuse, traffic violations, or retail theft. Now called victim offender mediation in many states, such efforts involve crime victims and their perpetrators in structured dialogues (Umbreit, Lightfoot, & Fier, 2001). Community therapists are challenged to work with these "nonvoluntary" clients, who initially may not be enthusiastic about dialogue. Such "restorative justice" work can use dialogue to help perpetrators and victims engage in conversations that can lead to reparative agreements (that might involve the perpetrator giving back in positive ways to the community and to the victims). I think such agreements are often preferable to punishments, which may serve to further alienate and embitter the punished.

Treatments for Community Poverty

Most of my clients have relationship poverty and are more alone than they want to be. As a community therapist, I often think that if I had a magic wand, the one thing I would give my clients is community. Many adult men, for example, have few, if any, close friends. One community therapy for this issue is a men's group.

One intervention I like to use in the first weeks of a new men's group is to spend an entire session on each man's life story. One participant called this "dialogue slowed way down." The week before, I ask for a volunteer to tell his story the next week. Then, when that session begins, the storyteller speaks for at least half of the session while the entire group just listens. The other men cannot make comments or ask questions until he is finished. This technique seems to deepen the relationships between the men, as they learn to really listen and speak from the heart. This conversation will take eight sessions if there are eight participants. The facilitator can also participate if he wishes.

As the community therapist facilitating a men's group, I feel that my responsibility is to help the men transform their own sociohistorical trauma into an awareness of their own privilege and into new behaviors based on that awareness. The dialogue process thus builds upon the storytelling work described above and then moves toward consciousness raising and social action. I have especially enjoyed occasionally bringing the men's group together with a women's group for a dialogue, which gives both groups some ideas that they can take back to their regular ongoing dialogues.

Dialogue and Public Health

Another issue that communities share today is concern about obesity, food, and health. Dialogue can help people form mutually helpful relationships. I was asked to give a talk to a group of adults at a health center on dieting and obesity. I sat down with the people in a circle and began by asking them why they think that most researchers say that the majority of people who diet eventually regain their lost weight. Everyone in the room admitted to having at least one "failed" diet. We spent the rest of the night having a dialogue about their experiences of dieting. I asked them at the end if the conversation was helpful, and all the participants said that they appreciated the chance to talk and listen with each other. They left feeling less alone, less "crazy," and more supported.

Bridging Intergenerational Divides

Most of our communities also have intergenerational divides, in which aging people lack meaningful relationships with younger persons. The community therapist can work with leaders to invite together a mix of younger and older participants for a series of dialogues.

One of the most interesting dialogues that happened in my dialogue models class one year involved a multigenerational conversation that included a group of adolescent break dancers, a group of young adults, and some aging participants. Each of my students had helped to bring in a group of participants, and the mix happened to create a wonderful "vibe" in the room. The grownups first asked the younger people questions, such as, "What do you think of adults?" and "What do you think about the world?" Later, the younger people returned the favor, asking the adults such questions as, "What was the '60s like?" and "Did you ever try drugs?"

Another dialogue I did featured a small circle of about six older men, who happened to be both social workers and best friends who had met together in an informal support group for over 10 years. All in their 60s, they had many stories to tell my MSW students, stories about love, work, and life. I much prefer this kind of conversation to a panel discussion because the visitors themselves talk in more real ways among themselves while the group listens. Later, the large group has an opportunity to make comments and ask questions.

APPLICATIONS IN WORKING WITH INSTITUTIONS

Perhaps dialogue belongs in the core mission statements and curricula in all our schools and churches. Throughout this book, I have argued that a mark of a mature, educated, enlightened person is his ability to have a conversation with everyone, especially with those who seem most different from him.

Dialogue in School Curricula

Perhaps all children and adolescents should be required to take dialogue classes, in which they practice dialogue with each other and with other groups. Such classes can be conducted both face to face and online. In most school lunchrooms today, our students sit at separate tables, segregated by such elements of diversity as race, culture, or age.

I have found that most high school students, for example, enjoy dialogue as much as adults. I think about the movie *The Breakfast Club* (Hughes, 1985), in which five high school students who all belong to different subcultures are thrown together for a day and start to form relationships with each other. A community therapist can use dialogue techniques to offer high school students a similar experience. Students in a high school can be asked to identify the subgroups in their school and then can be divided into small dialogue circles that have at least one or two representatives from each subgroup as members. The facilitator can then ask the students to start to talk about their experiences, perhaps by asking such *Breakfast Club* questions as, "What is something you can do well?" "What is your family like?" or "What is it like to be a member of your subgroup?"

Dialogue in Church Curricula

What if our churches began bringing their congregations together with other church congregations for regular dialogues? The purpose of such dialogues would not be to influence or compete but to mutually understand and respect.

In such dialogues, members can do warm-ups that help reduce the initial discomfort and perhaps underlying lack of trust that may exist between groups. Then more substantive issues can be discussed. Some examples of these are provided in Table 15.3.

Large Organizations

Many of us spend time in institutional settings, such as school, church, and business. The teacher, clergy member, or business leader can use dialogue to promote individual and

Table 15.3 Some Topics for Religious Group Dialogues

Topic Area	Dialogue Issues
Religion and spirituality	What do the terms *religion* and *spirituality* mean to you? How are they different or similar for you? Are you more religious or more spiritual?
Beliefs and feelings	What do you think and feel about other faiths? What do you think and feel about other faiths represented in the room?
Stereotypes	What are stereotypes you have heard about your own faith and people who have your own faith? What are stereotypes you have heard about other faiths represented in the room and about people who hold these other faiths?
Traumatic behaviors	What behaviors have you experienced from people with other faiths that were harmful or traumatic to you? What behaviors of your own have caused harm to people with other faiths?
Helpful behaviors	What behaviors have you experienced from people with other faiths that were helpful or transformative for you? What behaviors of your own have been helpful to people with other faiths?

community well-being. As in any dialogue, successful relationship building requires an openness to explore the sharing of power and the development of mutual trust. Such commitments do not always happen.

For example, I was asked once to attend a meeting that involved both leaders and members of a large organization. There had been considerable conflict within the organization, and three of us attended this meeting as facilitators, with about 50 participants. We had met earlier with a small committee of leaders and members, and the decision was made to ask people to talk in small groups about what they saw as the issues in the organization. We each took about 15 members in small-sized groups. It quickly became apparent that most people did not feel safe talking about how they really felt in the small groups. Members were afraid that the leaders would hear about their comments and then retaliate against them. We discussed this challenge with the members. In this particular case, the members decided to stop the dialogue process temporarily.

Another time, I was asked to facilitate a conversation between faculty in a college where there had been a religious divide for decades. The faculty as a whole had never had an open conversation about this divide. I knew many of the faculty, so I was concerned about how much my leadership would be accepted. Fortunately, I had the support of the institutional leader. After she introduced me as the facilitator, people seemed to give the dialogue a chance. I asked a group of faculty who identified as belonging to the dominant religion to sit in a small circle in the middle of the room. Then I sat with them and asked them to each tell a story about their experiences in the college. The outside circle listened quietly until it was their turn to volunteer to enter the small fishbowl circle. The third round was an open dialogue with everyone in the group. Although the evaluations of the dialogue were very positive, the administration was not willing to follow up with further dialogues.

APPLICATIONS IN WORKING WITH THE ECOSYSTEM

My impression is that most of my clients are also disconnected from the ecosystems that they live in, whether they are urban, suburban, or rural residents. We might not, for example, notice the night sky because of light pollution, we may be out of touch with the weather because we live in our cars and homes, and we might not be aware what the equinox or solstice is.

The community therapist can help people reconnect with their own bodies, with other living things, and with their natural environments. As shown in Chapter 10, there is increasing evidence to support the idea that our mental health is associated with the well-being of the ecosystems that support all life.

What kinds of dialogues can people do with their local ecosystem? Table 15.4 illustrates four types of community-environment dialogues.

Table 15.4 Community-Environment Dialogue Models

Dialogue Model	Brief Description
Dialogue on environmental issues	Participants take on the voices of the different positions humans take on the environment (e.g., ranchers and wolf advocates).
Dialogue with other living things	Participants take on the voices of humans and other beings (e.g., endangered species, forests, etc.).
Dialogue with ecosystem elements	Participants take on the voices of ecosystem elements (e.g., water, earth, air) and humans.
Combined dialogue with issues, living things, ecosystem elements	Participants take on voices of humans, other living things, and ecosystem elements.

Dialogue on Environmental Issues

In this dialogue type, participants take on the different "voices" that people have regarding environmental issues. Dialogue can help bridge the divides that often exist between these groups of people (e.g., off-highway vehicle [OHV] owners and environmentalists). I like to start the dialogues with stories about a common interest. I might have the OHV owners and environmentalists tell stories about their sacred landscapes.

Dialogue With Other Living Things and Dialogue With Ecosystem Elements

In these dialogues, participants do psychodramas that cross the divides that exist between living things (e.g., between people and other animals, between people and plants). Some members can volunteer to play the voices of any living thing, such as whales, birds, fish, insects, trees, "weeds," and bacteria. The other members play the voices of themselves, as human beings. In one conversation, for example, a woman played the voice of the weeds in her lawn. She said, "I am a beautiful dandelion but you do not appreciate me. You poison me with spray that makes your own children sick when they play on the grass. I am actually good to eat, especially in the springtime." Then another woman in the group replies to the dandelion.

Dialogue with ecosystem elements is similar, except that people take on the voices of parts of our environment, rather than living things. In one conversation, a man played the earth beneath the freeway. He moans and says, "I am dying under the concrete! All my living things are longing for sunshine and air. But I will emerge eventually. Everything changes, and even freeways eventually crumble."

Combined Dialogue

In this final dialogue model, the participants may include all the voices from the first three models. For example, in the same dialogue, there may be one participant playing the forest, another a lumberjack, another an environmentalist, and so on.

APPLICATIONS IN WORKING WITH THE GLOBAL SYSTEM

Local communities can dialogue about global issues in many ways. People can do "role-plays" where they psychodrama global issues, taking the "voice" of different sides of the issue. People can also do "real plays," in which participants share their own attitudes and feelings. I always prefer doing real plays when I can, because they seem to generate deeper and more transformational dialogues.

The topics listed in Table 15.5 suggest some of the many global issues that can be dialogued. Most of these issues represent divides that exist in our global community, that challenge our ability to cooperatively deal with the global survival threats we face today. Although the evidence is still growing, I believe we will discover that all of the mental health issues that confront us are associated with the state of mankind's current struggle to survive and prosper.

In all of these topic areas, the basic dialogue approach is about the same. Participants in the group take turns taking on one of the voices involved in a global community divide. For example, half of the class doing such a dialogue might agree to take on the voice of immigrants from Latin America who recently moved to the United States. The other half might take on the voices of land owners living in southern Arizona and Texas. The facilitator asks each group to talk about what their perspective is about "illegal immigration." Then the participants might switch after 20 to 30 minutes or so and take on the other voice. Finally, the group has a dialogue about what they thought and felt during the first hour.

Table 15.5 Global Community Dialogue Topics

Examples of Divides in Global Community
Wealthy and poor
Nation and the Other nation
Military strength and peace promoters
Religion and Other religion
Conservation and big energy
Left and right
Government and big business
Religion and science

Still emerging are increasingly effective opportunities to use communication technologies for dialogue that include people who are actually located in different parts of the world. Eventually, people will be able to engage in dialogue from their homes, schools, or businesses, with other people in real time, using technologies that project our images and voices in ways that mimic real, here-and-now interactions. In other words, with such advanced technology, I might not be able to tell if you are actually sitting in the room with me or if the images I see and sounds I hear are being projected through technology.

We will eventually be able to assemble a "virtual" circle of people for a dialogue, who are actually sitting in their chairs, in different and distant locations across the globe. I might facilitate, for example, a dialogue on global warming with people from Africa, South America, Asia, and Europe. In such a dialogue, we all would be able to see three-dimensional images of each other, and the technology also would translate our languages so we could understand each other. As communications technology continues to improve in these directions, all of the techniques described in this text eventually will be able to be used across vast distances, in the same way that we can use these techniques today as we actually sit together in our dialogue meetings.

EXPERIENTIAL LEARNING 15.3

(1) What community dialogue topics do you think would be most needed in your own community?

(2) How do you think of mental health and mental illness? What do you think/feel about the author's views?

(3) What do you think of the premise that individual well-being is always interconnected with collective well-being? Explain.

(4) Try out one of the models described in the family, local community, institution, ecosystem, and global community sections.

(5) Do you think that future dialogues that use the kind of technology described in the last two paragraphs would be as effective as today's dialogues that involve real face-to-face interactions? Why or why not?

REFERENCES

Bussey, M., & Wise, J. B. (2007). *Trauma transformed: An empowerment response.* New York: Columbia University Press.

Calton, T. (2009). Treating schizophrenia without drugs? There's good evidence for it. www .psychminded.co.uk/news/news2009/april09/schizophrenia-psychosis-medication003.htm

Everett, B., & Gallop, R. (2000). *The link between childhood trauma and mental illness: Effective interventions for mental health professionals.* Thousand Oaks, CA: Sage.

Friedman, M. S. (1983). *The confirmation of otherness, in family, community, and society.* New York: Pilgrim Press.

Gyllenhaal, S. (Director). (1995). *Losing Isaiah.* United States: Paramount Pictures.

Herbert, R. (2012, May/June). Memories of tomorrow. *Scientific American Mind,* pp. 66–67.

Herson, M., Turner, S. M., & Beidel, D. C. (2007). *Adult psychopathology and diagnosis.* New York: John Wiley.

Hughes, J. (Director). (1985). *The breakfast club* [Motion picture]. United States: Universal Studios.

Kronenberger, W. G., & Meyer, R. G. (2001). *The child clinician's handbook* (2nd ed.). Boston: Allyn & Bacon.

Mackler, D. (2012, October). *The underlying principles of various successful psychosis-oriented programs.* Paper presented at the ISPS-US Thirteenth Annual Meeting, Chicago, IL.

McNally, R. J. (2011). *What is mental illness?* Cambridge, MA: Belknap/Harvard University Press.

Nelson, J. (Director). (2001). *I am Sam* [Motion picture]. United States: Box Office Mojo.

Sakauye, K. (2008). *Geriatric psychiatry basics.* New York: W.W. Norton.

Umbreit, M. S., Lightfoot, E., & Fier, J. (2001). Legislative statutes on victim offender mediation: A national review. University of Minnesota: Center for Restorative Justice & Peacemaking. http:// www.cehd.umn.edu/ssw/rjp/resources/Program_Development/Legislative_Statutes_VOM_ National_Review.pdf

Violence Prevention Initiative. (2006, September 13). Facts on violence: Violence against women, government of Newfoundland and Labrador. http://www.gov.nf.ca/vpi/facts/women.html

Yalom, I. (2005). *The theory and practice of psychotherapy* (5th ed.). New York: Basic Books.

Index

Acceptance and commitment therapy (ACT), 127
Activist dialogue, 53
Acute stress disorder (ASD), 7
Adolescent dialogue, 210–212
    basics, 210–211
    bioecological dialogue, 211
    experiential learning, 212
    fishbowl exercise, 211
    gender divide, 211
    techniques, 211
    teen-adult divide, 211
Adversarial dialogue, 53
Aggressive participants:
    dialogue process, 97–98
    social justice dialogue, 185–186, 190–191
Aging-people dialogue, 216–218
    basics, 216
    dialogue training group (DTG), 217
    experiential learning, 218
    life-death dialogue, 217
    transgenerational dialogue, 216–217
Alternative dispute resolution (ADR), 200
Amygdala, 142, 167
Anger response:
    dialogue practice, 43
    personal transformation, 28
    social justice dialogue, 186
Anxiety, 225
Artistic-scientific approach, 67t, 75–78
Assessment:
    dialogue outcomes, 67t, 75–78
    engagement phase, 87t, 89–91
    sociohistorical trauma, 9t, 21
Attachment theory, 18

Big Dreams exercise, 209
Bioecological dialogue:
    adolescent dialogue, 211
    bioenergetics, 162
    body image dialogue, 165
    body-mind connection, 162

complementary and alternative medicine (CAM), 162
    dance and movement therapy (DMT), 163
    dance traditions, 162–163
    deep ecology dialogue, 166–169
    ecofeminism, 167
    ecosystem dialogue, 168
    experiential learning, 162, 163, 166, 169
    grouping arrangements, 163–164
    neurobiological approach, 167
    peace and conflict studies (PCS), 199
    pictorial dialogue, 168
    psychodrama, 168
    sacred landscape dialogue, 168
    seasonal dialogue, 168
    sexuality dialogue, 165–166
    whole-body dialogue, 161–163
    whole-body expression, 164
    whole-body listening, 165
    whole-body techniques, 163–166
Bioenergetics, 162
Biopolitics, 19
Bipolar disorder, 226
Blessings, 157
Body dialogue:
    body image, 165
    body language, 59
    body-mind connection, 162
    body parts, 35, 37f
    whole-body dialogue, 161–163
    whole-body expression, 164
    whole-body listening, 165
    whole-body techniques, 163–166
    See also Dance and movement therapy (DMT)
Borderline personality disorder, 225–226
Brain research. *See* Neurobiological approach
Breakfast Club, The (1985), 232
Buddhism, 152
Bullying, 209
Business approach, 79t, 81–82

Canada, 18, 30
Case-formulation approach, 129
Check-in procedure, 94
Check-out procedure, 94
Chemical imbalance, 14
Child custody issues, 229
Children's dialogue, 207–210
  basics, 207–209
  behavioral reinforcement, 209
  Big Dreams exercise, 209
  bullying, 209
  emotion dialogue, 209
  experiential learning, 210
  ground rules, 208*t*
  listening skills, 209
  self-knowledge, 208*t*
  self-skills, 208*t*
  self-values, 208*t*
  techniques, 209
  turn-taking supervision, 209
Christianity, 152, 162, 163
Cingulate cortex, 20, 37–38
Co-facilitation, 97
Cognitive-behavioral dialogue:
  acceptance and commitment
      therapy (ACT), 127
  behavioral experiments, 134–135
  behaviors, 125–135
  case-formulation approach, 129
  characteristics of, 126–128
  cognitive-behavioral group
      therapy (CBGT), 128
  cognitive-behavioral therapy (CBT), 126–129
  cognitive intimacy, 124
  communication skills, 133–134
  community divides, 125
  courageous conversation, 124–125
  dialectical behavioral therapy (DBT), 127
  diversity work, 132
  experiential learning, 126, 130, 133–134, 135
  food fantasy exercise, 130–131
  memes, 124
  motivational interviewing (MI), 127
  nonjudgmental awareness, 132
  peace and conflict studies (PCS), 197–198
  practice-based evidence (PBE), 128–129
  safe conversation, 123–124
  scientific evidence, 128–129

second force psychology, 127
  story, 130
  values exercise, 131
  warm-up exercises, 129–131
Cognitive dimension, 60, 74–75
Cognitive intimacy, 124
Collaborative behavior model, 52, 53
Collaborative communication theory, 48–49
Collaborative inquiry, 78
Collective dialogue, 107, 113–121
Commitment, 90–91
Communication skills, 133–134
Communicative justice, 181
Communicative social action, 54
Community development theory,
      50–51, 52, 119–120
Community divides:
  bridging approach, 173–174
  cognitive-behavioral dialogue, 125
  defined, 173
  dialogue models, 174*t*
  dialogue process, 89–90
  experiential learning, 175, 178
  gender divide, 105, 125, 175, 211
  job-ranking divide, 178
  political divide, 176–177
  religious divide, 175–176
  sexual orientation divide, 177–178
  social action activity, 179
Community-of-diversity theory, 67*t*, 68
Community therapy:
  anxiety, 225
  applications, 224–237
  bipolar disorder, 226
  borderline personality disorder, 225–226
  child custody issues, 229
  community therapist, 223
  criminal offenders, 230
  defined, 222–223
  depression, 225
  ecosystem applications, 234–235
  educational settings, 232
  experiential learning, 224, 229, 236–237
  family applications, 227–229
  global applications, 235–237
  individual applications, 224–227
  institutional applications, 232–234
  local community applications, 229–232

mental health, 220–221
mental illness, 220–221
multiple family dialogue, 229
narcissistic personality disorder, 225–226
organizations, 232–234
pervasive developmental disorder (PDD), 227
political divides, 227–228
poverty, 230–231
psychosis, 226–227
public health, 231
religious dialogue, 232, 233*t*
restorative justice work, 230
road rage, 230
sexual orientation, 228
sociohistorical trauma response, 221–224
transgenerational dialogue, 231–232
Complementary and alternative
    medicine (CAM), 162
Conciliation, 200
Conflict. *See* Peace and conflict studies (PCS)
Consciousness levels:
    facilitator development, 68–69
    personal consciousness, 34, 35*f*, 68–69
    prepersonal consciousness, 34, 35*f*, 68–69
    relational transformation, 34, 35*f*
    transpersonal consciousness, 34, 35*f*, 68–69
    See also Ego state model
Conscious-use-of-self theory, 67*t*, 71–73, 77
Constriction response, 8–10
Contact zones, 13
Coritsol, 142, 143
Countertransference, 72, 76, 78–79
Couples dialogue, 113–115
Courageous conversation, 124–125
Criminal offenders, 230
Cultural dialogue, 119–121
Cultural differences:
    contact zones, 13, 17
    sociohistorical trauma, 9*t*, 13, 16–17
        Cultural evolution theory:
    memes, 14–15, 19–20
    sociohistorical trauma, 9*t*, 14–15
Curry-Smid, Shauntele, 84

Dance and movement therapy (DMT), 163
Dance traditions, 162–163
Daniels, Debra S., 62
Dating issues, 213

Debriefing session:
    dialogue process, 98–99
    social justice dialogue, 193
Deep ecology dialogue:
    bioecological dialogue, 166–169
    relational transformation, 38–39
Defense mechanisms, 114
Depression, 225
Developmental dimensions dialogue, 35, 36*f*
Developmental systems theory, 9*t*, 10–11
DHEA, 142
Diagnostic Statistical Manual of Mental Disorders
    (DSM), 10
Dialectical behavioral therapy (DBT), 127
Dialectic of trauma, 8–10
Dialogic, participatory, experiential (DPE)
    approach, 49
Dialogue facilitator. *See* Facilitator development
Dialogue models class, 196*t*, 203–205
Dialogue practice:
    activist dialogue, 53
    adversarial dialogue, 53
    cognitive dimension, 60
    collaborative behavior model, 52, 53
    collaborative communication theory, 48–49
    communicative social action, 54
    community development theory, 50–51, 52
    defined, 47
    dialogic, participatory, experiential (DPE)
        approach, 49
    ecobiopsychosocialspiritual approach, 59–60
    emotional dimension, 59
    experiential learning, 45, 56, 58, 60
    ground rules, 46
    historical context, 47–48
    human relations dialogue, 53
    ideological reconciliation model, 52, 53
    in diversity work, 47*t*, 55
    in education, 47*t*, 48–50, 56–58
    in health care, 47*t*, 55
    in organizations, 47*t*, 48, 54
    in peace and conflict studies (PCS), 47*t*, 53–54
    in philosophy, 47*t*, 53
    in political science, 47*t*, 51
    in psychology, 47*t*, 52–53
    in religion, 47*t*, 50–51, 61
    in social work, 47*t*, 51–52
    interactive dialogue, 49

intergroup dialogue, 49, 53–54, 56–58
international examples, 55–56
multidisciplinary approach, 47–56
neurobiological impact, 59
nonviolent rhetoric, 53
physical dimension, 59
problem-solving dialogue, 53
racism, 52–53, 56–58
reflexive dialogue, 54
relational transformation, 38
serial monologue, 49
social construction theory, 52
social development dimension, 60
spiritual dimension, 60
theoretical perspective, 43–45
vignette, 61, 62
Dialogue process:
    action-processing-action cycle, 94
    aggressive participants, 97–98
    check-in procedure, 94
    check-out procedure, 94
    co-facilitation, 97
    community divides, 89–90
    creating space, 91–92
    debriefing session, 98–99
    dialogue training group (DTG), 96–97
    difficult conversations, 93
    engagement/assessment phase, 87t, 89–91
    evaluation/follow-up phase, 87t, 94–96
    experiential learning, 91, 95, 99
    facilitator mistakes, 98
    goal-setting, 90
    ground rules, 91
    group assessment, 95, 96t
    group commitment, 90–91
    group referrals, 95
    group renegotiations, 95
    group size, 94
    inclusive approach, 88–89, 171–172
    issues, 88t, 96–99
    meta-communication, 94
    models, 88t
    needs identification, 89–90
    opening up, 92–93
    participant recruitment, 90
    participant supervisors, 96
    phases, 87t, 89–96
    practice areas, 89t

relationship/community-building phase,
    87t, 91–94
social action, 94–95
structure, 97
vignette, 99
Dialogue training group (DTG):
    aging-people dialogue, 217
    dialogue process, 96–97
    social justice dialogue, 187–188, 193
Distributive justice, 181
Diversity work:
    cognitive-behavioral dialogue, 132
    dialogue practice, 47t, 55
Divides. See Community divides
DNA, 11

Ecobiopsychosocialspiritual approach:
    cognitive dimension, 60, 74–75
    dialogue practice, 59–60
    emotional dimension, 59, 74
    facilitator development, 67, 73–75
    physical dimension, 59, 73–74
    social development dimension, 60, 75
    sociohistorical trauma, 5, 7, 9t, 19–20
    spiritual dimension, 60, 75
Ecofeminism, 167
Ecosystem dialogue:
    bioecological dialogue, 168
    combined dialogue, 234t, 235
    community therapy, 234–235
    ecosystem elements, 234t, 235
    environmental issues, 234
    other living things, 234t, 235
    relational transformation, 38–39
    See also Bioecological dialogue
Education:
    community therapy, 232
    dialogue practice, 47t, 48–50, 56–58
Ego state model:
    child role, 34, 35f, 68–69, 109–111,
        140–141, 198t
    experiential-humanistic dialogue, 140–141,
        145, 146
    facilitator development, 68–69
    observing self, 34, 35f, 68–69, 109–111,
        140–141, 198t
    parent role, 34, 35f, 68–69, 109–111,
        140–141, 198t

peace and conflict studies (PCS), 198*t*
psychodynamic dialogue, 109–111
relational transformation, 34, 35*f*
Emotional intelligence, 82
Emotions:
    children's dialogue, 209
    ecobiopsychosocialspiritual approach, 59, 74
Empathy:
    experiential-humanistic dialogue, 139, 144
    neurobiological approach, 33, 37–38
    relational transformation, 37–38
Empowerment response:
    ethnocultural factors, 30
    personal transformation, 28–31
    transformational learning theory, 29–30
Empty-chairs technique, 109, 111
Engagement/assessment phase, 87*t*, 89–91
Environmental influences, 6, 10–11
    See also Bioecological dialogue; Ecosystem
        dialogue
Epi-environmental influences, 6, 10–11
Epigenetic influences:
    relational transformation, 38
    sociohistorical trauma, 6, 10–11
Estrogen, 142
Evaluation/follow-up phase, 87*t*, 94–96
Evangelicals for Environmental Responsibility, 30
Evidence-based practice (EBP), 76
Evidence-based treatment (EBT), 76
Evolutionary theory, 9*t*, 11–12
    See also Cultural evolution theory
Existentialism, 67*t*, 69
Experiential-humanistic dialogue:
    cognitive-emotional dynamic, 137–138
    dialogue techniques, 143–147
    ego state model, 140–141, 145, 146
    emotional primacy, 138
    emotional sharing, 143–144
    experiential-humanistic therapy
        (EHT), 138–139
    experiential learning, 138, 139, 144, 147
    facilitator empathy, 139, 144
    facilitator genuineness, 139, 144
    facilitator warmth, 139, 144
    Gestalt therapy, 140
    horizontal psychodrama, 145
    listening skills, 144
    neurobiological approach, 142–143

peace and conflict studies (PCS), 198–199
psychodrama, 139–142, 145–147
real-play technique, 143
role-play technique, 143
scientific evidence, 141–142
story, 140–141
talking-from-heart, 137
theatrical psychodrama, 147
three-dimensional psychodrama, 146
two-dimensional psychodrama, 145–146
vertical psychodrama, 145

Facilitator development:
    artistic-scientific approach, 67*t*, 75–78
    business approach, 79*t*, 81–82
    cognitive maturity, 74–75
    collaborative inquiry, 78
    community-of-diversity theory, 67*t*, 68
    consciousness levels, 68–69
    conscious-use-of-self theory, 67*t*, 71–73, 77
    countertransference, 72, 76, 78–79
    dialogue assessment, 67*t*, 75–78
    ecobiopsychosocialspiritual approach,
        67, 73–75
    ego state model, 68–69
    emotional intelligence, 82
    emotional maturity, 74
    evidence-based practice (EBP), 76
    evidence-based treatment (EBT), 76
    existentialism, 67*t*, 69
    experiential learning, 70, 76, 78, 82
    facilitator competency, 80–81, 82, 185
    facilitator materialism, 70
    facilitator training, 79
    feedback process, 77
    group work, 79–81
    hypothesis testing, 73, 77
    importance of, 67
    Jungian approach, 67*t*, 69
    me-to-we shift, 68–70
    mindfulness, 72–73
    monitoring process, 77
    multidimensional development theory,
        67*t*, 73–75
    multidisciplinary approach, 78–82
    participatory facilitation, 79*t*, 82
    personal reflection, 82–83
    person-centered model, 79

physical maturity, 73–74
practice-based evidence (PBE), 77
process evaluation approach, 78
projection, 71–72, 76
psychodynamic theory, 67t, 68–69
psychology approach, 79t, 81
relationship dialogue, 70–71
scholar practitioner, 77
social maturity, 75
spiritual maturity, 75
stereotypes, 72, 76
technical facilitation model, 79
theoretical perspectives, 67t, 68–78
transactional analysis (TA), 68–69
transactional leadership, 81
transference, 72
transformational leadership, 81
transpersonal theory, 67t, 68–69
vignette, 83–85
Family dialogue:
    community therapy, 227–229
    facilitator development, 80
    psychodynamic dialogue, 115–116
Feedback process, 77
Female brain, 142
Films, 9t, 16
First force psychology, 105, 127
Fishbowl exercise:
    adolescent dialogue, 211
    middle-age adult dialogue, 214–215, 215
    partners dialogue, 215
Forgiveness, 36–37
Fourth force psychology, 150
Frontal lobe, 33, 38

Gamma-aminobutyric acid (GABA), 14
Gender divide, 105, 125, 175, 211
Genetic influences, 6, 10–11
Genuineness, 139, 144
Gestalt therapy, 140
Global Dialogue Institute, 51
Globalization:
    community therapy, 235–237
    transpersonal dialogue, 152–153
Group psychotherapy, 48
Group work, 79–81
Guided imagery, 156
Guilt response, 186

Harrison, Renee, 22
Healing, 27–28
Health care dialogue, 47t, 55
Hippocampus, 142, 154, 167
Historical trauma, 10
HIV virus, 31–32
Holocaust survivors, 11, 17
Human relations dialogue, 53
Hyperarousal response, 8–10
Hypothesis testing, 73, 77

Ideological reconciliation model, 52, 53
Imagination techniques, 155–156
Inclusive approach:
    dialogue models, 171–172
    dialogue process, 88–89
Institutional dialogue, 117–118
    See also Organizations
Intentions, 155
Interactive dialogue, 49
Interdisciplinary studies, 9t, 19
Interfaith Health Program, 50
Intergenerational dialogue. See Life-span
    approach; Transgenerational dialogue
Intergroup contact hypothesis, 182
Intergroup dialogue, 49, 53–54, 56–58,
    187–188
Intergroup Dialogue as Pedagogy Across the
    Curriculum (INTERACT), 57–58
Internal dialogue, 107, 109–113, 118, 119
International Association of
    Facilitators (IAF), 81
International Institute for Sustained
    Dialogue, 48
Interphysic dialogue, 212t
Intimate relationships:
    couples dialogue, 113–115
    partners dialogue, 215
    relational transformation, 36–38
Intragroup dialogue, 188
Intraphysic dialogue, 212t
Intrusion response, 8–10
Intuition, 59

Japanese Americans, 17
Jefferson, Wazir, 83
Job-ranking divide, 178
Jungian approach, 67t, 69, 150

Knowledge:
    children's dialogue, 208*t*
    social justice dialogue, 185

Latinos, 16–17
Learning brain, 13–14
Legal justice, 181
Life-death dialogue, 217
Life-span dialogue:
    adolescents, 210–212
    aging people, 216–218
    children, 207–210
    experiential learning, 210, 212, 216, 218
    middle-age adults, 214–216
    young adults, 212–213
Limbic brain, 142
Listening skills:
    children's dialogue, 209
    experiential-humanistic
        dialogue, 144
    social justice dialogue, 185
    whole-body listening, 165
Literary studies, 9*t*, 15–16
Living funeral technique, 157

Male brain, 142–143
McGill Domestic Violence Clinic, 80
Mediation, 196*t*, 200–201
Meditation, 153, 154
Memes:
    cognitive-behavioral dialogue, 124
    cultural evolution theory, 14–15, 19–20
    supermemes, 14–15
Memory system:
    explicit memory, 12–13
    implicit memory, 13
    sociohistorical trauma, 5, 9*t*, 12–13
Mental health dialogue. *See* Community
    therapy
Meta-communication, 94
Middle-age adult dialogue, 214–216
    basics, 214
    child-aging parent, 215
    experiential learning, 216
    fishbowl exercise, 214–215, 215
    parent-younger child, 214–215
    partners dialogue, 215
    transgenerational divide, 214

Mindfulness:
    facilitator development, 72–73
    neurobiological approach, 20
    transpersonal dialogue, 151, 153–155, 157
Mindsight, 33
Mirror neurons, 37–38
Monitoring process, 77
Motivational interviewing (MI), 127
Müllerian inhibiting substance (MIS), 143
Multiculturalism:
    empowerment response, 30
    multicultural competence, 183*t*, 191–192
    racism, 52–53, 56–58
    stereotypes, 72, 76
Multidimensional development theory,
    67*t*, 73–75
Multidisciplinary approach:
    dialogue practice, 47–56
    facilitator development, 78–82
    sociohistorical trauma, 7–8

Narcissistic personality disorder, 225–226
National Coalition for Dialogue and
    Deliberation, 48
National Farm Worker Ministry, 30
National Issues Forum, 48
Native Americans:
    cultural buffers, 16
    literary studies, 16
    multidisciplinary approach, 7
    psychodynamic dialogue, 104, 119,
        120–121
    resilience, 30
    social justice dialogue, 184
    transgenerational trauma, 17
    vignette, 21–22
Neurobiological approach:
    amygdala, 142, 167
    bioecological dialogue, 167
    chemical imbalance, 14
    cingulate cortex, 20, 37–38
    coritsol, 142, 143
    DHEA, 142
    dialogue practice, 59
    empathy, 33, 37–38
    estrogen, 142
    experiential-humanistic dialogue,
        142–143

female brain, 142
forgiveness, 37
frontal lobe, 33, 38
gamma-aminobutyric acid (GABA), 14
hippocampus, 142, 154, 167
learning brain, 13–14
limbic brain, 142
male brain, 142–143
mindfulness techniques, 20
mirror neurons, 37–38
Müllerian inhibiting substance (MIS), 143
neurodiversity, 143
neurogenesis, 154
neuroplasticity, 33
oxytocin, 142, 143
parietal lobes, 37–38
post-traumatic stress disorder (PTSD), 13–14
prefrontal cortex, 33, 154
progesterone, 142
prolactin, 143
serotonin, 14
sociohistorical trauma, 9t, 13–14
spirituality, 33
survival brain, 13–14
testosterone, 142
thalamus, 20, 167
translation defense, 33
transpersonal dialogue, 33, 151–152, 154
vasopressin, 142–143
Neurodiversity, 143
Neurogenesis, 154
Neuroplasticity, 33
Nonviolent rhetoric, 53

Oppression, 183t, 188–191
Organizations:
community therapy, 232–234
dialogue practice, 47t, 48, 54
institutional dialogue, 117–118
Owens, Mark, 61
Oxytocin, 142, 143

Parietal lobes, 37–38
Participatory facilitation, 79t, 82
Partners dialogue, 215
Peace and conflict studies (PCS):
alternative dispute resolution (ADR), 200
bioecological dialogue, 199

cognitive-behavioral dialogue, 197–198
conciliation, 200
conflict, 195
curriculum areas, 196t, 202–203
defined, 196
dialogue models class, 196t, 203–205
dialogue practice, 47t, 53–54
dialogue techniques, 196t, 197–205
ego state model, 198t
experiential-humanistic dialogue, 198–199
experiential learning, 197, 199, 202, 205
mediation, 196t, 200–201
peace, 195
peaceful conflict resolution, 196t, 197–199
peacemaking dialogue, 195–196
psychodynamic dialogue, 197
reconciliation, 196t, 201–202
sociohistorical trauma, 196
tag-team circle, 201
transpersonal dialogue, 199
violence, 195
People with disabilities, 104
Perry, Emily, 40
Person-centered model, 79
Pervasive developmental disorder (PDD), 227
Philosophical dialogue, 47t, 53
Physical dimension, 59, 73–74
See also Body dialogue
Pictorial dialogue, 168
Poetry, 47–48
Political dialogue:
biopolitics, 19
community divide, 176–177, 227–228
community therapy, 227–228
dialogue practice, 47t, 51
sociohistorical trauma, 15
Posttraumatic growth:
personal transformation, 31–33
religious/spiritual transformation, 32–33
resilience, 32
transpersonal psychology, 33
war trauma, 20
Post-traumatic stress disorder (PTSD):
cultural differences, 16–17
defined, 10
Holocaust survivors, 17
Latinos, 16–17
memory system, 13

neurobiological approach, 13–14
resilience process, 32
war trauma, 11, 16–17, 18
Western medical model, 7
Poverty, 230–231
Practice-based evidence (PBE):
  cognitive-behavioral dialogue, 128–129
  facilitator development, 77
Practice dialogues, 184–185
Prefrontal cortex, 33, 154
Privilege, 183t, 187–188
Problem-solving dialogue, 53
Process evaluation approach, 78
Progesterone, 142
Projection:
  facilitator development, 71–72, 76
  psychodynamic dialogue, 111, 113
Prolactin, 143
Protein production theory, 11
Psychic trauma, 10
Psychodrama:
  bioecological dialogue, 168
  experiential-humanistic dialogue,
    139–142, 145–147
  young-adult dialogue, 213
Psychodynamic dialogue:
  collective dialogue, 107, 113–121
  community development theory, 119–120
  couples dialogue, 113–115
  couples example, 114–115
  cultural dialogue, 119–121
  cultural example, 120–121
  defense mechanisms, 114
  defined, 105
  ego state example, 110
  ego state model, 109–111
  experiential learning, 107, 111, 112, 113,
    115, 116, 118, 121
  facilitator role, 108–109
  facilitator self-work, 121
  family dialogue, 115–116
  family example, 116
  first force psychology, 105, 127
  institutional dialogue, 117–118
  institutional example, 117, 118
  internal dialogue, 107, 109–113, 118, 119
  peace and conflict studies (PCS), 197
  projection, 111, 113

projection example, 113
psychodynamic story, 106–107
scientific evidence, 106–121
shame, 114
stages of, 103–105
stories, 103, 117
transference, 111–112
transference example, 112
transparent internal dialogue, 118
Psychodynamic theory, 67t, 68–69
Psychology approach:
  dialogue practice, 47t, 52–53
  facilitator development, 79t, 81
  first force psychology, 105, 127
  fourth force psychology, 150
  second force psychology, 127
  transpersonal psychology, 33
Psychosis, 226–227
Psychosocial trauma, 10
Psychosynthesis, 150
Public Conversation Projects, 52
Public health, 231

Racism, 52–53, 56–58
Real-play technique, 143
Reconciliation, 196t, 201–202
Referrals, 95
Reflexive dialogue, 54
Refugees, 31, 39–40, 130
Relational transformation:
  body parts dialogue, 35, 37f
  consciousness levels, 34, 35f
  deep ecology dialogue, 38–39
  developmental dimensions dialogue, 35, 36f
  dialogue practice, 38
  ecosystem dialogue, 38–39
  ego state model, 34, 35f
  empathy, 37–38
  epigenetic influences, 38
  forgiveness, 36–37
  intimate relationships, 36–38
  personal transformation, 34–39
  story approach, 38
Relationship/community-building phase, 87t, 91–94
Relationship dialogue, 70–71
Religious dialogue:
  community divide, 175–176
  community therapy, 232, 233t

dialogue practice, 47*t*, 50–51, 61
posttraumatic growth, 32–33
See also Spiritual dialogue; Transpersonal
    dialogue
Renga, 47–48
Repetition compulsion, 8
Residential school syndrome, 30
Resilience:
    Native Americans, 30
    personal transformation, 27, 32
    posttraumatic growth, 32
Restorative justice work, 230
RNA editing, 11
Road rage, 230
Role-play technique, 143
Rules:
    children's dialogue, 208*t*
    dialogue practice, 46
    dialogue process, 91

Sacred landscape dialogue, 168
Safe conversation, 123–124
Schmid, Muriel, 100
Scholar practitioner, 77
Scientific approach:
    cognitive-behavioral dialogue,
        128–129
    experiential-humanistic dialogue,
        141–142
    psychodynamic dialogue, 106–121
    sociohistorical trauma, 8–10
    transpersonal dialogue, 151–152
Search for Common Ground, 48
Seasonal dialogue, 168
Second force psychology, 127
Self-knowledge:
    children's dialogue, 208*t*
    social justice dialogue, 185
Self-skills:
    children's dialogue, 208*t*
    social justice dialogue, 185
Self-values:
    children's dialogue, 208*t*
    social justice dialogue, 185
Self-work, 121
Serial monologue, 49
Serotonin, 14
Sexuality dialogue, 165–166

Sexual orientation:
    community divides, 177–178
    community therapy, 228
    social justice dialogue, 182
Sexual trauma, 9, 10
Shame response:
    psychodynamic dialogue, 114
    social justice dialogue, 186
    toxic shame, 186
Skills:
    children's dialogue, 208*t*
    social justice dialogue, 185
    See also Communication skills; Facilitator
        development; Listening skills
Social action:
    community divides, 179
    dialogue practice, 54
    dialogue process, 94–95
    social justice dialogue, 183*t*, 193
Social construction theory, 52
Social development dimension, 60, 75
Social justice dialogue:
    aggressive participants, 185–186, 190–191
    anger response, 186
    communicative justice, 181
    debriefing session, 193
    dialogue beginnings, 183*t*, 184–186
    dialogue modes, 189*f*, 190*f*
    dialogue topics, 183*t*
    dialogue training group (DTG), 187–188, 193
    distributive justice, 181
    experiential learning, 183, 192, 194
    facilitator competency, 185
    group allies, 183*t*, 192–193, 194
    group commitment, 184
    group commonalities, 184
    group motivations, 191–192
    group obstacles, 192
    guilt response, 186
    intergroup contact hypothesis, 182
    intergroup dialogue, 187–188
    intragroup dialogue, 188
    legal justice, 181
    listening skills, 185
    multicultural competence, 183*t*, 191–192
    oppression, 183*t*, 188–191
    practice dialogues, 184–185
    privilege, 183*t*, 187–188

rationale for, 182
research studies, 182
self-knowledge, 185
self-skills, 185
self-values, 185
sexual orientation dialogue, 182
shame response, 186
sharing stories, 188–190
social action, 183*t*, 193
social justice work, 181
sociohistorical trauma impact, 182–183
warm-up exercises, 184
Social work:
    dialogue practice, 47*t*, 51–52
    transpersonal dialogue, 152
Sociobiology, 19
Sociohistorical trauma:
    biopolitical studies, 19
    constriction response, 8–10
    cultural differences, 9*t*, 13, 16–17
    cultural evolution theory, 9*t*, 14–15
    defined, 5
    developmental systems theory, 9*t*, 10–11
    dialectical symptoms, 8–10
    ecobiopsychosocialspiritual approach,
        5, 7, 9*t*, 19–20
    environmental influences, 6, 10–11
    epi-environmental influences, 6, 10–11
    epigenetic influences, 6, 10–11
    evolutionary theory, 9*t*, 11–12
    experiential learning, 6, 8, 11, 19, 20
    facilitator assessment, 9*t*, 21
    films, 9*t*, 16
    genetic influences, 6, 10–11
    historical trauma, 10
    hyperarousal response, 8–10
    influences on, 5–6, 10–11
    interdisciplinary studies, 9*t*, 19
    intrusion response, 8–10
    literary studies, 9*t*, 15–16
    mathematical formula for, 7–8
    memory system, 5, 9*t*, 12–13
    multidisciplinary approach, 7–8
    neurobiological approach, 9*t*, 13–14
    political dialogue, 15
    psychic trauma, 10
    psychosocial trauma, 10
    repetition compulsion, 8

scientific approach, 8–10
sociobiology studies, 19
theoretical perspectives, 7–20
transgenerational dialogue, 9*t*, 17–19
vignette, 21–22
world history studies, 9*t*, 15
South African Truth and Reconciliation
    Commission (TRC), 201
Spectrum model, 150
Spiritual dialogue:
    ecobiopsychosocialspiritual approach,
        60, 75
    posttraumatic growth, 32–33
    See also Religious dialogue; Transpersonal
        dialogue
Spiritual Transformation Scientific Research
    Program, 32–33
Stereotypes, 72, 76
Story approach. *See* Psychodynamic dialogue
Sufism, 162
Survival brain, 13–14

Tag-team circle, 201
Technical facilitation model, 79
Testosterone, 142
Thalamus, 20, 167
Toxic shame, 186
Transactional analysis (TA), 68–69
Transactional leadership, 81
Transference:
    facilitator development, 72
    psychodynamic dialogue, 111–112
Transformation:
    anger response, 28
    defined, 27–28
    empowerment response, 28–31
    experiential learning, 31, 33, 38
    from healing, 27–28
    mindsight, 33
    posttraumatic growth, 31–33
    relational transformation, 34–39
    resilience, 27, 32
    vignette, 39–40
Transformational leadership, 81
Transformational learning theory, 29–30
Transgenerational dialogue:
    aging people, 216–217
    attachment theory, 18

community therapy, 231–232
middle-age adults, 214
sociohistorical trauma, 9*t,* 17–19
Translation defense, 33
Transparent internal dialogue, 118
Transpersonal dialogue:
    dialogue techniques, 155–157
    disidentification drawing, 156*f*
    experiential learning, 151, 153, 155
    fourth force psychology, 150
    global spiritual traditions, 152–153
    guided imagery, 156
    historical context, 149–150
    imagination techniques, 155–156
    individual blessings, 157
    individual intentions, 155
    Jungian approach, 150
    living funeral technique, 157
    meditation, 153, 154
    mindfulness, 151, 153–155, 157
    neurobiological approach,
        33, 151–152, 154
    peace and conflict studies (PCS), 199
    psychosynthesis, 150
    religion versus spirituality, 150–151
    scientific evidence, 151–152
    social work, 152
    spectrum model, 150
    talking-from-spirit, 149
    truth experiences, 157
Transpersonal psychology, 33
Transpersonal theory, 67*t,* 68–69
Truth experiences, 157
Two Rivers (2007), 184

Values:
    children's dialogue, 208*t*
    cognitive-behavioral dialogue, 131
    social justice dialogue, 185
Vasopressin, 142–143
Vietnam War, 16–17, 18
Violence:
    collective level, 1–2
    experiential learning, 3
    individual level, 1
    nonviolent rhetoric, 53
    peace and conflict studies (PCS), 195

Warmth, 139, 144
War trauma:
    dialectical symptoms, 9
    posttraumatic growth, 20
    post-traumatic stress disorder (PTSD), 11,
        16–17, 18
Western medical model, 7, 28
Women:
    child custody issues, 229
    diversity dialogue, 55
    ecofeminism, 167
    gender divide, 105, 125, 175, 211
World Café, 48
World War II, 17, 20

Young-adult dialogue, 212–213
    basics, 212
    dating issues, 213
    interphysic dialogue, 212*t*
    intraphysic dialogue, 212*t*
    psychodrama, 213

About the Author

David Derezotes is currently Professor at the College of Social Work, University of Utah, where he is Chair of Mental Health and Practice and Director of the Bridge Training Clinic. He also teaches in the Peace and Conflict Studies program, the URLEND program, and the Religious Studies program at the university. His other texts include *Spiritually-Oriented Social Work Practice* (2006), *Revaluing Social Work: Implications of Emerging Science and Technology* (2005), and *Advanced Generalist Social Work Practice: An Inclusive Approach* (2000). He is involved in a number of campus and community dialogue projects in Utah, including Bridging the Religious Divide, the Dialogue Training Group, and the White Male Privilege Group.